The Aching Hearth
Family Violence in Life and Literature

The Aching Hearth
Family Violence in Life and Literature

Edited by
Sara Munson Deats, Ph.D.
and
Lagretta Tallent Lenker, M.S.

University of South Florida
Tampa, Florida

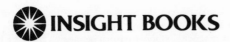 **INSIGHT BOOKS**

Plenum Press • New York and London

AA20706

Library of Congress Cataloging-in-Publication Data

The aching hearth : family violence in life and literature / edited by
  Sara Munson Deats and Lagretta Tallent Lenker.
      p.   cm.
  Includes bibliographical references and index.
  ISBN 0-306-43761-9
    1. English literature--History and criticism. 2. American
  literature--History and criticism. 3. Family violence in
  literature. 4. Family violence.   I. Deats, Sara Munson.
  II. Lenker, Lagretta Tallent.
  PR149.F34A64 1991
  820.9'355--dc20   91-6279
                                                                   CIP

ISBN 0-306-43761-9

© 1991 Plenum Press, New York
A Division of Plenum Publishing Corporation
233 Spring Street, New York, N.Y. 10013

An Insight Book

Printed in the United States of America

We lovingly dedicate this book to Gordon and Mark, who have shown us throughout the years that mutuality in marriage can be a reality as well as an ideal.

Contributors

Rosalie Murphy Baum, Ph.D., Assistant Professor, Department of English, University of South Florida, Tampa, Florida 33620

Ralph M. Cline, Ph.D., Director, International Baccalaureate Program, Hillsborough Country Schools, Tampa, Florida 33602

C. Gordon Deats, Freelance writer and sculptor, Tampa, Florida 33620

Sara Munson Deats, Ph.D., Professor, Department of English, and Director, Graduate Studies, Department of English, University of South Florida, Tampa, Florida 33620

Harriet A. Deer, M.A., Professor, Department of English, University of South Florida, St. Petersburg, Florida 33701

Irving Deer, Ph.D., Professor, Department of English, University of South Florida, Tampa, Florida 33620

Rita Slaght Gould, Ph.D., Author, St. Petersburg, Florida 33703

Maryhelen C. Harmon, Ph.D., Associate Professor, Department of English, University of South Florida, Tampa, Florida 33620

Fredricka Howie, M.A., Teacher, Department of English, Ft. Myers High School, Ft. Myers, Florida 33916

James Rolland Keller, M.A., Instructor, Department of English, St. Petersburg Junior College, St. Petersburg, Florida 33733

Lagretta Tallent Lenker, M.S., Humanities Coordinator, Division of Lifelong Learning, University of South Florida, Tampa, Florida 33620

Nicholas Mazza, Ph.D., Associate Professor, School of Social Work, Florida State University, Tallahassee, Florida 32306

Carlos A. Perez, Ph.D., Psychotherapist in private practice, Tampa, Florida 33617

Helen Houser Popovich, Ph.D., President, Ferris State College, Big Rapids, Michigan 49307

William H. Scheuerle, Ph.D., Dean of Undergraduate Studies and Professor of English, University of South Florida, Tampa, Florida 33620

Phillip Sipiora, Ph.D., Assistant Professor, Department of English, University of South Florida, Tampa, Florida 33620

Lisa S. Starks, Ph.D. candidate, Department of English, University of South Florida, Tampa, Florida 33620

Nancy Jane Tyson, Ph.D., Associate Professor, Department of English, University of South Florida, Tampa, Florida 33620

Emma Waters-Dawson, Ph.D., Associate Professor, Department of English, St. Petersburg Junior College, St. Petersburg, Florida 33733

Bonnie L. Yegidis, Ph.D., Chairperson and Associate Professor, Department of Social Work, University of South Florida, Tampa, Florida 33620

Acknowledgments

The editors gratefully acknowledge the support of the University of South Florida School of Extended Studies and Learning Technologies and the Division of Sponsored Research for funding the conference that led to the creation of this volume. James Heck and Frank Lucarelli, directors of the agencies named above, deserve special thanks, as do Kim Wills and Kate Oliver of the Division of Sponsored Research. In the University of South Florida Division of Lifelong Learning, Lee Leavengood has shown continual support and encouragement, and Beth Williams has provided superb technical assistance. Gordon Deats has made invaluable contributions, including a close reading of the entire text and a highly appropriate title for the entire volume. We are also grateful for the opportunity to work with quality professionals— Norma Fox, Frank Darmstadt, Herman Makler, and the Plenum team.

Finally, we thank our families, Gordon Deats and Mark, Megan, and Mark Lenker, for their love and patience during the completion of this and many other time-consuming projects.

Contents

1

Introduction

Sara Munson Deats and Lagretta Tallent Lenker

Rationale

Throughout Western civilization, the hearth universally symbolizes safety, warmth, and comfort; no other inanimate feature of domestic life can conjure such pleasurable and reassuring images as does the hearth. When visualizing a hearth, we picture a cheerful, cozy place, a quiet refuge where a loving family gathers in the evening for happy, contented communion. If a home has a heart, surely it must beat within the hearth. The rude realm of realities, however, does not conform to our expectations, and the hearth does not protect us. An American resident is "more likely to be physically assaulted, beaten, and killed in the home at the hands of a loved one than any place else, or by anyone else" (Gelles and Straus 1988, 18; see also Steinmetz and Straus 1974, 3; Widom 1989, 1).

During our early years, even in homes with happy hearths, we all learn about fear, and a healthy apprehension can be beneficial. Our senses warn us to beware of very hot surfaces, like stove elements, and our imagination cautions us about leaning too far out a window. Also, most of us, as children, experience nightmares without suffering permanent emotional scars. When the dream monsters get too close to catching us, we may awaken with a jolt of momentary panic, but the terror fades because we remember that a haven awaits nearby. We can run down the hall and leap for sanctuary into the comforting arms of mother, father, grandpa, or grandmother. But consider the plight of the children who awake from a bad dream, run terrified for refuge, and embrace a parent, only to realize that they are caught in the arms of a monster far worse than the demons of their dreams, and that the monster most threatening to their existence is their mother, their father, or both. What deep, permanent emotional scars are left on those bewildered, hurting children?

When we become adults, we wish to have our own hearths. Most of us view marriage as a natural and desirable condition, and in most cases, when a man and a woman marry they expect to enjoy a life improved by the relationship. We expect burdens to be more easily managed if shared by two—both the important basic tasks of gaining food, clothing, and shelter and the lesser, more mundane chores of preparing dinner, picking up the dry cleaning, and vacuuming the carpet. We believe joys will be greater if multiplied by two, and we hope sorrows will be lessened if divided by two. Ideally, a married couple should have a loving partnership in which each member feels a responsibility for the happiness and welfare of the other. Surely all of us desire, when fulfilling our ambitions, to bask in the pride reflected from our spouse. When we grieve, we seek solace in the comforting embrace of our marriage partner. When we feel anxiety or fear, we regain composure from the protective compassion of our mate. We expect to be enhanced by marriage, to become more confident, and to feel more secure.

Tragically, many wives and some husbands discover after the festive ceremony that the bonds of matrimony have become tight, brutal shackles, that their new home is a cruel prison, and that they have slipped the wedding band on the hand of a sadistic jailer. In happy homes where couples share a pleasant union, the wife, perhaps needing encouragement or simply seeking a moment of mutual affection, may lean her face close to her husband's and receive his tender kiss. In too many dark households, however, when the wife lifts her face toward her husband, she can never be sure whether she will feel his lips touch her face or the ruthless impact of his closed fist crashing into her cheekbone.

Former U.S. Surgeon General C. Everett Koop, in a recent address to the American College of Obstetricians and Gynecologists, identified spouse abuse, specifically wife battering, as one of the most critical problems confronting our society today, "an overwhelming moral, economic, and public health burden that our society can no longer bear." According to Koop, battered women currently constitute "a population at risk." "As many as 15 million adult women have been victims of battering, rape, and other forms of physical and sexual assault. Each year, a million or more women are added to that total" (1989). Alarming statistics furnished by the American College of Obstetricians and Gynecologists state that "a woman is battered at least once every 15 seconds in the U.S."; that "battering is the single largest cause of injury to women in the U.S."; and that "in 1986, 30% of female homicide victims were killed by their husbands or partners" ("The Abused Woman," *Fact Sheet* 1989). Psychologist Terry Davidson further estimates that 50% of American marriages are marred by some form of wife beating (1978, 3), and data from the *ACOG Report* on "The Battered Woman" confirm this statistic (1989, 1). Other estimates conclude that physical abuse between spouses occurs at least once in 30% of all marriages and that severe abuse may be a chronic occurrence between 13% of all spouses (Straus 1977, quoted by Widom 1989, 1). A somewhat more optimistic picture is offered in a recent comparison study by Richard Gelles and Murray Straus, who found the incidence of reported husband-to-wife violence to be 121 per 1000 in 1975 and 113 per 1000 in 1985 (1988, 250). The considerable difference between the statistics of Gelles and Straus and those of Davidson and the *ACOG Report* may be due to the conditioned reluctance of wives to report physical abuse by their husbands or to the difficulty of defining exactly what constitutes physical abuse. Nevertheless, whichever statistics we accept, spousal violence is clearly a problem of enormous gravity.

Not only does spousal violence occur more frequently than many of us would suspect, but it is also more pervasive, affecting all social and economic levels. Both Koop and Luella Klein, past president of the ACOG, explode misleading myths about battered women by insisting that battered women may be from any segment of society:

> Woman battering is not confined to low socio-economic groups.
> It's not something that only happens to poor women. It can and
> does happen everyday to poor, middle-class, and well-to-do

women. It happens to blacks. It happens to whites. It happens to
Hispanics. It happens to any racial and economic group. And it is
time that it is stopped. (Klein 1989, 2)

Perhaps a word should be said here concerning the violence of
wives against husbands. In the comparison study quoted above,
Gelles and Straus found little difference in the incidence of wife or
husband battery; wife-to-husband violence was reported in 116 out of
1000 cases in 1975 and in 121 out of 1000 cases in 1985 (1989, 251).
However, although according to Gelles and Straus, research uni-
formly shows that about as many women hit men as men hit women,
the greater average size and strength of men and their greater aggressiveness insures that the battering husband will inflict more pain
and injury than the battering wife. Furthermore, Gelles and Straus
point out that nearly three-fourths of the violence perpetrated by
women is committed in self-defense; more often than not, a wife who
beats her husband has herself been beaten, and she strikes back for
self-protection (1988, 90).

The frequency and pervasiveness of child abuse in our society is
equally alarming. Magazines and newspapers often publish pho-
tographs of pathetic victims of devastating childhood diseases, but
seldom do articles warm of the terrible damage regularly caused by
parents. Yet each year abusing parents kill more children than do
leukemia, cystic fibrosis, or muscular dystrophy (Gelles and Straus
1988, 40). Young boys and girls are counseled for their safety to stay
away from potentially dangerous places and dark alleys and to avoid
all strangers. In reality, however, more children are injured by violence
in the home than in any other place (Gelles and Straus 1988, 18). In
1989, nearly 1000 children were killed by people who were supposed to
protect and nurture them. In the city of New York alone, in 1988,
abusing parents snuffed out the lives of more than 100 of their own
children (Gelles and Straus 1988, 38). The comparison study of Gelles
and Straus found the incidence of reported parent-to-child violence to
be 630 per 1000 in 1975 (63%) and 620 per 1000 in 1985 (62%). Thus,
almost two-thirds of the parents interviewed in both studies reported
at least hitting their children. Furthermore, 14% of the parents interviewed in 1975 and 10.7% in 1985 reported engaging in actions against
their children that Gelles and Straus term severe violence.

To return to a discussion of spouse abuse, R. Emerson and Russell Dobash offer a valuable caveat when they warn that understanding the syndrome of wife battering cannot be achieved by simply compiling personal and family statistics, or even by analyzing individual cases. Instead, they prescribe an in-depth "analysis of the society in which wife beating occurs and the cultural beliefs and institutional practices that contribute to this pattern" (1979, 12). According to many social and behavioral scientists, these factors include the legitimation of violence as an acceptable solution to problems (Roy 1977, xii; Dobash and Dobash 1979, 22; Schechter 1982, 215; Walker 1984, 37) and the hierarchical structure of the family that authorizes male dominance and female subordination (Dobash and Dobash 1979, 22-24; Schechter 1982, 215; Walker 1984, 2, 9, 37).

When discussing wife battering, it is useful to place this phenomenon within the larger context of family violence, since social and behavioral scientists have demonstrated that violent abuse of spouse and child are intricately intertwined and that the same cultural beliefs and institutional practices that contribute to wife battering—particularly the legitimation of violence and the hierarchical structure of the family—also encourage child battering (Gelles and Straus 1988, 90–91; Steinmetz and Straus 1974, 15, 20–21; Walker 1984, 37; Whitehurst 1974, 316–19). Specialists in the field postulate that both excesses are learned responses and that there is a disturbing reciprocity between these two types of violent behavior (Davidson 1978, 116; Gelles and Straus 1988, 90–91; Yegidis, p. 25 in this volume).

The primary models of behavior for children to imitate during the first five years of their lives are their parents or their parent surrogates. An action performed by the parent not only gives the child a template to copy, it also provides the child with an example of the moral standards by which that family is governed. If a parent strikes a weaker member of the family, the child usually assumes that, at least within the family, social morality allows the strong to hit the weak. The stronger parent may hit the weaker mate, and both may hit the children. These beatings help develop the child's concept of a correct pattern to learn and eventually to imitate. When the child grows to adulthood, gets married, and has children, the grown child may be convinced that within the family unit beatings are a natural and sometimes even an admirable method of managing the household and training children. Newspaper accounts of severe family violence often report quotes by the arrested member. The husband says, "She

wouldn't stop nagging me so I had to belt her," or a mother complains, "I couldn't get the baby to quit crying so I hit her again." In
these and other similar cases, the perpetrator of violence will often try
to explain the reason for inflicting violence but will see no necessity in
justifying violence as an acceptable action.

Of course, not all abused children automatically become abusing
adults, but a number of studies indicate that the majority of abusing
adults were either abused as children or witnessed the abuse of other
members of the family unit. Gelles and Straus posit that observing
one's parents hit one another is a more powerful contributor to the
probability of becoming a violent adult than being oneself a victim of
violence (1988, 91), and, in a study conducted in 1988, Bonnie Yegidis
concludes that viewing parental violence is just as important in establishing a later pattern of inflicting abuse as is the direct experience of
being abused as a child (p. 25 in this volume). Gelles and Straus affirm
that three lessons are learned by the child subjected to an environment of violence, whether as a spectator or as a target. First, the child
will believe that those who love you will hit you and you can hit the
people you love; second, the child will be impressed with the moral
rightness of hitting those whom you love; and, third, the child will
accept violence as a permissible solution if other means of dealing
with stress or getting one's way do not work (1988, 91). Having
learned these lessons, the child may grow up to become either an
abusing spouse or an abusing parent or both.

However, the widely held belief that abuse begets abuse has
been questioned in two recent studies of family violence. Rita and
Blair Justice, in their recent study, *The Abusing Family* (1990), conclude
from current research that although many abusive parents were
themselves maltreated as children, even severely abused children
may not grow up to be abusive parents. Justice and Justice argue that
a more thorough study of the coping mechanisms typical of these
"resilient" children is one legitimate way of both treating and preventing child abuse (1990, 151–56). Cathy Widom further challenges
the research supporting the theory that abuse begets abuse (1989).
Widom argues that the "evidence for the notion that abuse breeds
abuse is methodologically problematic and limited by an overdepen-
dence on self-report and retrospective data" (1989, 9). She submits
that additional research that distinguishes more carefully between

types of abuse, between neglect and abuse, between witnessing and experiencing abuse, and between a number of other variables is necessary before firm conclusions can be drawn (1989, 42–50). We note the qualifications of Justice and Justice and the caveat of Widom and present the theory that abuse breeds abuse as a persuasive hypothesis only.

Yet whatever the relationship between spouse and child abuse, both are unacceptable behavior in a civilized society. Expanding Klein's statement on wife battering to include all forms of family violence—not only wife battering but also husband battering and child battering—the contributors to this volume agree that this brutal practice, one as durable as human civilization, must be stopped. They also concur that in order to modify human behavior, the motivations producing the behavior must be understood. Finally, they believe that our literary heritage may provide one of the most valuable resources in our culture for comprehending the underlying causes of family violence as well as other human actions, both normal and aberrant.

This project affirms the assumption that the humanities transmit profound reflections on human life that have shaped our heritage. The rationale for this book is predicated on the assumption that literature bears a vital relationship to situations experienced by individuals in a given society. On one hand, literature mirrors the conventional mores and attitudes of its own social milieu; it may also reflect the concepts of a vestigial culture or anticipate the tenets of an emerging culture. Additionally, the way in which individuals perceive the world is largely determined by the language they use to describe the phenomena they experience as reality. Thus language constructs as well as encodes the conventional perceptions of individuals in a given society; it intervenes in history even as it reflects history. It follows, therefore, that literature, the only art form composed entirely from words, not only mirrors society's conventions but also creates them.

Moreover, the theories of philosophers, psychologists, and clinicians, as well as the attitudes of ordinary citizens, have, throughout the years, been informed—perhaps even determined—by the insights of literary artists. At least four contemporary commentators— Susan Snyder, Leonard Shengold, Edwin Shneidman, and Elaine Showalter—have outlined the reciprocal relationship between literature and psychology. The work of all four of these scholars validates the theory that not only does art often imitate life, but life also imitates art. An affirmation of this reciprocal relationship underlies the rationale of this book.

To the degree that it records credible human behavior, at least the behavior accepted as credible or normal by a particular audience (since "normality," it can be argued, is a social construct), a work of fiction can be studied as a case history to explore the syndrome of family violence, even as Shneidman (1989, 15–47) has employed literary figures as case histories in his study of contemporary suicide, and Shengold has focused on both the lives and works of Anton Chekhov, Charles Dickens, Rudyard Kipling, and George Orwell in his analyses of child abuse (1989, 68–117, 181–283). Literary artists from Geoffrey Chaucer and William Shakespeare to William Faulkner and Alice Walker have probed the occurrence of family violence with sensitivity and insight, and a study of these fictional works can expand our understanding of the motivations and attitudes underlying this deplorable but pervasive social practice.

Additionally, as objective case histories, episodes or characters from literature may provide a means of dialogue with troubled families. Literary works can be vehicles for anonymous discussion about a variety of problems facing the family, or they can furnish a readily available, nonthreatening tool for use in one-to-one and/or group sessions with families or individuals. Literature may thus help families to speak the unspeakable and thereby break the vicious cycle of family violence.

Literature often speaks out boldly against the deleterious ideologies and gender stereotypes that encourage both spouse and child battering, sometimes obliquely, through negative portrayals in fictional works (*Othello, Jane Eyre, Oliver Twist, The Iceman Cometh, The Great Gatsby,* "Barn Burning," and *The Color Purple*), sometimes straightforwardly, in significant essays (Mary Wollestonecraft's *The Vindication of the Rights of Women;* John Stuart Mill's *The Subjection of Women*). Conversely, however, literature often implicitly legitimizes these patriarchal stereotypes as universal and natural (*Gone with the Wind*). Other works may appear to support the status quo while simultaneously offering alternative perspectives, thereby subtly subverting the traditional institutions that they appear to affirm (*The Taming of the Shrew*). All of these types of literature—those works that inscribe these destructive ideologies as natural and universal, those that question them as deviant and detrimental, and those that both subvert and affirm them—are useful vehicles for study, offering positive and negative ideological models. Negative models can make us aware of the pervasiveness of these harmful ideologies, helping us to question the authorization of violence, the masculine hegemony, the hierarchical family structure, and the gender polarization that have encouraged the enslavement and victimization of wives and children. Positive models can provide us with patterns for rethinking and transforming our attitudes and those of society. Thus literature, by imitating "reality" (or at least the ideology perceived as "reality" by a particular culture), can provide a mirror in which these ideologies may be viewed and "deconstructed," while simultaneously offering patterns and tools for reconstructing a more egalitarian and pacific society.

Definitions

Misunderstanding frequently arises from unclear definition of terms, and never more so than in the area of family violence. In using both the terms "spouse abuse" and "battered wife," we are generally following the definitions from the *ACOG Technical Bulletin* article on "The Battered Woman" (1989). The *Bulletin* states that "domestic violence and spouse abuse are terms referring to violence occurring between partners in an ongoing relationship, regardless of whether they are married" (1989, 1). In addition, the "battered woman" is defined in the *ACOG Technical Bulletin,* and throughout this collection of chapters, as "any woman over the age of 16 with evidence of physical abuse on at least one occasion at the hands of an intimate male partner" (1989, 1).

Most civilized persons would agree, in theory at least, that the use of force between adults with the intent of inflicting pain is inappropriate behavior. However, because of the widespread acceptance of corporal punishment as an appropriate method for disciplining children—spare the rod and spoil the child—child abuse becomes a much more difficult term to define. For example, Justice and Justice note, "In Texas, for instance, there has been a law on the books since 1974 that says 'the use of force but not deadly force against a child' by a parent or a stepparent is justified 'when and to the degree the actor

reasonably believes the force is necessary to discipline the child'"
(1990, 5). Much of the controversy has centered on the question:
"Where does 'legitimate' force end and violence begin?" For the purposes of this study, we will not attempt to distinguish between force
and violence. Rather, we will follow Gelles and Straus (1988, 54) in
defining violence as any act of force—from pushing and shoving to
shooting and stabbing—carried out with the intention of causing
physical pain or injury to another person (54–55). However, the question as to when violence to children becomes abuse remains one of
the most hotly debated issues in the clinical literature. We will not,
therefore, attempt to define the amorphous term "child abuse," but
throughout this book will use the term to describe specific acts of
omission and commission that are harmful to children.

Lastly, it should be noted that, although both the terms "spouse"
and "child abuse" are generally associated with violence, there are
undoubtedly types of serious and painful abuse that do not employ
physical force. Therefore, the chapters in this book frequently use the
terms "spouse" and "child abuse" to describe psychological as well as
physical harassment.

Dobash and Dobash warn of the danger of substituting the more
neutral and egalitarian terms "marital violence" and "spouse abuse"
for the more descriptive and specific term "battered wife." They argue that the former terms "imply that each marital partner is equally
likely to play the part of perpetrator or victim in a violent episode;
that the frequency and severity of the physical force used by each is
similar; and that the social meaning and consequences of these acts
are the same" (1979, 11–12). Dobash and Dobash further protest that
the use of this more egalitarian terminology, albeit well-meaning,
may in practice "mask the centuries of oppression of women" and
thus may actually contribute to women's further oppression by neu-
tralizing the very words employed to describe the pervasive practice
of wife beating (1979, 12). The commentators in this book certainly
have no desire to "contribute to the oppression of women" and have
tried to draw a precise distinction between more general spouse
abuse—which would include both psychological and physical mistreatment as well as abuse committed by both or either spouse—and
physical violence perpetrated by the husband upon the wife. Realiz-
ing that 95% of all serious physical violence is committed by men
against women (*ACOG Fact Sheet* 1989), we have generally referred to
all physical abuse as "wife battering," except in the rare instances

(Washington Irving's tales, some of Faulkner's novels) in which the perpetrator is female. However, because the chapters in this volume treat a wide variety of family violence, including psychological mistreatment committed by spouses of both genders as well as both physical and psychological child abuse, we have employed the term "family violence" in the title, since this term more accurately indicates the comprehensive scope of this book.

Another highly connotative designation needing careful definition is the term "patriarchy." The contributors to this volume use this term to describe the particular social system that has prevailed throughout Western civilization since the beginning of history, a "social organization marked by the supremacy of the father in the clan or in the family, the legal dependence of wives and children, and the reckoning of descent and inheritance in the male line" (*Webster's New Collegiate Dictionary*). In employing this term, we are fully aware that this hierarchical social system victimizes men as well as women and children, socializing males into aggressive behavior even as it socializes females into acquiescence to violence (Dobash and Dobash 1979, 22) and children into both aggression and passivity. We believe that the gender polarization and the hierarchical structure of the traditional patriarchal family limit the freedom of men, women, and children, and we seek the creation of a more egalitarian and peaceful society as a way of liberating both sexes from the compression of role stereotyping, from the burden of dominance or subordination, and from the horror of psychological spouse abuse, conjugal violence, and child abuse.

History

Many of the chapters in this volume were first read as papers at a conference entitled "Spouse Abuse: Literary Perspectives," presented in Tampa, Florida, on April 7 and 8, 1989. The idea for the conference was conceived after we experienced great success in a one-day interdisciplinary seminar cosponsored by the Florida Endowment for the Humanities and the University of South Florida's Division of Lifelong Learning and College of Public Health, entitled, "Youth Suicide Prevention: Lessons from Literature." This seminar, held in October 1986, was attended by a standing-room only audience, comprised of parents, educators, mental health professionals, law enforcement personnel, high school teachers, and others who work with young people. The program subsequently won a national award for creativity in Continuing Education programming, and received extensive media coverage in newspapers and on radio and television in Tampa, Orlando, Detroit, and Chicago. The papers presented by the panel were published in 1989 by Insight Books/Plenum Press, and the editors of the book have received letters commenting on the collection from a dozen states in all areas of the nation.

In order to maintain the momentum generated by the suicide and literature project, we applied for and received a grant from the Division of Lifelong Learning and Sponsored Research at the University of South Florida to present a similar conference on "Spouse Abuse: Literary Perspectives." This conference, presented on April 7 and 8, 1989, received an enthusiastic response from a capacity audience composed of professors, students, high school teachers, psychologists, social workers, counselors, and public health officials. In this intensive one-and-a-half-day seminar, a panel comprised of professors from three Florida Universities (University of South Florida, Florida A&M University, and Florida State University), the Dean of the College of Arts and Letters at the University of South Florida, the President of Florida Atlantic University, mental health personnel involved in working with battered wives and abusive partners, high school teachers, social workers, and a state representative discussed many of the works included in this volume, exploring the implications of employing literature as an innovative therapeutic instrument for working with troubled families in dealing with this most personal, almost unspeakable subject. The seminar studied the value of using fictional works as case studies, since they provide impersonal, objective vehicles for discussing personal feelings while allowing the subject to maintain a degree of anonymity. The panel also addressed the gender stereotypes inscribed in literature and the media that encourage unhealthy marital relationships that often lead to spouse abuse. Lastly, the speakers examined positive images of gender relations depicted in literature and the media that might provide remedies for this devastating social sickness. The lively exchange of ideas, and sometimes even heated controversy generated by the seminar, convinced us of the legitimacy of our approach and led us to seek a wider audience for our ideas. Further research on the relationship between spouse and child abuse encouraged us to expand our topic. The result is this book, *The Aching Hearth: Family Violence in Life and Literature.*

Content

Following the format of the conference, this study is organized according to various perspectives, which, in our opinion, contribute to the impact of literature on family relationships, and thus on family violence: the clinical perspective, the literary perspective, and the perspective of the media or popular culture.

The first chapter in the book by Bonnie Yegidis, a published authority on spouse and child abuse, surveys the current clinical literature on family violence in America in the 1980s, thereby establishing the social context within which the literary works in this volume will be considered. In the second chapter, Nicholas Mazza provides a bridge between the clinical and literary perspectives by assessing the value of literature as a tool for clinical treatment of battered wives. Mazza, a practicing therapist, professor, and author of numerous articles on poetry therapy, discusses his use of poetry, both preexisting and composed by the client/victim, as an instrument for both healing and education. According to Mazza, poetry can be an effective technique for building trust, providing feelings of security, improving communication, and raising self-esteem. Shame and stigma are often associated with the role of a battered woman; these victims often feel isolated and alone. Sharing a poem or a piece of recorded music and accompanying lyrics with a group of individuals who have experienced similar trauma can help to validate and universalize feelings while also providing the anonymity often necessary for candid communication. In addition, poems or fiction identifying human rights issues or advocating gender sensitivity may expand the consciousness of the victim. Finally, creative writing (poems, short stories, diaries) offers a vehicle for the victim to express repressed emotions and perhaps through the structuring of art to gain some measure of control over a disordered life. In his chapter, Mazza includes some original poems by battered women that validate his approach. To read these poignant verses is to have one's consciousness raised; to write them was an act of courage and affirmation.

The third chapter introduces the literary perspective that dominates this study. The literary analyses in the book, which all appear in print for the first time, represent a broad spectrum of genres (poetry, drama, the novel, the short story), of time periods (from medieval to contemporary), of tones (tragic, comic, melodramatic, ironic), and of points of view. The focus on destructive family relationships provides the nexus uniting these disparate texts. The chronological arrangement of these chapters vindicates the editors' assumption that family violence is an institution as old as history, although, unfortunately, also as current as today's newspaper. The inclusion of multiple literary modes substantiates our conviction that this disturbing human problem transcends genre as well as era. The criteria for selection of literary works includes not only both variety and sensitivity in the treatment of this explosive issue but also familiarity to a general audience and pertinence to contemporary research on family violence.

The poems, plays, novels, and short stories discussed in this volume also reveal widely diverse perspectives on marital abuse. The type of abuse varies from the brutal slaying of Desdemona and Emilia in *Othello* and Hickey's wife Evelyn in *The Iceman Cometh*, to the vicious battering of Celie in *The Color Purple*, to the deprivation and harassment of Kate in *The Taming of the Shrew*, to the psychological torture of Jim in *All God's Chillun Got Wings* and Antoinette in *Wide Sargasso Sea*, to the subtle manipulation of Nora in *A Doll House*. Yet although a number of the works examined record types of physical abuse, only a few (*Othello, Sons and Lovers, The Great Gatsby,* "Barn Burning," *The Iceman Cometh,* and *The Color Purple*) focus on wife battering—and all of these works but one were written during the modern period—an index perhaps of the paucity of wife-beating episodes in canonical texts, and thus of the pervasiveness of the taboo imposed on this incendiary issue by society, at least until the past few decades. Significantly, two of these vastly different texts (*Othello, The Color Purple*) also link wife battering with another until recently taboo subject, racial bigotry, while two other works associate psychological spouse abuse with racism (*Wide Sargasso Sea, All God's Chillun*). Indeed, many of the works analyzed depict primarily, or exclusively, psychological spouse abuse ("Patient Griselda," *The Scarlet Letter, A Doll House, Wide Sargasso Sea, Before Breakfast, All God's Chillun, Another Part of the Forest, The Little Foxes*), although sometimes the psychological persecution is so intense that it results in madness (*Wide Sargasso Sea*), suicide (*Light in August, Before Breakfast*), or the death of the spouse from other causes ("The Birthmark," *The Little Foxes*). However, whether portraying physical or psychological spouse abuse, the majority of these literary texts delineate the devastating effects of this harassment on the degeneration of the family and the individual. Similarly, although some of the works portray the abusive husband and others limn the abusive wife, many balance and contrast abusive mates of both genders (Boccaccio and Chaucer's tales, *Taming of the Shrew, The Great Gatsby*, Faulkner's novels, O'Neill's plays, Hellman's plays), reminding the reader that although battering remains almost exclusively a masculine crime, psychological abuse is no respecter of gender. Additionally, works by at least three authors illustrate the collusion of the abusive and abused mate in a destructive conjugal symbiosis (Ibsen, Lawrence, Faulkner). Finally, one novel (*Jane Eyre*) probes only potentially abusive liaisons, while examining the ideology that renders such damaging matrimonial relationships almost inevitable.

Although our study focuses primarily on conjugal abuse, a number of the works discussed present vivid depictions of child abuse, both physical and psychological (*Jane Eyre, Oliver Twist,* "Rappaccini's Daughter," Faulkner's novels, *The Color Purple*), and frequently these works stress the relationship between conjugal and parental cruelty. *Jane Eyre* and *The Color Purple* portray child abuse as one element in the deleterious patriarchal system that both novels indict, the system that also makes spouse abuse almost inevitable. Faulkner's novels relate both spouse and child abuse to the linking of love with violence so characteristic of the social system he describes, while also poignantly dramatizing the plight of the emotionally or physically abandoned child. Two of the short stories by Hawthorne ("Rappaccini's Daughter," "The Birthmark") also delineate a striking parallelism between the motivations and circumstances producing spouse and child abuse. Other works, while not centering on child abuse, explore the deleterious effects of conjugal discord on the development of the children (*Sons and Lovers*, Faulkner's novels, O'Neill's plays, Hellman's plays). Of all the works analyzed in this study, only Dickens's novels focus exclusively on child abuse, presenting a gallery of haunting portraits of bullied, battered, overworked, and undernourished children.

Although all of these chapters are motivated by a positive teleology, the works explored are not necessarily affirmative. The authorial attitudes toward spouse abuse in the various literary works differ as dramatically as the types of abuse presented. Some works portray spouse abuse as tragic and terrible; others depict it comically; frequently the abusive situation invokes ironic handling. In his survey of the American literature canon, Ralph Cline discovers a provocative phenomenon: American writers, at least, invariably treat wife abuse (both battering and psychological torment) seriously, whereas husband abuse almost always invites humor. Furthermore, in the works analyzed in this collection, the battered wife sometimes escapes triumphantly from her abusive partner (*The Color Purple, Another Part of the Forest*), or, at least, achieves the courage to defy her abusive mate (*Othello*); in rare instances, the abusive and abused spouses achieve reconciliation ("Patient Griselda," "Wife of Bath's Prologue"); often, however, the stories describe an endless cycle of continued abuse (*Sons and Lovers*, Faulkner's novels, O'Neill's plays, Hellman's plays); and occasionally the solution remains problematic (*The Taming of the Shrew, A Doll House*). Also, some of the works analyzed (*Jane Eyre, Oliver Twist*) provide examples of the "resilient" children noted by Justice and Justice, who are able to overcome the harmful effects of child abuse.

The last methodology, the popular culture perspective, analyzes the influence of the media on the construction of societal attitudes toward gender, marriage, and spouse abuse. Although acknowledging that there is little conscious approval of spouse abuse in the popular arts, Harriet and Irving Deer observe that the treatment of some of the most popular media heroines of the last 50 years suggests an unconscious acceptance of closed patriarchal patterns of value that contribute to the victimization of wives. The most popular of these heroines, Scarlett O'Hara, is depicted as deserving punishment (marital rape, physical injury, miscarriage, and psychological humiliation) because she disrupts traditional conjugal systems and defies gender stereotypes. Two popular television heroines, Lucy Arnez and Gracie Allen, embody significant characteristics of the patriarchal stereotypes that encourage spouse abuse. Conversely, the traditional use of women as objects of abuse, not only physically but in the conventions of language, is submitted to incisive scrutiny in Kubrick's recent film, *Full Metal Jacket*. In contradistinction to *Gone with the Wind*, which endorses negative patriarchal values, and the Lucy and Gracie series, which at least partially affirm these attitudes, Kubrick's film suggests the power of the popular arts to reappraise, and perhaps to reconstruct, traditional ideologies.

Established clinical approaches to the practice of family violence inform all the analyses in this collection, whether they adopt a clinical, literary, or popular culture perspective. In his discussion of *Sons and Lovers*, psychologist Carlos Perez outlines the four models dominating contemporary research on spouse abuse: intrapsychic, behavior response, social learning, and systems theory. Most of the chapters in this collection are eclectic in nature, adapting material from a number of these clinical approaches in their analyses of the literary treatments of conjugal cruelty.

Several commentators, following the intrapsychic model, concentrate on the individual personality traits of the abusive and abused spouses or parents, attempting to explain familial persecution in terms of the manifestation of pathological characteristics. Sara Deats posits that the leading characters in Shakespeare's *Othello* show a remarkable conformity to the personality profiles of the intractable spouse abuser (Iago), the treatable spouse abuser (Othello), and the battered wife (Desdemona) as delineated by psychologist Terry Davidson (1978, 23–28, 50–54); Maryhelen Harmon finds an uncannily precise counterpart to Lenore Walker's battered wife and abusing spouse in the persecuted wife and egotistical, insecure husband of Hawthorne's "The Birthmark" (Walker 1984, 12, 27–28, 206); Lisa Starks sees a striking analogy between Antoinette in Rhys's *Wide Sargasso Sea* and Walker's profile of the battered wife (1984, 75–86); Phillip Sipiora discovers in the character of Tom Buchanan in Fitzgerald's *The Great Gatsby* a classic example of Davidson's wife beater (1978, 29–30); and Lagretta Lenker identifies Lavinia in Hellman's *Another Part of the Forest* and Birdie and Regina in *The Little Foxes* as exact prototypes of the abusive and abused spouses as sketched by both Davidson (1978, 27, 52) and Walker (1984, 11, 27–28, 87). Furthermore, Helen Popovich and James Keller demonstrate that in all his depictions of spouse abuse, O'Neill etches emotionally deprived characters suffering from deficient self-esteem, who cannot form or maintain loving adult relationships.

Behaviorists discount intrapsychic processes and focus instead on stimulus–response reactions. Although this approach is tangential to most of the analyses in this volume, many of the contributors follow Maria Roy (1982, 3–5) in identifying frustration and powerlessness as catalysts, if not causes, of family violence.

Despite their references to personality profiles and environmental stress, however, the majority of the commentators emphasize the social learning model—the model favored by Bonnie Yegidis (1989) as the most useful in treating and preventing family violence—the belief that violence is strictly a learned behavior and that abusive tendencies are acquired by imitating role models and are reinforced through social approval. Popovich, Keller, and Lenker demonstrate that in the plays of O'Neill and Hellman the sins of the fathers are visited upon the sons and daughters of future generations, as offspring of both genders mimic the tyrannical behavior of their fathers; Rosalie Baum finds a similar cyclic movement in the novels of Faulkner; and Starks observes the degree to which Antoinette reenacts her mother's destructive behavior in *Wide Sargasso Sea*.

In an expansion of the social learning model, other contributors accentuate the social norms that legitimate violence and reinforce the authoritarian control that males exert over females and adults over children in the power structure of society. Rita Gould traces the development of these norms in medieval society, their detrimental effect on the position of women, and their reflection in the literature of the period. Deats attributes the violence in *Othello* to both the negative gender stereotypes of Renaissance society and the deleterious relationships endemic to the patriarchal family, and Starks finds the same destructive ideology operative in *Wide Sargasso Sea*. Harriet Deer, in her innovative reading of *The Taming of the Shrew*, interprets the play as exploring the relationship between theatrical and societal stereotypes and the way in which the creative player, both on the stage and in life, must learn to experiment with and expand limiting dramatic and social conventions. Nancy Tyson reads *Jane Eyre* as a passionate indictment of Victorian attitudes toward courtship and marriage, on the one hand, and children, on the other, views that provide an impediment to genuine love because they encourage the victimization of women by men and children by adults. William Scheuerle interprets *Oliver Twist* as a similar indictment of the stereotypic reduction of children to property and their consequent exploitation in the nineteenth century. Frederika Howie shows how inappropriate role stereotyping distorts the relationship of Nora and Torvald in *A Doll House*. Cline identifies the same pernicious societal attitudes in American literature, particularly stressing the oppression inherent in the double standard of patriarchal marriage. Baum links the maladaptive traits of many of Faulkner's characters to deleterious ideals embedded in Southern culture: the machismo association of power with manliness contributes to the intertwining of violence with love so pervasive in Faulkner's novels and the stereotype of the Southern Belle encourages the narcissism, repression, and masochism so typical of many of Faulkner's female characters. Emma Waters Dawson expands masculine hegemony to include white dominance, interpreting *The Color Purple* as an exposé of the racism and sexism of American society that encourage the persecution of black women by their mates. Finally, Harriet and Irving Deer explore the construction, problematizing, and deconstruction of traditional gender concepts by language and the media.

Focusing on somewhat different, but equally harmful social attitudes, Sipiora relates the aimless drifting of the "peripatetic profligates" in *The Great Gatsby* to the sense of futility experienced by Americans after World War I, seeing in *Gatsby's* psychologically and physically battered lovers and spouses emblems for the battered lives of the "lost generation."

Lastly, Howie, Perez, and Baum find in Henrik Ibsen's controversial play *A Doll House*, in D.H. Lawrence's much debated novel *Sons and Lovers*, and in a number of Faulkner's often analyzed narratives an illustration of the systems theory model, which focuses on the family system as a complex, organic whole in which all deviant behavior derives from the interplay of all forces operating to maintain that system. According to this model, physical and psychological abuse result not exclusively from personality traits, environment frustration, or even familial role models or societal mores, but from the power relationships of individuals within the family.

Not only the four clinical models discussed above but other important clinical theories on family violence find support and illustration in the literary works examined in this volume. The coherence between clinical research and literary representation further validates the reciprocal relationship between literature and social conventions upon which this book is predicated.

At the beginning of human evolution, humanity created language and through language and ritual constructed society. Language, a self-replicating structure, returned the favor and continually recreates humanity and society in the programmed image. Yet the society it constructs is one eternally plagued by war, devastated by crime, consumed by violence. Language and meaning must change if society would change, and this transformation must begin at the beginning of consciousness, in the home. In order to achieve this, humanity must alter the way it regards and discusses marriage and the family. In changing its way of thinking and talking about the family, it will, we submit, alter the way it acts within the family. Utopians dream of a world free of war, a world devoid of crime, a world purged of violence. But such lofty ideals can never be realized until society eliminates crime, violence, and abuse from the most basic social unit, the home, and from the symbol of security and belonging, the hearth. We fervently hope that this book will contribute to that endeavor.

References

"The Abused Woman *Fact Sheet.*" *American College of Obstetricians and Gynecologists News Release* January 3, 1989.

"The Battered Woman," *American College of Obstetricians and Gynecologists Technical Bulletin* 124, January 1989.

Davidson, Terry. *Conjugal Crime: Understanding and Changing the Wifebeating Pattern.* New York: Hawthorne Books, 1978.

Dobash, R. Emerson, and Russell Dobash. *Violence Against Wives: A Case Against the Patriarchy.* New York: Free Press, 1979.

Gelles, Richard J., and Murray Straus. *Intimate Violence.* New York: Simon & Schuster, 1988.

Justice, Blair, and Rita Justice. *The Abusing Family,* rev. ed. New York: Insight Books/Plenum Press, 1990.

Klein, Luella. "Statement." *American College of Obstetricians and Gynecologists News Release* January 3, 1989.

Koop, C. Everett. "Remarks." *American College of Obstetricians and Gynecologists News Release* January 3, 1989.

Roy, Maria, ed. *Battered Women: A Psychosociological Study of Domestic Violence.* New York: Van Nostrand Reinhold, 1977.

Roy, Maria, ed. *The Abusive Partner: An Analysis of Domestic Battering.* New York: Van Nostrand Reinhold, 1982.

Schechter, Susan. *Women and Male Violence: The Visions and Struggles of the Battered Women's Movement.* Boston: South End Press, 1982.

Shengold, Leonard. *Soul Murder: The Effects of Childhood Abuse and Deprivation.* New Haven: Yale University Press, 1989.

Shneidman, Edwin. "The Suicidal Psycho-Logics of *Moby-Dick.*" In Sara M. Deats and Lagretta T. Lenker, eds., *Youth Suicide Prevention: Lessons from Literature,* pp. 15–47. New York: Plenum Press, 1989.

Showalter, Elaine. "Representing Ophelia: Women, Madness, and the Responsibilities of Feminist Criticism." In Patricia Parker and Geoffrey

Hartman, eds., *Shakespeare and the Question of Theory*, pp. 77–94. New York: Methuen, 1985.

Snyder, Susan. "*King Lear* and the Psychology of Dying." *Shakespeare Quarterly*, 33: 449–460, 1982.

Steinmetz, Suzanne K., and Murray A. Straus. "Intra-Family Violence." In Suzanne K. Steinmetz and Murray A. Straus, eds., *Violence in the Family*, pp. 3–25. New York: Harper & Row, 1974.

Straus, Murray. "Normative and Behavioral Aspects of Violence Between Spouses." Paper presented at the Symposium on Violence in Canadian Society, Simon Fraser University, 1977.

Straus, Murray. "Stress and Child Abuse." In C. H. Kempe and R. E. Helfer, eds. *The Battered Child*, 3d ed, pp. 86–103. Chicago: University of Chicago Press, 1980.

Walker, Lenore. *The Battered Woman Syndrome*. New York: Springer, 1984.

Webster's New Collegiate Dictionary. Springfield, MA: Merriam, 1979.

Whitehurst, Robert N. "Alternative Family Structures and Violence-Reduction." In Suzanne K. Steinmetz and Murray A. Straus, eds., *Violence in the Family*, pp. 316–319. New York: Harper & Row, 1974.

Widom, Cathy Spatz. *The Intergenerational Transmission of Violence*. Occasional Papers of the Harry Frank Guggenheim Foundation, no. 4. New York, 1989.

Yegidis, Bonnie. "Family Violence: Contemporary Research and Practice Issues." Paper presented at the 13th Annual Conference on Professional Social Work Development, National Association of Social Workers, Florida Chapter, Tampa, FL, 1989.

2

Speaking the Unspeakable
Family Violence in America in the 1990s

BONNIE L. YEGIDIS

Introduction

During the last 20 years, the professional literature in the social and behavioral sciences addressing family violence has increased markedly. The published research has focused on nearly all aspects of the problem, such as developing incidence data, identifying profiles of abusers and victims, developing explanations of why people are abusive, and so on.

The purpose of this chapter is to provide an overview of how extensive family violence is in contemporary American society, to discuss the psychosocial factors associated with family violence, and to present a summary of the educational, legal, and psychosocial strategies that might stop the family violence cycle.

Family Violence: How Extensive Is It?

Just how much of a problem is family violence in society today? Actually, this has been a difficult question to address because acts of family violence are not typically observed by others. By its nature, family violence takes place in the privacy of the home. In America, we have come to view our homes as our private domain, a place where we can behave as we wish without interference from the outside. This affirmation of the sanctity of the American home has prevented researchers from accurately determining the extent of the problem. Violence against a family member often goes unobserved by others.

Another difficulty in determining an accurate estimate of the problem involves the lack of a standard operational definition of what constitutes family violence. Definitions vary from state to state, from one region of the country to another, and from culture to culture. In one family a slap on the wrist might be considered violence, while in another a whipping with a strap may not.

These two factors, the private nature of the behavior and the lack of a standard definition for what denotes family violence, conspire to make the development of reliable incidence data difficult. At least two large-scale national surveys, however, have been conducted to try to estimate the national incidence of family violence. A summary of the findings from these studies follows.

In 1975, Straus and Gelles used a national probability sample of 2143 people to conduct in-depth interviews for this purpose. In 1985, the study was repeated, using a probability sample of 6002 households interviewed by telephone. The researchers have compared the violence rates over this decade and report the following. For parent-to-child violence, the rate of overall reported violence shows a slight decline for the last 10 years, from 630 per 1000 children in 1975 to 620 per 1000 children in 1985. Thus 62% of the population (or almost two-thirds) reported at least hitting their children. For marital violence, there has also been a slight decrease in reported violence from 121 per 1000 couples in 1975 to 113 per 1000 couples in 1985. These differences are not statistically significant. However, severe child assault is also down approximately 17%, and severe wife assault has decreased about 8% for this same period of time (Straus and Gelles 1986). The decline in reported severe child assault very likely is attributable to the national focus on child abuse reporting and treatment that has evolved since the early 1970s. Every state currently has a mandatory reporting law for child abuse.

With respect to spouse battery, the authors report that while both husbands and wives tend to commit violence against their spouses at about the same rate, the damage that men do to women is greater and often requires medical attention. This is due in part to the difference in physical strength. In addition, they have shown that violence by wives tends to be retaliatory in nature; that is, that women become abusive for reasons of self-defense.

Thus, as of 1985, reported family violence is still relatively high. However, the trend is for a decrease in the two major forms of family violence: child abuse and spouse battery.

The Effects of Family Violence

Social scientists, human service professionals, and the public alike are all concerned with preventing and treating family violence. This is so because the research of the last two decades has documented that the effects of family violence on individuals and families are devastating.

We know now that family violence tends to run in families. Thus being reared in a violent home increases the likelihood of later abusive behavior. The vast majority of literature has shown that children reared in violent homes tend to be violent to their own spouses and children (Parker and Schumaker 1977; Petersen 1980; Silver, Dublin, and Lourie 1969; Steinmetz 1977). This cycle of violence is difficult to interrupt without fairly extensive social and psychological intervention.

In addition, the literature has demonstrated that victims of violence tend to be depressed and suffer from low self-esteem (Sturkie 1987; Hughes 1988). They also suffer the physical problems and symptoms that are a direct result of having been battered. These physical and psychological difficulties prevent them from developing healthy interpersonal relationships and often cause them to abuse themselves or others. In addition, a new literature is emerging that suggests that young victims of sexual abuse may develop problems of self-abuse and eating disorders.

Finally, victims of family violence may become homicide or suicide victims. A recent issue of *Criminology* magazine showed that 12% of all killings in the United States from 1976 to 1985 involved spouses, former spouses, or lovers (as reported by Malcolm 1990). Thus, there is the distinct possibility that family violence may result in the death of either the abuser or the perpetrator (Browne 1987).

Social Factors Associated with Family Violence

The research of the 1970s identified the major sociological correlates of family violence. Abusive families tend to be socially isolated and poor, experiencing multiple sources of environmental stress. They have poor capacities for survival and coping. Characteristically, they are likely to be overrepresented as racial or ethnic minorities with educational limitations and occupational difficulties (Yegidis 1989). As Garbarino has said, "Being poor is bad for families" (1977).

This particular set of social factors leads to difficulties in interpersonal relations. Abused families have few resources, either economic or personal, and hence they have limited options for dealing with stress and frustration. Of course it does not follow that all impoverished families tend to use family violence as a coping mechanism. The mediating variable is the psychological reality of the family members. This will be discussed in the next section.

Psychological Factors Associated with Family Violence

Most research on the psychological environment of violent families shows that the adult members of the family feel powerless to effect changes in their lives. They tend to be immature, poor copers with low self-esteem and strong dependency needs. This means that they rely on others to take care of them. When these dependency needs are met, they are comfortable. But if they are unable to get others to take care of them, their hostility breaks through. In addition, violent families display poor communication skills, recurrent family and marital stress, inappropriate behavior expectations of the victim, role confusion or role reversal, and an overreliance on physical punishment for disciplining. Thus, violent families tend to be stressed both interpersonally and intrapersonally. They have difficulty coping with life's demands and are poorly prepared to meet their needs and the needs of their families.

Moreover, there is a strong association between family violence and alcohol abuse. Alcohol has been shown to be an immediate antecedent of wife abuse in approximately 25% of reported instances (Kantor and Straus 1987). Alcohol and/or drug abuse reduces the inhibitions that one might ordinarily have about being abusive toward a family member. In other words, being drunk or drugged allows one to do more easily what one wishes. However, most research that has examined the relationship between alcohol and family violence has consistently concluded that alcohol is neither a necessary nor a sufficient explanation for family violence, although it is one factor strongly associated with it.

The Predominant Theory of Family Violence

One can enumerate as many as 16 theories that have been used to explain family violence (Lewis 1983). However, one theory predominates as perhaps the most useful in terms of prevention and treatment; this theory is known as social learning theory. According to Bandura (1977), social learning is conceptualized by both a modeling component and the concept of "reciprocal influence." Reciprocal influence means that we influence our environments and can therefore in part shape our futures. O'Leary (1988) has applied this theory to the study of violent families and has developed five major variables that taken together explain family violence from this perspective. These variables are: (1) the effects of modeling on behavior, (2) the role of stress, (3) the use of alcohol, (4) the presence of relationship dissatisfaction, and (5) aggression as a personality style. A summary of these factors and a description of how each contributes to creating a violent family is presented below.

1. The effects of modeling on behavior. Modeling is the observation of physical aggression by parents or the direct experience of having been abused oneself. Modeling increases the likelihood that one will use violence to resolve difficulties, since this has been the course of action used by one's parents. In a study of spouse battery which I conducted a few years ago, I discovered that viewing parental violence was just as important in establishing a later pattern of abuse as was the direct experience of child abuse (Yegidis 1989).

2. The role of stress. There is an extensive literature in psychology describing the relationship between stress, frustration, and aggression (see, for example, Staub 1971; Farrington 1980). While the presence of stress in and of itself does not cause violence, it may function as a stimulus to arouse some individuals. Thus, in the face of a stressor and perhaps influenced

by having viewed parental aggression, one might choose a violent course of action.

3. The use of alcohol. The relationship between alcohol and violence has already been presented. Research on this topic suggests that there may be two important aspects to this relationship, both the disinhibiting effect that alcohol has on behavior and an expectancy effect. The expectancy effect means that people expect to act a certain way when they are under the influence of alcohol and may behave this way, even if they are not really drunk.

4. The presence of relationship dissatisfaction. Obviously, some degree of marital or family discord must be present for violence to occur. Analyses of typical spouse-battering events show that there is first a tension-building state, then an eruption that is typically verbal (an argument), and finally the violent encounter (Hilbermann 1980). Research examining the relationship between psychological abuse and physical abuse has concluded that psychological aggression precedes and predicts physical violence (Murphy and O'Leary 1989).

5. Aggression as a personality style. Individuals with aggressive personality styles become angry more often than others and express their anger as aggression. These individuals are thus more likely to be abusive to family members than other people are. These individuals also tend to minimize or deny this kind of behavior, which means that they are not easily accessible to psychological intervention.

A synthesis of these five factors provides a framework for explaining family violence from the social learning perspective. This framework also lays the foundation for intervention strategies.

What Can Be Done to Stop Family Violence?

There are a number of different types of educational, criminal justice/legal, and psychosocial strategies designed to stop the family violence cycle. A summary of these strategies follows.

Educational Strategies

In most communities, educational programs exist that have as their primary goal teaching people to be more effective as parents. These programs teach participants about the kinds of behaviors that are normal for children at particular developmental stages. This is important content because abusive parents typically have inappropriate expectations of their children. For example, they may get angry with a nine-month-old baby for not responding to them when they say "no." In addition to material on child development, these programs typically teach parents how to discipline their children without using violence. Specific curricula on this topic vary widely, but frequently this content refers to structuring the environment so that children can play safely and teaching parents behavioral management through reinforcement contingencies. An example of the latter would be removing privileges for children who misbehave. Often these educational programs also teach parents self-management skills. This refers to helping parents learn to manage stress more productively, learn anger management strategies, and develop better interpersonal communication skills. These interventions are primarily educational. They often are offered by community social service agencies, such as family service or mental health agencies.

Other kinds of educational programs are more long-term in nature. For example, school programs that teach young people about the effect of drugs and alcohol on behavior or about family planning play a role in developing healthy family lives. Also, family life education programs help people develop more realistic attitudes about children and family responsibilities and should also promote healthy family functioning.

Criminal Justice Strategies

In many states the statutes, criminal justice, and legal procedures have been modified to protect victims of family violence. As reported earlier, all states currently have mandatory child abuse reporting laws. These laws make it a crime for a person in a caregiving/teaching role not to report child abuse when there is the suspicion. Also, the laws protect people from liability if the report is made in good faith.

In addition to mandatory reporting of child abuse, many states have made marital rape a crime. And a number of states have a reporting "hotline" for abused elders.

Changes in statutes are important because they signify a change in social attitudes. The change communicates to abusers that their behavior will no longer be tolerated by society and that criminal sanctions will be brought to bear against them. This is a message that abusers need to hear because often they believe they can behave with impunity with family members.

In addition, a number of states and/or local police municipalities also have a policy of mandatory, prompt, or preferred arrest for perpetrators of domestic violence. These policies enable law enforcement personnel to arrest an abuser if there is cause to believe that an act of abuse has occurred or will likely occur. In addition, these policies remove the victim from the role of complainant; the state becomes the complainant. This is significant because often victims of family violence refuse to press charges against their husbands. Thus, in these cases, the state may prosecute perpetrators of abuse even if the spouse chooses not to. This sends a message to the abuser, "Your behavior is unacceptable and will not be tolerated."

In addition to these arrest procedures, some communities have also been able to arrange mandatory, court-ordered treatment for the abuser. This kind of an arrangement typically means that the alleged abuser can either receive a sentence from the judge or participate in a psychoeducational program designed to treat batterers. Obviously, if the goal of intervention is to stop the battering cycle, then psychological treatment is frequently necessary.

Psychosocial Strategies

There are a number of programs designed to "treat" both victims and perpetrators of family violence. Spouse abuse shelters are now a resource in most communities. These programs provide a safe refuge for battered women and their children. Typically, victims remain in a shelter program for several weeks, while they secure legal advice, help in getting concrete services (such as food or housing), and medical attention. In addition, shelter programs usually offer at least some of the educational programs described earlier in this section, such as self-management skills and parent education, as well as social support for the victims. Increasingly, shelter programs are also offering a component of treatment for abusers. They may offer this as part of the shelter program or provide it on an outpatient basis.

In addition to shelter programs, most communities employ mental health providers to offer individual, group, and/or family therapy for abusive people. The literature on treatment effectiveness has generally concluded that marital or family therapy is only effective once the violence is already under control (Deschner 1984). Once the abusive behavior ceases, then relationship difficulties may be addressed, and couples may be taught to communicate and resolve problems more constructively.

For most kinds of abuse, group treatment has been used very successfully. Support groups for victims are also important. Not only do these groups provide friendship, but they help victims to see that they are not alone and that their reactions to abuse are valid. These kinds of experiences are therapeutically valuable and cannot as easily be offered in individual counseling. Of course, some victims and some abusers will also need individual treatment to help them resolve their difficulties. This decision is most appropriately made by a mental health professional trained in psychosocial assessment.

This, then, is the profile of family abuse in America in the 1980s. The comparison study of Straus and Gelles (1986) suggests with guarded optimism that some of the intervention strategies outlined in this essay may be having an effect. Yet there is much more to be done. An honest confrontation with this critical societal problem is one of the central challenges facing America today—a challenge affecting not only social workers, counselors, psychologists, and law enforcement personnel, but the entire community.

References

Bandura, A. *Social Learning Theory.* Englewood Cliffs, NJ: Prentice-Hall, 1977.

Browne, A. *When Battered Women Kill.* New York: Free Press, 1987.

Deschner, J. P. *The Hitting Habit: Anger Control for Battered Couples.* New York: Free Press, 1984.

Farrington, F. "Stress and Family Violence." In M. Straus and C. Hotaling, eds. *The Social Causes of Husband-Wife Violence.* Minneapolis: University of Minnesota Press, 1980.

Garbarino, J. "The Human Ecology of Child Maltreatment." *Journal of Marriage and the Family* 39 (4): 721–735, 1977.

Hilbermann, E. "Overview: The Wife Beater's Wife Reconsidered." *American Journal of Psychiatry* 137: 1336–1347, 1980.

Hughes, H. M. "Psychological and Behavioral Correlates of Family Violence in Child Witnesses and Victims." *American Journal of Orthopsychiatry* 58 (1): 77–90, 1988.

Kantor, G., and M. Straus " 'The Drunken Bum' Theory of Wife Beating." *Social Problems* 34 (3): 213–230, 1987.

Lewis, B. *The Development and Initial Validation of the Wife Abuse Inventory.* University Microfilms International, no. 8329175, 1983.

Murphy C., and K. D. O'Leary. "Psychological Aggression Predicts Physical Aggression in Early Marriage." *Journal of Consulting and Clinical Psychology* 57 (5): 579–582, 1989.

Parker, B., and D. Schumaker. "The Battered Wife Syndrome and Violence in the Nuclear Family of Origin: A Controlled Pilot Study." *American Journal of Public Health* 67 (8): 760–761, 1977.

Petersen, R. "Social Class, Social Learning and Wife Abuse." *The Social Science Review* 54: 390–416, 1980.

Silver, L., C. Dublin, and R. Lourie. "Does Violence Breed Violence? Contributions from a Study of the Child Abuse Syndrome." *American Journal of Psychiatry* 126: 404–407, 1969.

Staub, E. "The Learning and Unlearning of Aggression." In J. Singer, ed., *The Control of Aggression and Violence.* New York: Academic Press, 1971.

Steinmetz, S. *The Cycle of Violence: Assertive, Aggressive, and Abusive Family Interaction.* New York: Praeger, 1977.

Straus, M., and R. Gelles. "Societal Change and Change in Family Violence from 1975–1985 as Revealed by Two National Surveys." *Journal of Marriage and the Family* 48: 465–479, 1986.

Sturkie, K., and J. Flanzer. "Depression and Self-Esteem in the Families of Maltreated Adolescents." *Social Work* 32 (6): 491–495, 1987.

Yegidis, B. "Family Violence: Contemporary Research and Practice Issues." Paper presented at the 13th Annual Conference on Professional Social Work Development, National Association of Social Workers, Florida Chapter, Tampa, FL, March 31–April 2, 1989.

3

When Victims Become Survivors*
Poetry and Battered Women

NICHOLAS MAZZA

A Family Matter

She left in the middle of the night
battered and broken
leaving it all behind her
with her broken dreams.
"He's really sorry, you know."

Long sleeves and turtlenecks
A little too much make-up
Layers of resignation
Covering purple and scarlet reminders.
"He really couldn't help it."

Secrets to share with no one.
Carefully concealed
Visible to no one's eye
Like the bruise on her heart.
"He promised—no more."

---

* The title of this chapter is taken from the poem "Good-bye and Hello" by Jae Levine-
Schneider, (1989). The entire poem appears on pp. 42–44.

> A new day will dawn
> and she will return
> to his empire,
> like a queen to her king
> to play the scene over again and again.
> "But I still love him."
>
> (Judith M. Curran 1989, 279)

Judith Curran's poem vividly portrays the cycle of violence in abusive relationships that is so well documented in the professional literature. Barbara Mathias describes family violence as "the slap that is felt for generations" (1986, 20). There are many such visions associated with such terms as "spouse abuse," "battered women," "family/domestic violence," "victim," and "maltreatment," and few are as poetic as Curran's verse or Mathias's verbal image. Recognizing spouse abuse (including abuse between couples not legally married) as a serious form of family violence, this chapter will explore the surprisingly pertinent role of poetry in understanding and healing battered women.

Elizabeth Torre discusses drama as a consciousness-raising strategy for the self-empowerment of working women. She notes that drama "is a different way of approaching the truth" (1990, 51). Indeed, spouse abuse may be approached very differently by the various professionals or agencies providing service to the victim (e.g., therapist, police officer, physician, shelter worker). Poetry, like drama and other arts, provides another perspective or "way of approaching the truth." When the poet is also the victim, the perspective becomes even more compelling.

Battered women's experiences, reactions, and methods of coping with abuse can be expressed through the language and imagery of poetry. Kris Kissman notes that there are numerous examples of women's poetry that show how creativity can be used as a survival mechanism:

> Women who are isolated with their "secrets" of battering, rape and incest can tie into the collective and communal network of the written word which is rich in metaphors about women's experiences. (1989, 225).

The publication of poetry in women's shelter/program newsletters across the country is one example of how the network is being strengthened.

Treatment Approaches

Poetry therapy and related arts therapies can be useful adjunctive techniques in the treatment of victims of family violence (Mazza, Magaz, and Scaturro 1987). Crisis intervention is the most common form of treatment for the battered woman and necessarily involves such practical matters as ensuring the safety and well-being of the victim and her children. It should also be noted that the word "crisis" is a very subjective term and that many women at risk would not describe their situation as a crisis. For these women and their families, violence is the norm. Brief treatment that involves "the planned use of a number of therapeutic interventions aimed at the achievement of limited goals within a limited time frame" (Mazza 1987, 81) is another appropriate form of treatment for battered women. Given that the helping professional may be working with the victim for only a brief time, poetry therapy can serve as a catalyst to promote change, and as a means to extend the work of therapy beyond a particular session. It should be noted, however, that the use of the poetic in clinical practice with battered women must be consistent with both program objectives (e.g., build trust, provide a sense of security, raise self-esteem, develop self-empowerment) and therapeutic orientation. For the social worker, treatment goes beyond direct clinical practice to include social responsibility for identifying human rights issues and serving as an advocate for those victimized. The poetry and prose of battered women and those sensitive to their experiences offer a form of qualitative research that compels us to interventive and preventive action. Literary works dealing with spouse abuse challenge us to look at this "private problem" as a public issue. In short, clinical practice and social responsibility are intricately related. The following poetic techniques are useful in working with victims and the larger system of which they are a part.

Preexisting Poems

This technique involves reading a carefully selected poem to an individual or group and inviting reactions. Shame and stigma are often associated with being a battered woman; battered women thus frequently feel isolated and alone. Sharing either a poem or a pre-recorded piece of music with accompanying lyrics that corresponds to the victim's mood or problem can help validate and universalize the victim's feelings. The poetry can thus serve as a catalyst for self-disclosure and/or group discussion. Tracy Chapman's song "Behind the Wall" (1983) includes lines that deplore the futility of calling the police. This song is a valuable means of allowing victims the opportunity to share their own experiences. By beginning to talk about the song, they inevitably talk about themselves. By emotionally identifying with the song, battered women are able to validate their own experience (e.g., feeling trapped), seek alternative solutions (e.g., in a crisis situation, you might not have time to rely on the police), or dispel myths (e.g., some police departments have a pro-arrest policy and are sensitive to victim problems).

"The Road Not Taken" by Robert Frost is an excellent poem to use in dealing with the pressures of choice a battered woman experiences in trying to decide whether to act or to refrain from taking any new action (e.g., separate from her husband, go to a shelter, seek therapy, call the police). The following three lines are particularly effective:

> Two roads diverged in a wood, and I—
> I took the one less traveled by,
> And that has made all the difference. (1964, 131)

The poem can be employed to review with the victim the choices she has made in the past regarding personal, family, and social matters. If she has left her husband in the past, what prompted the decision? What was the outcome? Looking at her current situation, what are her alternatives? If she chooses to stay, what is her safety plan?

Many abused women are able to make an emotional identification with the poem, "After a While." The following lines are particularly noteworthy:

> After a while you learn/The subtle difference
> between/holding a hand/and chaining a soul.

> So you plant your own garden/and decorate
> your own soul/instead of waiting
> for someone to bring you/flowers.
> And you learn/that you really can endure
> that you really are strong
> and you really have worth. (© 1971 Veronica A. Shoffstall)

The above poem instills hope by identifying common feelings that abused women experience. The poem also calls victims to action and affirms their self-worth.

Creative Writing

The use of written self-expression has relevance for both assessment and treatment. Journal/diary entries and poetry provide the victim with a vehicle to express emotion and gain a sense of order and control. The following lines from "Scars," a poem written by a battered woman, demonstrate the far-reaching impact that abuse has on the woman in a later relationship:

> Once again, I hear the sound
> inside me, of shattering glass
> . . . .
> It isn't You. Forgive me, please . . . (A. K. 1988/89, 1)

Creative writing could also be prestructured through the use of sentence stems such as "When I am alone. . . " or "If you knew me. . . " One technique is to create collaborative poems whereby each group member is given the opportunity to contribute one or more lines to the poem. The following is an excerpt of a collaborative poem written by a women's group that included several victims of spouse abuse:

> my control
> is my protector
> of my feelings
>
> it is also my cage
>
> looking for a balance
> where?
>
> inside . . . (Mazza 1988, 490)

The collaborative poem generates a feeling of accomplishment and fosters group cohesion. It validates the group's feelings. Copies of the collaborative poem may be made for discussion in a subsequent session. Group members may choose to discuss the poem further, or, at the very least, they have validation of the previous week's work.

The use of journal writing is an especially powerful tool in working with battered women. Raymond Fox (1982) and Alice Glarden Brand (1979) note a number of the advantages of employing personal documents in therapy, such as the log, diary, or journal. This technique encourages internal examination, increases attention upon self-reporting and observation, provides continuity between therapy sessions, promotes competence through the discipline required to write about oneself, facilitates expression of feelings, and offers a creative outlet. The journal and other writing assignments require that work take place outside the therapy session; however, the review of such material at the discretion of the client allows her control and the opportunity for continuity between sessions.

Metaphors, Imagery, and Language

Using poetic expression, imagery, or symbols derived from the client's language and experience can also serve a therapeutic function. The May/June (1986) issue of *The Family Therapy Networker* was subtitled, with accompanying artwork, "Lifting the Shade on Family Violence" (Mathias 1986). This image vividly captures the sense of secrecy and isolation obscuring spouse abuse and compels us to expand our vision. In a clinical situation, a person who frequently refers to "home" could be asked to draw, write, or talk about a house. What does it look like? Who is in it? In working with victims of abuse, very powerful images often emerge (e.g., being beaten, shattered glass, verbal abuse, arrival of a police car, terrified children). Healing involves the discharge of powerful emotions in a safe environment, with appropriate support and guidance.

Clinical Issues

Lenore Walker's (1979, 1984) research identifies a three-phase cycle of violence that the battered woman experiences:

1. The tension-building phase. In this phase the woman has some control over the incidences of violence and can perhaps prevent violence by meeting the batterer's domestic demands (e.g., keep the children quiet, make the proper meal). The demands, however, increase and it becomes more difficult to

keep the batterer calm. Judith Curran's poem, "Just Like Dad" makes reference to this stage: "She should know better than to burn the roast./ or say something stupid/ or leave the house without him/. . . " (1989, 278).

2. The acute battering incident. It often occurs without warning. Tracy Chapman's song, "Behind the Wall" (1983), includes a reference to screaming in the night that is followed by silence and the arrival of an ambulance.

3. The kind-loving contrition. This is often referred to as the "honeymoon" or "hearts and flowers" stage. Tension is reduced following the explosion. The man asks for forgiveness and promises never to hit her again. In Judith Curran's "A Family Matter," the following lines close the first three stanzas: "He's really sorry, you know/. . . /He really couldn't help it/. . . /He promised no more." The last stanza affirms the cycle:

> A new day will dawn
> and she will return
> to his empire,
> like a queen to her king
> to play the scene over
> again and again.
> "But I still love him." (1989, 279)

Lenore Walker (1987) notes that there are five basic areas that must be recognized by the helping professional working with battered women: manipulation, expression of anger, dissociation, denial, and compliance. I will proceed to examine each area from a poetic perspective.

Manipulation

Battered women often maintain unrealistic expectations regarding their ability to calm the batterer by doing everything perfectly. Failure to succeed evokes guilt. Natasha Josefowitz's poem, "Can't Do It All" addresses the issue of making choices. It closes with the lines, "Not everything worth doing/is worth doing well" (1983, 10). The inability or reluctance of the victim to express emotion could also be addressed through the popular song recorded by Melissa Man-

chester, "Don't Cry Out Loud." It includes the lines; "Just keep it inside/ learn how to hide your feelings/. . . " (Allen and Sager 1976).*
An exploration of the victim's reaction is necessary because it is possible for her to construe these lines as advocating that she control her feelings.

The battered woman is often reluctant to share information openly in a therapeutic setting as she has learned to try to resolve problems on her own and to protect the batterer. Poetry offers a way for the victim to express herself while, at the same time, maintaining control over what to keep to herself and what to share.

Expression of Anger

Poetry can provide the structure for battered women to express the anger and rage that they have contained in order to protect themselves and their children. The lines from Langston Hughes's poem, "Harlem"—"What happens to a dream deferred?/. . . /maybe it just sags/ Like a heavy load. /Or does it explode?" (1970)—could offer the opportunity for the battered woman to discuss her own personal experiences and perhaps identify what keeps her from exploding. Or, if the battered woman does fight back, the poem could become a springboard to a discussion of the feelings and events leading to her present circumstance. The following stanza is from Deborah Eve Grayson's "Raggedy Ann Takes a Stand":

> After 18 years of
> belittling and battering,
> of hiding in closets
> and behind locked doors,
> she stood in death-silent defiance
> serving him divorce papers,
> her diamond shining shameless
> like the blade of a shrewd stiletto. (1985)

The reference to the stiletto is, of course, symbolic. This poem shows a victim taking a constructive and seemingly successful new action to combat the abuse and affirm herself. In some situations, the battered woman, feeling trapped, threatened, and overwhelmed, resorts to killing (Browne 1987). The following lines of verse are from a victim who is serving a life sentence for the shooting death of her abusive and alcoholic husband: "I have just. . . /returned. . . /from the. . . / visiting room. . . /and I watched/ as my children. . . /walked away. . . / and so. . . alone. . . /I weep. . . (D.B. 1989)

Dissociation or Splitting

In order to cope with overwhelming pain of being abused, many women report a mind and body split whereby they separate the pain from the beating while the battering is occurring. This fragmentation is a defense mechanism that sometimes helps the victim to survive; however, it also often leads her to question her own mental health. It is important for the therapist to support the victim while helping her to gain self-control and integrate mind and body. David Loggins's song "So You Couldn't Get to Me" (1974) expresses, through images of an island and a room, the need to get away from a hurtful partner. The song could assist the therapist in making a crucial connection with the victim's experience and perhaps through the use of a creative writing exercise help the victim to recognize the pain and begin the rebuilding integrative process.

Denial or Minimization

This is a defense mechanism that allows the victim to endure the abuse and cope with the ensuing depression. It also reduces the victim's self-esteem. The denial also encourages the hope that somehow the batterer will change and the honeymoon phase will return. Asking the victim to keep a log or journal will provide a measure of reality that can be useful in a therapeutic situation. Employing sentence stems such as "I used to be . . . But now I'm . . . " (Koch 1970, 156) can also be a valuable technique to help instill hope and a vision.

Compliance and Willingness to Please

Compliance and an attempt to please people in authority positions are other common behaviors employed by battered women to try to prevent violent episodes. This general compliance also includes rescuing behavior (e.g., covering up for him). Nikki Giovanni's poem, "Woman," refers to a series of efforts on the part of the woman to engage her partner (lover). For example, "she turned herself into a bulb/ but he wouldn't let her grow" (1980, 71). The poem concludes with the woman's affirmation of her own decision-making.

Voices from the Shelters

Published poems and songs by popular artists can offer much in exploring the plight of battered women, providing hope to the victims and educating the public. However, one area that warrants special attention is the poetry published in the newsletters of women's centers and shelters across the country. Arleen Hynes notes that "the most accessible source of material that expresses women's feelings about violence and its effects will be found in the newsletters published by women's shelters" (1987, 115). A comprehensive review of the collection of newsletters at the National Victim Center Library in Fort Worth, Texas, indicates that many of newsletters relating to spouse abuse publish poetry. Further review also indicates that a number of the shelters incorporate the arts, including literature, in working with the victim's children.

The following poems by Jae Levine-Schneider, a former resident of the Haven Hills Shelter, were published in the *Haven Hills News* (Spring, 1989), a newsletter sponsored by the Family Violence Center of San Fernando Valley in Canoga Park, California.

Good-bye and Hello

Look one last time
Around this room
And see the bonfire
Burning bright
In the gathering of
What was once
Dying embers
Flickering flames
Ignited by care's kindling

We came to you
Hoping to find
A fairy godmother

Who would wave
Her magic wand
To save us
But you taught us instead
That the power
To go home to ourselves
Was in the tapping
Of our own ruby shoes

We were broken winged birds
You mended our feathers
Then urged us, trembling
Out of the nest
And watched with pride
As, to our amazement,
We soared

You've been the lighthouse
Guiding us safely
Through confusion's fog
You became winter's overcoat
In the storm
Our highway's crossing guard
A warm hand pressed
To tear stained cheeks

You showed us that battered
Doesn't have to mean beaten
And that fear becomes courage
When victims become survivors
We emerged from despair's isolation
Into the compassion and friendship
That took the loneliness
Out of being alone
We've supported each other's struggles
Shared sadness and frustration
And heard for the first time
The beautiful sound
Of our own laughter

You were the gardener
Who saw in us
The seeds of flowers
Needing watering to bloom

And now your garden surrounds you
An array of brilliant colors
Blossomed by your nurturing
Survival's rainbow

It's hard to end
What we've become together
But you've been woven into
The fabric of our hearts
It will be your voice we hear
Each time we say, "Yes, I can"
And our courage will be what you see
Each time you look into
A frightened woman's eyes
We can't say good-bye to you
That word just seems too sad
So we're turning on
Your answering service instead
So you will still be there
Saying hello

Under Control

I thought
That if I kept my feelings to myself
I could touch and go
And not get hurt
I thought
That if I didn't expect anything
Getting nothing wouldn't disappoint
me
I thought
That if I didn't permit entrance into
my life
It wouldn't feel empty
When no one but me was in it
I thought
That if I was only what I thought he
wanted
He would want who he thought I
was
I thought
That if I ran first

I wouldn't feel rejected
When he didn't run after me
I thought
That if I learned not to cry
I would never feel sadness
again
I thought
That if I could act as if
I didn't care
I wouldn't
I thought
That I'd never let my cracked
heart
Bleed again
I thought
Wrong

Dead Roses

Guilt sells a lot of flowers
And I've tossed more
Than my fair share
Of dead roses
In the trash
Meant to erase
Pain's face
The scum unscrubbed
From crystal vases
Is all that remains
Of what I once
Believed was love

"Good-bye and Hello" sensitively captures the pain and despair experienced upon entering the shelter, the relationships within the shelter that fostered hope, the realization of individual strength in facing great difficulties, the power of receiving and giving support, and the journey toward survival. In short, the poem provides a vision and a voice for those who have suffered the abuse and others who care about ending the violence.

"Under Control" accurately dispels the myth that a woman has control over a man's violent behavior. In this poem the victim tells her story of trying to control her feelings and her environment, hoping that she would be protected and somehow endure. She closes the poem, "I thought/Wrong."

"Dead Roses" portrays the cyclical nature of spouse abuse. The poem relates specifically to the third "hearts and flowers" stage in which the man asks for forgiveness and the relationship continues only to lead to the next tension-building phase and the subsequent violent episode. In addition to providing insight into the experience, the poem also expresses a healthy anger and affirms the closure of the relationship.

Poetic Perspectives

Irene Hanson Frieze (1987) observes that the beliefs of battered women and the lack of external resources are often the reasons why battered women stay in abusive relationships. The following poetic perspectives drawn from victim newsletters, popular poetry, and personal communications illustrate those reasons.

Beliefs

- The violence is temporary.
    "didn't hurt that much/ and I know it was just/ one of those things . . . " (Anonymous)
- Husband's problem would get worse if she left him. He needs her.
    "Guilt sells a lot of flowers" (Jae Levine-Schneider, Haven Hills News, Canoga Park, CA, 1989)
- Responsibility to keep the marriage together.
    "In the beginning love was simple/ It was meant to last/ But the pain endured so love could last/. . . / The woman held on; the man let go. . . " (by Jennifer Nelson, *The Sojournal,* Phoenix, AZ, 1989)
- Violence is the male norm.
    "Bashed again/ my fault . . . " (Anonymous)
    and
    "I hope that when I get married,
    my wife is a perfect cook
    and beautiful and smart and never makes mistakes,

so I won't have to hurt her too bad" (from "Just Like Dad" by Judith Curran 1989, 278)
- She is incompetent and could not function alone.
  "I do not need to be secured by you/ I am secure with myself" (by R. Annette Harris, shelter worker, *Rosewood*, Pittsburgh, PA, 1989).
  and
  "I thought love would adapt itself/ to my needs/. . . / Such needful love has to be chopped out/ or forced to wilt back" (from "Did This Happen to Your Mother?" by Alice Walker 1979, 2–3).

External Resources

- She does not have the monetary resources to survive independently.
  "You showed us that battered
  Doesn't have to mean beaten
  And that fear becomes courage
  When victims become survivors"
  (From "Good-bye and Hello" by Jae Levine-Schneider 1989)
- She is unable to protect herself against a violent retaliation.
  "All you hear; you do not speak
  To others in the street
  What did you say, Jenny Lee is dead.
  How did that happen to her now?
  Oh, someone told her hubby Bo. . .
  I told you that you do not speak
  of confidences,
  In the street" (from "Confidentiality" by Betty Lane, shelter worker/community organizer, 1988)
- She has no friends or family that can help. A shelter is unavailable.
  This is perhaps where the brightest hope shines:
  When victims become survivors/ in the warmth of sisterhood's embraces/ we emerged from despair's isolation/ into compassion and friendship. . ."
  (from "Good-bye and Hello" by Jae Levine-Schneider 1989)

Conclusions

The focus of this chapter has been limited to a consideration of poetry and battered women. However, although the number of reported victims is much smaller, and the physical harm less severe, a serious problem exists for male victims of spouse abuse. Also, the problem of mutually combative partners has not been addressed in this chapter. The place of poetry in the treatment of abused children has been addressed in another study (see Mazza *et al.* 1987); however, further research is needed. The perspectives and problems of the abuser warrant attention if we are to understand fully the dynamics of the abuse. An examination of literary works, particularly the poetry and music that children and adults are exposed to and create, may offer some of the most powerful research available to understand and reduce family violence. The theme of the 1988 Tenth Anniversary Conference Meeting of the National Coalition Against Domestic Violence, "The Battered Women's Movement: Bringing the Vision Home," offers a direction. Poetry offers a perspective and a promise in a journey toward peace in and out of the home.

Acknowledgment. The author would like to thank Cindy Lea Arbelbide, Librarian at the National Victim Center Library in Fort Worth, Texas, for her assistance in researching victim newsletters.

References

Brand, Alice Glarden. "The Uses of Writing in Psychotherapy." *Journal of Humanistic Psychology* 19: 53–72, 1979.

Browne, Angela. *When Battered Women Kill.* New York: Free Press, 1987.

Fox, Raymond. "The Personal Log: Enriching Clinical Practice." *Clinical Social Work Journal* 10: 94–102, 1982.

Frieze, Irene Hanson. "The Female Victim: Rape, Wife Beating, and Incest." In Gary R. VandenBos and Brenda K. Bryant, eds., *Cataclysms, Crises, and Catastrophes: Psychology in Action,* pp. 113–145. Washington, DC: American Psychological Association, 1987.

Hynes, Arleen. "Biblio/Poetry Therapy in Women's Shelters." *American Journal of Social Psychiatry* 7: 112–116, 1987.

Kissman, Kris. "Poetry and Feminist Social Work." *Journal of Poetry Therapy* 2: 221–230, 1989.

Koch, Kenneth. *Wishes, Lies, and Dreams: Teaching Children to Write Poetry.* New York: Harper & Row, 1970.

Mathias, Barbara. "Lifting the Shade on Family Violence." *Family Therapy Networker* 10: 20–29, 1986.

Mazza, Nicholas. "Poetic Approaches in Brief Psychotherapy." *American Journal of Social Psychiatry* 7: 81–83, 1987.

Mazza, Nicholas. "Poetry and Popular Music as Adjunctive Psychotherapy Techniques." In Peter A. Keller and Steven R. Heyman, eds., *Innovations in Clinical Practice: A Source Book,* vol. 7, pp. 484–494. Sarasota, FL: Professional Resource Exchange, Inc., 1988.

Mazza, Nicholas, Christina Magaz, and Joanne Scaturro. "Poetry Therapy with Abused Children." *The Arts in Psychotherapy* 14: 85–92, 1987.

Torre, Elizabeth. "Drama as a Consciousness-Raising Strategy for the Self-Empowerment of Working Women." *AFFILIA: Journal of Women and Social Work* 5: 49–65, 1990.

Walker, Lenore, E. *The Battered Woman.* New York: Harper & Row, 1979.

Walker, Lenore E. *The Battered Woman Syndrome.* New York: Springer, 1984.

Walker, Lenore E. "Assessment and Intervention with Battered Women." In Peter A. Keller and Steven R. Heyman, eds., *Innovations in Clinical Practice: A Source Book,* vol. 6, pp. 131–142. Sarasota, FL: Professional Resource Exchange, Inc., 1987.

Poems

B., D. "I have just . . . " *HAVIN Hotline* (newsletter). Kittanning, PA: Helping Abuse Victims in Need, Inc., 1989.

Curran, Judith M. "A Family Matter." *Journal of Poetry Therapy* 2: 279, 1989.

Curran, Judith M. "Just Like Dad." *Journal of Poetry Therapy* 2: 278, 1989.

Frost, Robert. "The Road Not Taken." In *Complete Poems of Robert Frost,* p. 131. New York: Holt, 1964.

Giovanni, Nikki. "Woman." In *Poems by Nikki Giovanni: Cotton Candy on a Rainy Day,* p. 71. New York: Morrow, 1980.

Grayson, Deborah Eve. "Raggedy Ann Takes a Stand." In Margaret Honton, ed., *The Poet's Job: To Go Too Far.* Columbus, OH: Sophia Books, 1985.

Harris, R. Annette. "I Do Not Need to Be Secured by You." *Rosewood* (newsletter), 116 (Jan.): 7, 1989. Pittsburgh, PA: Women's Center and Shelter of Greater Pittsburgh.

Hughes, Langston. "Harlem." In *The Premier Book of Major Poets,* edited by Anita Dore, 206. Greenwich, CT: Fawcett, 1970.

Josefowitz, Natasha. "Can't Do It All!" In *Is This Where I Was Going? Verses for Women in the Midst of Life,* p. 14. New York: Warner, 1983.

K., A. "The Scars." *The Sojournal* (newsletter), 5 (2) (Winter): 2, 1988/89. Phoenix, AZ: Sojourner Center.

Lane, Betty. "Confidentiality." *Rosewood* (newsletter), 112 (Jan.): 7, 1988. Pittsburgh, PA: Women's Center and Shelter of Greater Pittsburgh.

Levine-Schneider, Jae. "Dead Roses." *Haven Hills News* (Spring): 3, 1989. Canoga Park, CA: Haven Hills Inc., Family Violence Center of the San Fernando Valley.

Levine-Schneider, Jae. "Good-bye and Hello." *Haven Hills News* (Spring): 3, 1989. Canoga Park, CA: Haven Hills Inc., Family Violence Center of the San Fernando Valley.

Levine-Schneider, Jae. "Under Control." *Haven Hills News* (Spring): 3, 1989. Canoga Park, CA: Haven Hills Inc., Family Violence Center of the San Fernando Valley.

Nelson, Jennifer. "New Life." *The Sojournal* (newsletter), 5 (2) (Winter): 4, 1988/89. Phoenix, AZ: Sojourner Center.

Shoffstall, Veronica A. "After a While." Unpublished poem, 1971.

Walker, Alice. "Did This Happen to Your Mother? Did Your Sister Throw Up a Lot?" In *Good Night, Willie Lee, I'll See You In the Morning: Poems by Alice Walker*, pp. 2–3. New York: Dial press, 1979. (Reprint San Diego: Harvest/Harcourt Brace Jovanovich, 1984.)

Songs

Allen, Peter, and Carole Bayer Sager. "Don't Cry Out Loud." Irving Music Inc./ Unichappel, Inc./ BMI, 1976.

Chapman, Tracy. "Behind the Wall." SBK April Music Inc./ Purple Rabbit Music, 1983.

Loggins, Dave. "So You Couldn't Get to Me." Leeds Music Corp./ Antique Music (ASCAP), 1974.

4

Saints, Shrews, and Scapegoats
Misalliances in Medieval Literature

RITA SLAGHT GOULD

> . . . this idea came to him to test her patience with a long trial and
> intolerable things. He said unkind things to her, seemed to be
> angry, and said that his subjects were most discontented with
> her . . . (Boccaccio 1949).

During the last 100 years, more may have been written about spouse
abuse, but the domestic bully flourished equally well during the Middle Ages. Boccaccio's tale of Gualtieri's browbeating of patient Griselda in *The Decameron* eloquently demonstrates that the dehumanizing sport of "mate-baiting" has been practiced for a long time. Before
discussing spouse abuse in literature during the medieval era of Europe and England, I shall first circumscribe the time period, define
spouse abuse, and examine some contemporaneous attitudes that
might have contributed to this deplorable practice.

The Middle Ages dates arbitrarily from the fifth to the fifteenth
centuries. The period is often divided into a "dark ages" and an "age
of chivalry," the two separated by the Norman invasion in 1066 and
the consequent expansion that the invasion brought in the second
half of the eleventh century.

Spouse abuse existed in the Middle Ages, and, as in all periods of history, it was perpetrated more against women than against men. Historically, not only have women been unable to protect themselves against brutality, but, as their usefulness as food gatherers was curtailed by the female debilities of pregnancy, childbearing, and lactation, the judgment that men were innately superior "became formalized in customs, religion, and laws" (Langley and Levy, 1977, 30).

There are various types of abuse: physical, referring to harming the body; sexual, including forced sex or marital rape as well as the withholding of sex or affection; and emotional, which includes threat, humiliation, criticism, ridicule, and harassment (NiCarthy 1982, xxiv). Although sexual and emotional harassment appear more often in the literature of the medieval period than does bodily violence, there are also examples of physical abuse in the works discussed.

Why do men abuse their wives? The answer might lie in the cliché, "We hurt those we love the most"; or, more probably, it is rooted in the fact that men, inculcated from birth to develop the male gender characteristics of strength, authority, and independence, frequently become resentful, even angry, when a woman, the acknowledged "inferior partner," wields power over them. Women, at the same time, having been conditioned to submissiveness and dependence, are often unable to assert their demands (NiCarthy 1982, 3–13).

In order to discuss spouse abuse, it is necessary to examine this practice in a social context because the negative, conventionally accepted attitudes toward the female in the late Middle Ages greatly influenced the treatment of women. While one cannot blame spouse abuse solely on restrictive and negative attitudes toward women, because certainly all abuse did not stem from such prescribed concepts, these attitudes did offer a socially approved justification for abuse.

Although there was undoubtedly discrimination against women in the early Middle Ages, in this period a frontier environment demanded talents; consequently, women were frequently summoned to use all their abilities, both as wives and mothers, and also as administrators, educators, and religious leaders. As a result, there was some "legal recognition of their economic and marital rights" (Wemple 1987, 149). However, as early as *Beowulf*, written in the seventh or eighth century although dating from the first century A.D., one can see women reduced to objects of barter and diplomacy. In the tenth and eleventh centuries, a precarious equality prevailed; women's inheritances and property rights remained in force and practice. In the eleventh through the fourteenth centuries, however, gender became a more significant component in the organization of society, and women began to lose power and position as economic resources became concentrated under male dominion (Stuard 1976, 170). Brutality increased as witch hunts became sanctioned. Three factors in the Middle Ages influenced attitudes toward women: economic, religious, and "conventional."

Contributing to the increasing subjugation of women in the late Middle Ages was, first of all, the institution of the "Roman dowry," in essence a gift to the groom from the bride's family. As capital in the form of dowry was transferred from one family to another, families of marriageable daughters, concerned with the distribution of their assets, imposed marriage restrictions on their female offspring. While brides inherently owned their dowries, they had limited, if any, legal control over them (Stuard 1976, 160–165). And, in this period, divorce was almost unknown (Gies 1984, 185).

A second factor, Christianity, affected attitudes toward women. After three centuries of persecution, Christianity "rout[ed] the gods from the Pantheon and the Lares from the hearths" (Gies 1984, 36) and filled the void with its own doctrines. Church fathers, such as Augustine in the fifth century, codified tenets pertaining to all aspects of everyday life: marriage, divorce, and the protection of children from infanticide and sale.

As late as the twelfth century clerical marriages existed, but controversies arose as women were accused of diverting church revenue to their own or their heirs' uses. This view finally resulted in the condemnation of marriage for parish priests; and it led, as well, to a general distrust of women. Church elders began to respond more to regulations established by a male church hierarchy; and finally men alone were trained for priesthoods in male-only cathedral schools and universities. As a result, women, without similar opportunities for education, found themselves excluded from intellectual discussions, and were, therefore, unable to comment on current gender ideologies. Finally, "[t]he increased complexity and bureaucracy in church, state, and commerce demanded lawyers. In their hands, causal notions [of gender] became legal precedents" (Stuard 1976, 158–166).

In the thirteenth century, Thomas Aquinas, adopting scholarly classical arguments—particularly those of Aristotle—concerning the polar characteristics of men and women, defined man as created in the image of God, tending toward perfection, with woman as the opposite, lacking this tendency. It became fashionable in the medieval period to play with metaphors about the opposite natures of men and women. Although polarization of gender characteristics was not necessarily depreciative of women, such metaphors usually tended toward misogyny.

In much the same way, Christianity split the concept of woman, prefiguring temptation in Eve, the ideal in Mary. Eve, responsible for the fall of man, his suffering and mortality, represents temptation or desire in its most sinful form. Mary, on the other hand, symbolizes love of God, purity, and virginity. In the Middle Ages, from the twelfth through the fifteenth centuries, a cult of Mariolatry swept Europe (Gilbert 1985, 5). Thus, men were ultimately taught to adore women, yet to distrust them. Woman was either goddess or temptress, Madonna or whore.

Also important in the Middle Ages was the phenomenon of courtly love. Courtly love, a literary convention and/or social practice, was a code of attitudes toward love, emphasizing service and fealty to women and sometimes even adoration of "the lady." According to this code, a knight or courtier falls in love at first sight with a beautiful woman, usually married, and suffers silently until he finally expresses his feelings to her. Two conflicting attitudes coalesce in courtly love, one elevating the woman, the other diminishing her. On one hand, the woman is adored as a paragon of virtue. Thus, a man, focusing on a woman, can ultimately raise himself spiritually. As a woman is adored, however, she also becomes an object of desire, with an ultimate goal of physical consummation. Troubadours of the eleventh and twelfth centuries thus sang bawdy songs of love, coupling adoration with desire.

With attention, both positive and negative, focused on women, they were, understandably, lauded for acting in accordance with socially prescribed views of their natures: for fulfilling domestic duties, for obedience to husbands, for passivity, and above all, for restraint of sexuality. With such restraints enforced upon them, however, women naturally were concerned with controlling their fates.

In relating spouse abuse to the literature of the late Middle Ages, one aspect becomes apparent: marriages not based on the love and consent of both parties often resulted in the woman's denying the restraints expected of her. Furthermore, men, by attempting to control the lives of women—forcing their wills upon them—actually lost control, thereby suffering for their shortsightedness.

For example, there are a number of ribald tales in Chaucer and Boccaccio dealing with women who chafe in repressive situations; some stories present May–December marriages in which a wealthy, older man chooses a young bride. Susan Stuard explains that in the high Middle Ages "as dowry awards scaled up so did a husband's age at marriage, while the age at marriage of a wife dropped" (Stuard 1976, 162). Older husbands in these tales, unable to satisfy their wives physically, ultimately pay for this "abuse" of omission. Chaucer's Miller recites a story of a rich old oaf, a carpenter, who married a lusty young wife who "Could skip and sport as a young ram. . . ." Chaucer's Merchant recounts the tale of a knight, who after 60 years of satisfying his fleshly appetites, decided it was time to marry, stating that if a man "cannot always keep to a chaste life,/Religiously he ought to take a wife." His friends "contract" for a young girl, whom the Knight pictures lecherously, delighting in her youth and beauty. Boccaccio further relates the tale of Maestro Mazzeo della Montagna, a surgeon of advanced years, who marries a beautiful girl, she being unfortunately "cold most of the time, since she was not well covered in the doctor's bed." Each story ends with the wife's innovative trickery, which ultimately cuckolds the husband. In the medieval period, however, cuckoldry constituted an extreme form of abuse when one considers, in addition to a man's pain over his wife's infidelity, the importance to him of being assured that his property is passed to his legitimate heirs.

Because of repression, itself a form of abuse, the women in the stories discussed above turn to abuse themselves in the form of cuckoldry. They attempt, in the only ways open to them, to control their own lives and to satisfy the physical sides of their nature, rebelling against the restraints expected of them; and Boccaccio and Chaucer treat their dilemmas with considerable sympathy and understanding. But no character goes so far in her quest for mastery, nor affirms it so openly, as does Chaucer's indomitable Wife of Bath.

According to the Prologue of *The Canterbury Tales,* even the Wife of Bath's appearance demands attention. On her head, she wears a hat as "wide in circuit as a shield," and on her feet, scarlet stockings and "sharp-roweled spurs." The Wife is anything but passive; for example, in her home city of Bath, no other woman would dream of preceding her at the offering for fear of arousing her anger. Having been married five times from the age of twelve, and outliving each of her husbands, the Wife, knowing all about "love," pursues a sixth mate. Obviously she does not fear abuse, rather she has been the abuser, bragging of marrying old men for wealth, except for her last husband, 20 years her junior, whom she married for love.

The Wife is significant for her outspoken statements about repressive attitudes and her open defense of the physical aspects of marriage, as well as of multiple marriages. Only an individual with tremendous energy and strength of character could speak out as she does, particularly considering the medieval advocacy of woman's passivity. Even though she has had no children, the Wife of Bath ironically defends the physical act of procreation by quoting scripture: "God told us to increase and multiply," and "Tell me this also: why at our creation/Were organs given for generation?" She, further, ironically argues for multiple marriages by citing an example of polygamy: "Think of that monarch, wise King Solomon./It strikes me that he had more wives than one." And she argues against chastity: "But truth is, if no seed were ever sown,/In what soil could virginity be grown?"

Unlike other wives, the Wife of Bath turns her rebellion to overt dominion. She is the aggressor in all of her relationships, demanding love, obedience, and wealth from her husbands, chiding and nagging them for imaginary transgressions in order to maintain the upper hand. Only from her fifth husband does she receive actual abuse. She endures his diatribes concerning the exploits of wicked wives until finally one evening, totally exasperated, she rips three leaves from his book on misogyny and throws them into the fire. For this she receives a box on the ear, vicious enough to deafen her. But she turns this blow to her advantage, letting her husband think he has killed her, boxing him in return, and finally gaining the mastery over him that she so desires.

All writers do not treat the subject of cuckolding and wife beating in so lighthearted a manner as do Boccaccio and Chaucer. For example, writing in the fourteenth century in the *Inferno* of the *Divine Comedy,* Dante describes the adulterous affair of Paolo and Francesca, a couple who, following the courtly love convention, fall in love and satisfy their physical longing for one another, even though she is married to another man. This couple, discovered in their union and murdered by Francesca's husband Giovanni Malatesta, Dante places in the Inferno where no hope exists for salvation. They whirl about through eternity, close enough to one another to be constantly reminded of a love that has condemned them to eternal damnation.

The husband Malatesta, still living at the time the *Inferno* was written, was doomed by Dante to a deeper level of hell to sojourn with others who had performed acts of treachery against kin. The fact that the husband still lives after committing a double murder sheds some light on the negative attitudes in the Middle Ages toward compromised wives, and the resultant sympathy for cuckolded husbands. However, through the powerful sense of tragedy in the story of Paolo and Francesca, Dante reveals his sympathy for the lovers.

The polar opposite of the Wife of Bath's tale is the prototypic story of spouse abuse—Boccaccio's tale of Griselda, which stands, like the story of the suffering Job, as an exemplum of the virtue of uncomplaining acceptance. The story is problematic, however, revealing Boccaccio's ambivalence toward women's passivity, and exemplifying the importance of literature as a vital medium for speaking out against injustices.

Griselda, the wife of Gualtieri, suffers extreme cruelty from her husband, who takes from her all the advantages of her married position: her children, his affection, even her clothing. He further threatens to force her to serve him and the new wife he pretends he will marry. In *Conjugal Crime*, Terry Davidson points out that women who take abuse are often products of a conditioning that teaches them to respect the institution of marriage above all else. Appearances are important, proving superficially that their marriages are operating according to social expectations. When these women are mistreated, they feel guilty, wondering what mistakes they have made; and their confusion often results in passivity as they attempt to understand their mistreatment. Wives become accomplices to their own abuse when they do not rebel against maltreatment because, witnessing such passivity, husbands continue to abuse. Davidson writes, "Thus, a pattern is set. All the evidence is that when the first or second assault is not firmly dealt with, there will be more" (Davidson 1978, 51).

Griselda is expected from the outset of her marriage to be pleasing and obedient, and time proves her the most agreeable of women. Even though Gualtieri basks in his happiness over the virtuous patience of his bride, he decides to test the limits of her virtue; and because Griselda does not rebuke him after his first attack, a verbal one in which he states his displeasure with her, she abets further abuse. Without the least resistance, she reacts, telling him that he may do with her what he wishes because she is unworthy of the position to which he has courteously raised her.

The tale appears to valorize passivity for a number of reasons: Griselda does not complain, and she is ultimately rewarded with a reinstatement to her former position. Furthermore, the tale is the last of 100 stories in *The Decameron;* 100 is the number of perfection and also the number of cantos in Dante's *Divine Comedy,* a work illustrating the path to salvation. Thus, some critics have viewed this tale as a moral exemplum. Shirley S. Allen points out that Petrarch, writing in the fourteenth century in Italy, viewed the story as "a providential plan for testing Christian patience" (Allen 1981, 2). Other critics, such as Margo Cottino-Jones (1977), even view Griselda as a Christ figure.

Nevertheless, there are problems with accepting Griselda as a model of virtue. For example, Allen sees the ultimate restoration of the wife to her former position as "psychologically unconvincing and a violation of poetic justice," stating, "Such an extreme example of female submission embarrassed men even in the fourteenth century; to post-Freudian readers it suggests a diagnosis of masochism" (Allen 1981, 1). It is difficult to approve Griselda's passive response as her children are taken from her to be killed. While she may have an obligation to her husband, she has an obligation, as well, to the children she has borne. One is reminded of horrific contemporary accounts of women passively allowing their children to be abused by a brutal father. Griselda might, in fact, be condemned for her lack of spirit; her patience becomes weakness, even foolishness.

For these reasons, Allen points out that the Griselda tale has a purpose contrary to the apparent approbation of passivity: by reducing the situation of the tale to the ridiculous, artificial and suppressive marriage standards are undermined. Allen verifies this by pointing out that the narrator of the tale is Dioneo, whose name is a derivation of Dionysius, the Greek god of wine. The association of the spinner of this tale with a god who incited his followers to bacchic frenzy relates Dioneo and his tale to licentiousness and unruliness; Dioneo, himself, is gay, witty, and concupiscent, an unlikely candidate to relate a moral exemplum (Allen 1981, 4–6).

While spouse abuse of all types is unquestionably a serious problem, writers such as Boccaccio and Chaucer, rather than handling this abuse seriously, treat it in a humorous fashion, either in order to relieve the tensions aroused by restrictions that are contrary to human nature, or to expose these restrictions indirectly. In his book *Beyond Laughter*, Martin Grotjohn states, "humor is a triumphant joy and represents the victory of the pleasure principle. The ego, usually forced to submit to or modify the pleasure-seeking drives to the demands of reality, resolutely turns away from reality and enjoys uninhibited and guilt-free narcissistic existence" (Grotjohn 1957, 20). Laughter, as Mikhail Bakhtin in his theory of the carnivalization of literature explains, is a strong subversive force (1968, 1–58).

According to Freud, one source of humor is nonsense (Grotjohn 1957, 7); and situations in the stories of Chaucer and Boccaccio prove to be nonsensical, just as character traits are ridiculously exaggerated. Randy young brides cavort in farcical situations, satisfying their desires as nature dictates. A dull-witted old husband sits in a tub awaiting a deluge while his wife plots an assignation. Another aged mate, blinded by Pluto, upon recovering his sight spies his wife in the indelicate act of adultery high in a pear tree. A young lover, while the husband is away, inadvertently drinks a sleeping potion during his nightly visit and, appearing to be dead, has to be carried out of the house by the disconcerted inamorata and hidden in a chest. The Knight in the Wife of Bath's tale, forced to wed an aged hag, suffers in a comical reversal of the habitual plot pattern of an older man's marrying a younger woman.

While humor releases tensions caused by repressive practices, the genre of satire unmasks the injustices that arouse tensions. Satirists, in order to exorcise inequities, appear to unite with the disorder they expose, revealing a split between what should be and what is. Accordingly, in his Griselda tale, Boccaccio seems to advocate a woman's passivity even as he ridiculously exaggerates Griselda's patience, thereby undermining the virtue. Thus, the story of Griselda unveils repressive cultural assumptions even as it seems to favor them.

In medieval literature, therefore, although spouse abuse was treated humorously, even satirically, seriousness undergirded the ribaldry and levity of the tales. People of the period, needing answers

because of "economic hard times, chronic warfare, and continual concern over periodic plague epidemics" (Stuard 1976, 169), were willing
to believe the tenets of the church and scholarly institutions because
they offered answers to troubling questions. Prescribed institutional
ideologies became practice, allowing society to approve repressive
attitudes, particularly toward women. Perhaps only under the cam-
ouflage of humor and satire did authors of the period dare to attack
conventional attitudes toward gender relations.

Although both wives and husbands abuse one another in the
literature of the Middle Ages, the women of the stories dominate our
interest, exacting sympathy because of their creativity and vitality.
While abuse is certainly not approved by the authors, the reader
cannot but admire the Wife of Bath for her outspoken convictions, the
errant wives for creatively catering to their passions, perhaps even
Griselda for her hyperbolically patient submission to abuse.

Much of the literature of the Middle Ages therefore mocks abuse,
revealing inequities in the social system. Conventions that allow
Gualtieri to "purchase" Griselda from her poor father rather than to
woo her and, because of his mercantile marriage, to feel compelled to
test her virtue, are themselves at fault. Boccaccio's humorous coda to
the tale of Griselda's suffering reveals his sympathetic attitude toward
women and his condemnation of repression:

> It would perhaps not have been such a bad thing if he [Gualtieri]
> had chosen one of those women who, if she had been driven out
> of her home in a shift, would have let another man so shake her
> fur that a new dress would have come from it. (1949)

References

Allen, Shirley S. "The Griselda Tale and the Portrayal of Women in the *De-
cameron.*" *Philological Quarterly* 56: 1–11, 1981.
Bakhtin, Mikhail. *Rabelais and His World.* Trans. Helene Iswolsky. Cambridge,
MA: M.I.T. Press, 1968.
Boccaccio, Giovanni. *The Decameron.* Trans. Richard Aldington. New York:
Doubleday, 1949.
Chaucer, Geoffrey. *The Portable Chaucer.* Trans. and ed. Theodore Morrison.
New York: Viking, 1968.

Cottino-Jones, Margo. "Fabula vs. Figura." *The Decameron*. Trans. and ed. Mark Musa and Peter Bondanella. New York: Norton, 1977.

Davidson, Terry. *Conjugal Crime*. New York: Hawthorne, 1978.

Gies, Frances, and Joseph Gies. *Marriage and the Family in the Middle Ages*. New York: Harper & Row, 1984.

Gilbert, Sandra M., and Susan Gubar. *The Norton Anthology of Literature by Women*. New York: Norton, 1985.

Grotjohn, Martin. *Beyond Laughter*. New York: McGraw-Hill, 1957.

Langley, Roger, and Richard C. Levy. *Wife Beating: The Silent Crisis*. New York: Dutton, 1977.

NiCarthy, Ginny. *Getting Free*. Intro. Del Martin. Seattle, WA: The Seal Press, 1982.

Stuard, Susan Mosher. *Women in Medieval Society*. Philadelphia: University of Pennsylvania Press, 1976.

Stuard, Susan Mosher. "The Dominion of Gender: Women's Fortunes in the High Middle Ages." In Renate Bridenthal, Claudia Koonz, and Susan Stuard, eds., *Becoming Visible: Women in European History*, 2d ed. Boston: Houghton Mifflin, 1987.

Walker, Lenore E. *The Battered Woman Syndrome*. New York: Springer, 1984.

Wemple, Suzanne F. "Sanctity and Power: The Dual Pursuit of Early Medieval Women." In Renate Bridenthal, Claudia Koonz, and Susan Stuard, eds. *Becoming Visible: Women in European History*, 2d ed. Boston, Houghton Mifflin, 1987.

5

Untyping Stereotypes
The Taming of the Shrew

Harriet A. Deer

There is no question that *The Taming of the Shrew* incorporates spouse abuse. Its "knockabout" farce occurs chiefly at the expense of a wife who suffers verbal abuse, starvation, and material deprivation. Furthermore, the abusive husband seems to be more praised than blamed, for in the banquet scene with which the play closes, the wife appears to praise his right to control her and then to embrace dutiful obedience. Thus, the play seems to reinscribe many of the stereotypes that have been rejected by contemporary feminists. Whether one objects to the play's apparent condemnation of willful women or finds fault with its apparent praise of women who conform to men's rules for wifely conduct, *The Taming of the Shrew* seems to capitalize on the perception of women as marginal members of a hierarchical, masculine society. It therefore seems a potentially objectionable choice for a contemporary junior high school literature curriculum. Yet the play is taught without much protest by intelligent, sensitive people who would normally rebel against having to deal with such chauvinistic material. When one mentions that it may praise spouse abuse and the servitude of women, most teachers look puzzled and demur that since the abuse is all in fun, it should not be taken seriously.

One is therefore left with a contradiction, a play that capitalizes on spouse abuse and yet is palatable to late twentieth-century audiences. Given the uncritical reverence that Shakespeare is often accorded and the continuing prevalence of shrew stereotypes in our own time, one must first ask: Are we simply responding mindlessly to Shakespeare's name and to stereotypes so deeply seated in the grammar of farce that we accept them uncritically, or does the play elicit from us more complex responses than we recognize? Is there a possibility that the play may deftly undercut its surface chauvinism by making chauvinism itself the butt of the joke?

The play's most noticeable quality is not its chauvinism but its theatricality, and several sustained critical considerations of its theatricality have appeared. Thomas Van Laan's consideration in *Role Playing in Shakespeare* (1978, 21–52), J. Denis Huston's extended treatment in *Shakespeare's Comedies of Play* (1981, 58–94), and Sidney Homan's somewhat briefer observations in *When Theatre Turns to Itself* (1981, 31–54), all address the question of how a playwright uses the commonplaces of theatrical tradition to create something more than the commonplace. Their concern with theatricality springs from their postmodernist assumption that the models individuals live by—call them fictions or illusions—are creations of human beings, not facts of nature, and that one test of an artist is the extent to which he or she is aware of the act of model making and the limitations of the models used, both those inherited and those created. In other words, most postmodern criticism explores the creativity possible for the individual who knows how to play with models. If the individual is a playwright, then her or his great inherited model is the theater, and one of her or his major subjects is likely to be the significance of the theater and its conventions as ways of structuring our perceptions of the world. Even if individuals are merely participants in the dominant models of their time, their ability to play with and invent models is still analogous to the creative process of the playwright, and the problems of the dramatist are analogous to the problems of people who wish to control and invent the fictions that dominate their daily lives. Thus, the activity of the theatrical model maker and the activity of the individuals who are trying to find models for their daily conduct are not radically different in kind, and the process of model making in literature often reveals the process by which we make models in our lives.

Such an approach is particularly appropriate to Shakespeare's early comedies, since they are so openly about invention and conformity, and about the suffering that marginal people undergo when they must adapt to inappropriate conventions. In the early plays, Shakespeare is particularly concerned with women who have to conform to patriarchal marriage conventions whose implicit authoritarianism sanctions abuse in the name of conformity. Especially in *The Taming of the Shrew,* Shakespeare explores from many perspectives the idea that while slavish adherence to conventional theatrical models of plot and character may be dull and destructive—not only for both playwrights and actors but for society in general—using conventions as tools for discovering the lapses, inadequacies, and new possibilities in a society may transform them from devices encouraging inhumane homogeneity into lively sources for discovering ways to break free of that conformity.

Even within the Induction concerning Christopher Sly, Shakespeare seems interested in both the nature of theatrical invention and its humane implications. As the play begins, Christopher Sly, a low drunk, is thrust out of a tavern, and passes out. He is so marginal a part of his society that even the other drunks cannot tolerate him. A passing lord and his hunting party discover Sly. Taking him at first for dead, the lord then realizes he is merely dead drunk and decides to use this clod for the amusement of his party. From his deathlike stupor, the lord will resurrect Sly, clothe him like a noble, place him in the lord's bed tended by a page disguised as his genteel "wife," and convince him that he is a noble restored to his senses after long insanity. The lord's little masquerade is, then, primarily a source for condescending laughter about Sly, and a way of keeping Sly a clod rather than humanizing him.

The limitations of the lord's authoritarian imagination quickly become clear. Since the lord and his court have conceived a play with a central character who is almost totally passive, and since the courtiers think of themselves as observers, not participants, there is a limit to how far the play can be developed. Before the play is two scenes old, Shakespeare has suggested that the authoritarian imagination may be somewhat sterile. Fortunately, a troupe of strolling players happens by, for, without them, the lord's invention would come to an untimely end. The lord commands them to perform before

Sly as if he were the lord; after the play begins, the assembled courtiers and Sly are heard from only once more, during a brief interruption early in the main play.

The Induction seems to have so little influence on the course of the central *Shrew* play that critics have sometimes questioned why it is there at all.[1] Yet its presence is important, for it is the "frame" through which the play is viewed. It establishes connections among the treatment of marginal members of society, society's authoritarian assumptions, the creative imagination, and the problems of art. These are the same connections that Kate and Petruchio will explore during the course of the main play, and the frame play suggests the interpenetration of the fictions of art and the fictions by which human beings live. If we look at *The Taming of the Shrew* without taking into consideration the failure of conventional values and the abuse of marginal members of society in the Induction, then we miss the perspective that allows us to see how original Kate and Petruchio are, how Petruchio uses role-playing to educate Kate, and how Kate finally learns enough about patriarchal conventions to transform these conventions into tools by which she can control her world rather than be controlled by it.

The players have been commanded to contrive a play that is supposed to satisfy impossible requirements. First, the play is to continue the lord's weak joke by attempting to please Christopher Sly, yet Sly is totally unfamiliar with plays. When he is told he will witness a comedy, he asks, "What is this Comonty?" He hopes it will be like "Christmas gambolds and tumbling tricks" (Induction.2.141). His concept of entertainment includes only the simplest physical action and conflict. Appealing to him is difficult in itself. Yet, the players must also appeal to the nobles, for although the nobles want to watch Sly watching the play, they also expect to be entertained by the play, and the nobles expect that the play will include those ready-made, genteel, self-flattering stereotypes common to courtly theater, stereotypes that affirm the superiority of a hierarchical vision and of the authoritarian vision of the nobles. Although the two ideas of entertainment seem incompatible, their forced juxtaposition so shatters our preconceptions that it encourages us to explore both the vitality and the limitations of each idea, and to discover the necessity for broader perspectives.

The conflation of courtly and folk tastes is observable even in the sources for this play. The tale of the shrewish wife is usually associated with the use of physical farce, and it generally includes physical abuse of the shrew; in a popular English ballad, the shrew is even wrapped in a salted horsehide to induce obedience.[2] Shakespeare's softening of abuse from the coarsely physical to the more verbal and psychological is one of the most immediately noticeable alterations he makes in the old tale, and this suggests that he is more concerned with the realities of abuse than with the knockabout stereotypes associated with it. The Lucentio–Bianca subplot springs from the courtly love tradition,[3] and it stresses the conventions of courtly love—disguise, music, poetry, love at first sight, and true love versus materialistic marriage, to name only a few (Van Laan 1978, 21–52).

The two traditions—courtly and folk—are held together only by the particular theatrical imagination of the strolling troupe that devises the play. It is a *commedia* troupe, the kind of troupe whose roots stretch back in theater tradition at least as far as Plautus and forward at least as far as nineteenth-century Italy, where the still-surviving troupes serve as the inspiration for *I Pagliacci*. A *commedia* troupe is composed of actors who specialize in particular kinds of stock roles rendered familiar to their audience through long usage and prevalence in both folk and courtly literature. As the character types in *The Shrew* make evident, this particular troupe is composed of actors who are skilled in creating a number of stock characters prevalent in Renaissance literature: for example, it has several pantaloon actors (i.e., foolish older men), it has a very skilled coquette, a young lover type who handles witty language well, a miser type, at least one clown, a braggart type, and a shrew. *Commedia* players present plays, either by adapting their stock roles to already existing plots, or else by inventing plots that are appropriate for the characters that they know how to play. Thus members of a *commedia* troupe are part actor, part playwright, sometimes working with previously developed material but just as often "discovering" the turns of the plot as they face the problems of adapting their stock characters and *commedia* routines to a multitude of different plot situations.[4]

The troupe is an appropriate vehicle for combining farce and courtly traditions since, by Shakespeare's time, *commedia* actors had developed a broad range of stock characters that covered the spectrum of Renaissance social types and dramatic tastes. Some of their stock characters, the coquette and the young lover, for example, reflected the stock characters and plot expectations of courtly drama. Others, like the shrew and the braggart, reflected the demands of folk drama. And still others, like the servant types, could function in either courtly or folk drama, as do Lucentio's servant Tranio and Petruchio's servant Grumio. Since the actors in a *commedia* troupe are to some degree playwrights, they are inventors as well as interpreters of the dialogue and of the reactions of characters to each other within scenes. The nature of their trade makes them in some sense surrogate playwrights whose onstage struggles to create plays may mirror both the creative offstage struggles of playwrights to reconcile the stereotyped expectations of their society with their particular original visions and the problems these playwrights encounter in working with particular plots. Thus, the question for a *commedia* troupe is not *whether* but *how* to mix the apparently disparate traditions of folk and courtly drama. The demand placed on them to satisfy the tastes of both Sly and the courtiers challenges their inventiveness, and the varying levels of inventiveness with which they meet the challenge are connected not only with the kinds of conventions available to the various actors but also with their success in developing the social and humane implications of those conventions.

In his brilliant analysis of the play, Tom Van Laan points out three different levels of invention. The two lower levels are connected with the rather routine, aristocratic courtly love story concerning Bianca and Lucentio. The performers of this plot seem content to confirm the courtiers' assumptions concerning the superiority of nobility, the virtue of feminine dependence on and obedience to men, and the importance of maintaining the patriarchy. On the lowest level of invention are the hack actors, the minor characters who can barely stumble through their roles, let alone find fresh ways of treating them. Gremio, the pantaloon, is a good example of these. He is so stupid and inept that Lucentio can gull him almost effortlessly into permission to teach Bianca poetry, and he is so lacking in invention that when Lucentio's trick is revealed, he simply sinks into obscurity. He can neither complicate the plot nor test the validity of courtly values. He can only conform in the most unimaginative way.

Lucentio, playing the *amoroso*, represents a second, far more significant level, that of the *virtuoso* who practices his craft, not to understand and deepen the values and conventions implied in the stock characters he portrays, but rather to display his own style. He gains access to Bianca by employing a rather stale device, but he performs it with grace and wit; imitating Dante, he uses Ovid to court her, and his success seems in every way to confirm the stage audience's assumptions about the superiority of courtly conventions in the hands of a proficient performer. Although Bianca's character seems to be less developed, she is also proficient. She knows how to please her suitors, how to dissemble before her father, how to discriminate between Lucentio's love and the other suitors' interest in her dowry, and how to reap the rewards of conformity. Yet, despite their virtuosity, until the banquet scene both Bianca and Lucentio are purely conventional. Not until Bianca refuses to obey Lucentio does either of them seem anything more than a competent but uninventive courtly actor. Through Lucentio, Shakespeare gives the courtly tradition its due, allowing it virtuosity but denying it real vitality and imagination. Its demands for conformity make it the enemy of invention. His treatment of Bianca is more interesting, for during the banquet scene she violates the mindless conformity that Lucentio holds so dear. Bianca's conventional obedience may mask a capacity for rebellion about which she has remained silent throughout most of the play. Once married, she can afford to reject courtly ideals.

Kate and Petruchio represent the highest level of invention. Both theatrically and socially, they are marginal and antiromantic. The actor creating Kate is expert at shrewishness, temper tantrums, and brawling. His/her shrew character is outside the pale of polite society, marginal by definition. Petruchio is played by an actor who is an expert boor, more skilled at harangues and knockdown farce than at love. Because of his boorishness and bombast, he, too, is a somewhat marginal member of the aristocracy. Even the tale with which they are associated is only marginally romantic, for the shrewish wife is traditionally a "curst" woman who is brutalized into obedience by a husband more interested in securing peace than love. Nevertheless, however unpromising the material, these two folk characters from a crude folk tale are intended, on the one hand, to capture the interest of Christopher Sly and, on the other, to serve as the primary subjects of a romance suitable for a courtly audience. The necessity to concentrate on the Kate and Petruchio relationship becomes evident early in the play when the action is briefly interrupted by the nobles trying to waken Christopher Sly. The play has, to that point, been proceeding along routine courtly lines, far outside of Sly's experience, and he has gone to sleep. If he is to remain awake, that is, if the nobles are to have the fun of watching him watch a play, then the rough-and-tumble plot will have to be highlighted. But it must be brought into prominence in such a way that the taste of the courtiers for a love story is also satisfied.

Whereas the Lucentio–Bianca plot requires only expert handling of and conformity to predictable motives and situations, the Kate–Petruchio plot defies convention. Shrews and braggarts are not courtly lovers, and thrusting them into a romantic plot forces everyone to examine, on the one hand, the motives and assumptions that underlie shrewishness and verbal abuse and, on the other, the conventional expectations that wives should bring with them a dowry and should practice obedience and conformity. Although the conventions associated with shrews and boors seem intended to deny the possibility that either character might be able to love anyone else, the actors must use those conventions to create a love story. And although a shrew is per se an undesirable mate, this shrew must find a way to convince her audience that she will live happily ever after. The task is gargantuan, and it cannot be accomplished simply by rearranging existing rules. It requires that the actors rethink the potential of their roles and the assumptions implicit in the conventions associated with them. The task requires not only virtuosity, but the development of a highly independent creative imagination.

What I am suggesting is that the *Shrew* deals with more than playfulness, as Denis Huston suggests, or with levels of role-playing, as Van Laan argues. Both are important aspects of the play, but they are secondary to its exploration of the relationship between theatrical conventions and social values. The play deliberately develops an analogy between the difficulties that the skilled actor–playwright encounters when he or she tries to convert popular plots, roles, and acting techniques into new uses and wider meanings and the struggles of marginal human beings, both male and female, to convert the destructive and abusive conventions associated with Renaissance marriage and marginality into sources for new kinds of relationships. Just as the playwright must create vitality while still retaining the established conventions on which actor and audience depend for communication, so women in a patriarchal society must learn to use the conventions of conformity necessary to their survival as sources for affirming their own creativity and imagination. From one perspective, Shakespeare is talking about how players can put old dramatic conventions to new uses, and, from another, about how women (and men) performing conventional roles within a society also try to discover new possibilities for human relationships.

Kate and Petruchio make great sense if we think of them as stock actors who can perform their play only if they discover new possibilities within the routines and conventions they have always unquestioningly performed. Part of their solution is to center the plot not on routine courtship but on the search for conventions that would make courtship possible. At the beginning of the play, each actor is presenting his usual routines—Kate throwing tantrums and brawling with her sister, Petruchio boorishly announcing that he has "come to wive it wealthily in Padua." But braggart and shrew stereotypes cannot develop the romantic relationships that the plot requires. Romance conventions require that a character be able to care for at least one other person, yet the conventions of shrew and braggart are specifically structured to prevent the characters from noticing anyone else. The actors cannot discard their stock characters; those are the only acting conventions they are any good at performing. They must improvise until they can discover in the mannerisms and interactions of their characters some possibilities that can be used to develop more complex characters capable of multiple reactions. They must, in other words, particularize the shrew and braggart so that they can find out why this particular pair exist and what other qualities their behavior may imply.

Almost immediately the shrew and braggart begin to acquire specificity, because the plot requires that their stereotypes develop some motivation. The character playing Kate develops the idea that she resents her father's oft-repeated belief that she is simply marriage material to be awarded to a high bidder. She has rejected the marriage contract, but not the idea of marriage itself. She refuses to cooperate with her father or to adopt the manners that would make her desirable merchandise. But her shrewishness is a self-defeating strategy, for her unpleasantness, intended to fend off merely mercenary suitors, guarantees that the only reason anyone would marry her is for her fortune. Petruchio, like most of his society, regards marriage as a business proposition. He wants wealth. Yet, he does want a wife as well as a dowry, although his stream of expletives makes him the most inept of suitors. If Kate's shrewishness offends courtly suitors, then Petruchio's verbal assaults offend the courtly fathers of genteel daughters. Nevertheless, within the desire for marriage the pair can find enough common ground to improvise the beginnings of a romance. But how to sustain a romance? How to reconcile Petruchio's materialism with Kate's rejection of it? How to direct the process of improvisation and invention so that some kind of interaction can take place?

At first, Petruchio seems the more inventive player. He exploits the aspects of his behavior that most resemble those of Kate—that is, the conventions of boorishness associated with his stock character— to intensify and mirror back to Kate her own outrageous behavior. If she attacks him, he will attack her. If she affects disdain for marriage, he will arrive in antic dress for the wedding. If she makes unreasonable, arbitrary demands of others, he will treat her to extremely unreasonable behavior, arbitrarily refusing her food, rest, and proper clothing. If she throws tantrums, he will harangue her to death. Petruchio's mirroring technique is not a departure from his usual bag of acting tricks or his virtuosity as a braggart; in recognizing the resemblance between the abusive language of his stock responses and those of a shrew's, he is developing a tool for discovering new perspectives on the two roles, new ways of generating action when one would normally expect only impasse. From stock tricks, a kind of creativity is emerging. His well-practiced routines are put to the new purpose of forcing on Kate an awareness of the way her violent language and actions frustrate her desires.

Unfortunately, Petruchio's mirroring tactics create more self-awareness in Kate than they create in him. Although his acts allow Kate to understand a great deal about herself, they do not create similar insight in Petruchio. He is still a "controller," still boorish, still in danger of seeing Kate merely as an extension of his own ego, just as her father saw her merely as a tool for improving his family fortunes. Although he has found a way to be Kate's mirror, his ego and control of the plot prevent Kate from returning the favor. Yet, if Petruchio is to educate Kate, he must recognize and limit the destructive possibilities of his usual mode of acting. He must not go beyond education to sheer manipulation. Such recognition is difficult for Petruchio, since he is enjoying his lord-and-master role, and we sense that unless some new device intervenes, boorishness will overwhelm inventiveness. One device that helps Petruchio to retain some balance is his servant Grumio, who often mirrors his master's actions without his master's wit or awareness. Like Petruchio, Grumio also harangues others, particularly the tailor. But Grumio's harangues are directed toward hapless bystanders; his bamboozling of the tailor constitutes gratuitous abuse, and Petruchio, observing this, has to set matters right. Petruchio's intervention reminds him that Kate may be more like the unfortunate tailor than he had realized, and that his own abuse may go beyond education to a gratuitous exercise of power. The mirror Grumio can furnish is too simplistic and limited, however, to save Petruchio from his own ego. Grumio's actions are a form of burlesque, naive distortions of Petruchio's actions; they do not furnish the kind of sophisticated and intense mirror that Petruchio has given Kate.

One yearns to place Petruchio before such a mirror, for the performance strategies and the imaginative uses of boorishness by the actor playing Petruchio suggest that, placed before the right mirror, he might find creative alternatives to his egocentric desire to control everything and everyone around him. Yet Petruchio, the actor and the character, is so consumed with his desire to control that he seeks to impose on Kate his own vision of the world; on the road when they are returning to Padua for Bianca's wedding, he even invents tests for her to be sure she has learned his lesson; he is willing to let her walk every step of the way back to Padua unless she conforms to his demands.

Despite Petruchio's creativity in using the conventions of the boor to make Kate recognize the destructiveness of her shrewishness, he cannot see that the alternative to the shrew that he advocates is the courtly convention of the obedient and dependent wife. The character–actor improvising this courtship can imagine no relationship between man and woman that does not involve mastery and submission. He can devise no plot that does not, despite its inappropriateness, affirm the ideals implicit in the Lucentio–Bianca courtship plot. Thus, as the plot moves toward its conclusion, and despite the appreciation that he has displayed for Kate's high spirits, the Petruchio character is driven to rely on the courtly ideal of an obedient wife, and thus he seems willing to sacrifice Kate's spirit to coerce her obedience. The plot of depriving Kate of food, sleep, and clothing is far less destructive than the device of depriving her of her own vision. Whereas the first device leaves Kate with room to react and retain some kind of identity, the second device leaves the stage and the action entirely to Petruchio. Wanting to civilize Kate is one thing; wanting to displace her independence and vitality with a mere echo of himself is quite another. We are forced to ask whether Petruchio's "mirroring" technique is only a way of giving Kate new awareness, or whether it is also a way of forcing her to conform to his vision. We wonder whether controlling another person's imagination may not be the worst abuse that one spouse can inflict on another. Petruchio has pretended to mime Kate's routines as a way of freeing her from the destructive implications of the shrew character, but, in the end, we discover that he does not really want to free the character, he merely wants to substitute a compliant wife for the shrew, one who will agree to behave according to the ideal held by all Bianca's suitors. That desire is Petruchio's blind spot and the opening for which the actor playing Kate has been waiting.

During the entire play, the Kate actor–character has had difficulty converting the special tricks of the shrew to constructive ends. The logic of the plot has placed Petruchio in command, and the action has followed a pattern in which Petruchio acts, Kate reacts, and Petruchio then counteracts in such a way that she is forced to abandon one shrewish trick after another. She has been stripped of the shrew conventions that constituted her identity without being given the opportunity to find alternative conventions. In the scene on the road back to Padua, Petruchio's attacks become so outrageous that they finally reveal his desire not only to obliterate the shrew role, but to obliterate the independence and sense of self that gave the shrew role its originality and vitality. Petruchio is so determined to control the action that he commands Kate to swear that the sun is the moon, that an old man is a budding virgin; in other words, he wants her only to see the world according to the vision he allows her. He wants her to deny both the surface tricks of the shrew stereotype and the underlying sense of independence that has made her shrewishness a vital if unproductive activity.

Petruchio's demand cuts to the core of the character the shrew actor has developed during the play. Kate has been transformed into a motivated shrew; her shrewishness is presented as a defense against becoming a mere puppet, a mere reflection of the courtly values required by her entire society. Her excesses have proved to be counterproductive, and she has been auctioned off to Petruchio, but her motivation still remains. How can she turn the tables on Petruchio, and create through her actions a mirror of his expectations with such intensity and distortion that he recognizes how his expectations fundamentally rob her of the ability to act at all? If she cannot create a new awareness in Petruchio, then alternatively, how can she use his authoritarianism and egotism to create freedom for her own inventions? The question for Kate, the character, is the same as the question for Kate, the actor. The conventions for stage roles and the conventions for social roles seem to become interchangeable. The character's struggle to solve her marital problem is like that of the actor's or playwright's struggle to find a way of using conventions creatively rather than mechanically.

Kate's chance comes in the last act, when she finds a way to control Petruchio using his own illusions. The plot develops into a paradigm of a courtly "game" situation, a trial of the three new husbands based on their success in commanding their wives' absolute obedience. Petruchio, Lucentio, and Hortensio have all wagered that their wives will come when bidden. According to conventional expectations Bianca, as the courtly ideal, should immediately obey her husband's arbitrary command. But Bianca, now married, is no longer controlled by the "rules" of the coquette. She is therefore free to ignore her husband's command. Hortensio's wealthy widow is also free, and just as casual in answering his command as he was early in the play when he decided to marry her because it seemed easier than fighting for Bianca's hand.

Although the test has failed, the three husbands, instead of questioning whether their ideal of absolute obedience is either desirable or attainable, wait for Kate. She enters and in a remarkable tour-de-force performance mirrors back to Petruchio his own values and strategies. As he has often done to her, she delivers a long harangue, this time to the other two wives. As he desires, she delivers a conventional encomium on the values of obedience. Even the most uncritical viewer is amazed by Kate's "taming." The harangue and encomium are too good to be true; they have nothing to do with the rest of the play, with Kate's attitudes or experiences, with Petruchio's actions, or, for that matter, with the realities of Elizabethan marriage implied in Petruchio's capacity to deprive Kate of food, sleep, and clothing. Coming from Kate, they are so outrageous that they throw into relief the emptiness of the cliché responses demanded of her, and the lack of inventiveness of the actor and society who would approve such a demand. Just as Petruchio, earlier in the play, performed Kate's tantrums with even greater intensity than Kate did, so Kate is now performing, with an intensity that mocks credibility, the courtly rules of marriage that Petruchio seems to demand of her. The very exaggeration of the performance calls attention to the possibility that what we are seeing is so blatantly conventional that the viewers ought to beware. We begin to conceive the possibility that Kate, who has not lost her wits, is setting a trap, that her performance is a comment on, not merely an imitation, of Petruchio's own values. Our sense of such a possibility is increased when, with a single theatrical gesture, Kate commits an act so outrageous that only someone like Petruchio, who is utterly consumed with his own success, could accept it without question. Kneeling to him as if he were her God, her object of worship, she offers to let him tread on her hand.

Lucentio and Hortensio are awestruck. Here is surely the ideal of obedience that they have dreamed of. And Petruchio? We are not sure whether he has or has not gotten the point. Does Kate's hyperbolic performance of his courtly ideal reveal to him its destructiveness and emptiness? Does her performance reveal to him her wit, imagination, and independence? Does his roar of approval, "Why there's a wench! Come on, and kiss me, Kate" (5.2.180), signal his discovery of Kate's inventiveness? Or is Kate now to play on him the kinds of mirroring tricks he played on her? Is he Kate's partner or her fool? Will she merely control him or will they join in creative inventions? Is this the end of the play or the beginning of a new one? We are not sure. What we see is that the play's conclusion, which is often treated as Kate's conversion to a simple, mechanical conformity, has become problematic. What we see is that Kate, who appears so conventionally tamed, may have found a way to tame Petruchio. We see the clear possibility that she has used Petruchio's own conventions as a way of achieving control of the plot and her destiny. Seeing the play in that way puts fresh meaning and fresh doubts into the aristocratic wifely ideal: even as Kate pretends to be blindly obedient, she springs the trap implicit in the ideal of blind obedience, to wit, that he who believes in blind obedience is likely to be blindly enslaved by it.

Shakespeare has not created a play in which a "conversion" necessarily occurs, nor one in which the female characters *must* choose nontraditional roles. He has done something more important. He has found modes of questioning established values, of demonstrating that the systems of family values traditionally considered to be unified and justified are merely logocentric models that can be unmade just as well as they were originally made. In so doing, he has opened for the audience a world of the imagination in which the possibility of alternative relationships between husbands and wives, fathers and daughters, and masters and servants can be contemplated. What Shakespeare has done in this early play is to use the process of performance as a way of exploring the unstated values embodied in the traditional stereotypes on which stock characters are based, ways of testing their limits and their validity. By focusing on the difficulties that a group of actors encounter during the improvisational process of reconciling stock *commedia* characters with courtly plots, he has been able to probe the difference between static, closed assumptions and flexible, open ones. Employing a shrew and a braggart, he has been able to explore the patriarchal assumptions that underlie Elizabethan marriage and to show that spouse abuse is not an aberration, but an intense expression of those values that reduce Elizabethan wives to the status of appendages. Using the process of acting and playmaking as a microcosmic test of larger social assumptions, he has expanded the patriarchal assumptions underlying stock characters as sources for creative response without at the same time affirming those assumptions or their destructive effects. *The Taming of the Shrew* does indeed exploit spouse abuse as a major source of action and humor. But it does not encourage such behavior; rather it reveals how destructive and widespread is its hold on society.

Notes

1. Some critics have suggested that the Induction sets the tone for the play; it establishes that this is a play ostensibly for Sly and thus it cushions us from the inner play's brawling physicality. Van Laan (1978), Huston (1981), and Homan (1981) all suggest that the Induction calls our attention to the fact that we are witnessing a piece of theater, and thus shifts our attention from *what* happens to *how* it happens—from plot to style, performance, and invention—an observation fundamental to both their observations and mine. None of them, however, takes into account the main plot line of the Induction, which is simply that a lord invents a practical joke in the

form of a courtly play. His play runs out of steam because it cannot be developed, and it cannot be developed because both the playwright and his audience are so hedged in by assumptions about Sly's inferiority and their superiority that they cannot generate action; they can only generate a static emblem of their assumptions. For them, theater is merely a static, illustrative activity which confirms the aristocratic status quo, it is not a generative, exploratory one.

2. For a brief but very helpful discussion of sources for both the Kate–Petruchio plot and the Induction, see G. B. Harrison's (1968) introduction to the play.

3. Probably from George Gascoigne's translation of Ariosto's *Supposes*.

4. The extent to which Shakespeare is thinking in *commedia* terms is made clear in the Folio, where Gremio, Bianca's aged, greedy suitor, is first noted namelessly simply as "a pantaloon."

References

Harrison, G. B., ed. "Introduction to *The Taming of the Shrew*," in *Shakespeare: The Complete Works*. Harcourt Brace Jovanovich, 1968.

Homan, Sidney. *When the Theater Turns to Itself: The Aesthetic Metaphor in Shakespeare*. Lewisburg, PA: Bucknell University Press, 1981.

Huston, J. Denis. *Shakespeare's Comedies of Play*. Columbia University Press, 1981.

Shakespeare, William. *The Taming of the Shrew*. In G. B. Harrison, ed., *The Complete Works*. New York: Harcourt Brace Jovanovich, 1968.

Van Laan, Thomas F. *Role Playing in Shakespeare*. Toronto: University of Toronto Press, 1978.

6

From Pedestal to Ditch
Violence against Women in Shakespeare's Othello

SARA MUNSON DEATS

Today, most civilized persons would label wife battering an unspeakable crime, a crime that supposedly does not occur in educated middle-class or upper-class families. Yet until the nineteenth century, wife beating was authorized, even advocated by society, and even today, according to psychologist Terry Davidson, 50% of contemporary marriages are marred by some form of wife beating. A Harris poll taken in the 1970s concluded that physical violence against spouses occurs with equal frequency in all income groups, and this violence is overwhelmingly perpetrated against women (1978, 3, 6).

Central to the problem of wife battering is the legitimation of violence—against women, against children, against the elderly, against animals, indeed against all defenseless groups—as an acceptable method for solving problems. Many studies of this issue conclude that as long as violence continues to be authorized in our society, the helpless and vulnerable will continue to be victimized. Psychologist Maria Roy warns:

> In a violent society, all members are capable of violence against one another; men can injure women and children; women can harm children. In a society where violence is condoned and vic-

tims are blamed, accused of provocation, all members tolerating
the violence are potential perpetrators. (1977, Preface xii)

The deleterious attitudes toward women inscribed in patriarchal
ideology from prehistory to the present further contribute to the continued victimization of wives by their husbands. These often contradictory myths coalesced in the Middle Ages to create a paradoxical
image of women. On one hand, both women and children came to be
viewed as men's property—as daughters, women were often bar-
tered for financial or diplomatic advantage; as brides, women were
frequently married for economic or dynastic gain; as wives, women
were generally objectified as the emblems of a husband's honor. An-
thropologist Claude Levi-Strauss postulates that the exchange of
wives initiated civilization as we know it (1969, 493–496), and historian Lawrence Stone reminds us that husband and wife were traditionally considered one person and that person was the husband
(1977, 136). The very language of the marriage ceremony, "I pro-
nounce you man and wife," reveals that whereas the husband maintains his individual masculine identity in matrimony, the wife becomes an extension of her spouse, defined only in relation to her
husband (Furman 1985, 64–65). Thus, stripped of her individual identity, the wife is dehumanized into mere property, to be nurtured and
protected, or despoiled and destroyed, as the owner sees fit.

Another invidious assumption inscribed in patriarchal ideology
divides human personality into two contrary types: feminine and
masculine. This scheme depicts women as passionate rather than
rational, pliant rather than resolute, passive rather than active, helpless rather than competent; in short, as not fully mature, responsible
individuals. As psychologist Phyllis Chesler observes, the expectations for normal behavior in females in our society are those of a child
or a neurotic; if a man acted like a women is expected to act, he would
be adjudged to be sick or disturbed (1972, 66). It follows, therefore,
that these irrational, childish, irresponsible creatures must be guided
by their more rational, mature, responsible male mates and that they
will benefit from rigorous psychological or even corporal chastisement. Thus, this second assumption, like the first, legitimizes the
husband's natural ascendancy over the wife, implicitly authorizing
violence as a means of maintaining control over a mate perceived to

be recalcitrant or rebellious. R. Emerson and Russell Dobash see this attitude as pervasive in our society:

> Men are socialized into aggression, taught directly or indirectly that it is an appropriate means of problem-solving and of demonstrating authority. . . . This willingness to use force is coupled with a set of beliefs and standards regarding the appropriate hierarchical relationship between men and women in the family and the rightful authority of husbands over wives. Thus, all men see themselves as controllers of women, and because they are socialized into the use of violence they are potential aggressors against their wives. (1979, 22)

A third, equally pernicious assumption is the division of the female sex into two binary opposites. On one hand, woman is revered as a superior, supernal being, represented in sacred lore by the Virgin Mary, in the secular verse of the medieval and Renaissance periods as the "divine" courtly lady, and in later Victorian literature as the "angel-in-the-house." There is little evidence, however, that this reverence was ever more than a literary exercise. Failing to achieve this elevated status, a woman becomes the temptress or the shrew, the first abominated by the patristic tradition, the second, brutally punished in the medieval period and ridiculed in the literature from the Middle Ages to the present. Gender mythology thereby denies women a normal fallible humanity, dividing the feminine sex into either Marys or Eves, Madonnas or whores. And, of course, as any victim of our vestigial twentieth-century chivalry will probably agree, balancing precariously on a pedestal is almost as uncomfortable as being shoved into the ditch. But not quite.

Everything that I have stated seems particularly applicable to Shakespeare's lacerating study of racism and sexism, *Othello*. I have chosen to discuss *Othello* because, in my interpretation, this play epitomizes the legitimation of violence and the negative stereotyping of women that I believe underlie the phenomenon of wife battering.

The world of the play certainly depicts a society that authorizes violence as a solution to problems, particularly those involving male honor and male shame. As historian Lawrence Stone explained in a paper presented at the annual De Bartolo Conference at the University of South Florida in March 1989, female honor has traditionally been equated with chastity and female shame with unchastity, whereas male honor has been equated with virility, male shame with cuck-oldry. Psychologist Maria Roy suggests that "men, women, and chil-dren learn that physical aggression can be a very useful tool, and that given the right set of circumstances, everyone can be violent" (1977, xii). Othello lives in just such a turbulent society, and having been a soldier since the age of seven has been singularly schooled in a mili-tary code that condones force. The correct set of circumstances arise, and violence inevitably erupts.

Furthermore, the varying perspectives of Desdemona presented in the play offer a compendium of traditional deleterious feminine stereotypes. For Desdemona, whether adored or reviled, honored or battered, remains the play's cynosure, and like the colored glass in a kaleidoscope, her image changes with the shift in perspective from one male observer to another.[1]

Her conventional father Brabantio myopically sees her as the Elizabethan ideal, "a maiden never bold;/Of spirit so still and quiet that her motion/Blush'd at herself" (1.3.96–98).[2] He also considers her his property, his "jewel" to merchandise as he sees fit (1.2.198). When he judges his jewel flawed he casts it away, although the loss breaks his heart and leads to his death.

Cassio, Othello's lieutenant, is an ardent advocate of the Madon-na–whore dichotomy, as a comparison of his scornful treatment of the prostitute Bianca with his homage to the lady Desdemona clearly reveals. Cassio thus idealizes his General's wife as the incomparable courtly lady, through his poetic idiom transforming the "maiden nev-er bold" into the "divine Desdemona," who "paragons description and wild fame" (2.1.62–64).

While Cassio exalts Desdemona's spirituality, Iago, Othello's en-sign, gloats upon her carnality, depicting her not as a divine madonna but as a lascivious, "super-subtle Venetian" and potential whore. Yet Iago, the prototypic male chauvinist, degrades not only Desdemona, but the entire female sex. He falsely suspects his own wife Emilia of unfaithfulness, defaming her as both a strumpet and a shrew, and treats the courtesan Bianca with undisguised contempt. In his osten-sibly jocular exchange with Desdemona in Act 2, he concludes that even a paragon of womanhood serves no better function than to "suckle fools and chronicle small beer" (2.1.159). An advocate of the "barefoot and pregnant" school, Iago plays no favorites and demeans all women to the lowest common denominator—for him they are all weak, lustful creatures, at best worthy to bear children and keep petty household accounts, at worst, cunning whores. Yet, as Carol Neely observes, there are cracks in Iago's cynicism, and the play subtly reveals these lacunae in Iago's dialogue (1980, 218). Cassio, he admits, "hath a daily beauty in his life/That makes me ugly" (5.1.18–20); Othello, he acknowledges, "is of a constant, loving, noble nature" (2.1.287–88); even Desdemona, he concedes, is virtuous and good (2.3.354–55). Idealistic courtiers like Cassio, noble blacks like Othello, and virtuous ladies like Desdemona challenge Iago's cynicism, racism, and sexism, and in order to maintain his assurance of white, male superiority, he must destroy them.

Othello's perception of Desdemona is far more complex than that of Brabantio, Cassio, or Iago. On one hand, Othello emulates Cassio's worship of the heavenly Desdemona, idealizing her into a "disembodied Petrarchan divinity" (Calderwood, 1987). Typically, however, when convinced by Iago that his Madonna is tainted, Othello swerves to the opposite pole of the spectrum, echoing Iago's idiom and ideas and reducing his beloved to a whore. Othello's dialogue is infused with the ambivalence between adoration and vilification characteristic of the Madonna–whore perspective. Moreover, Othello affirms other traditional patriarchal stereotypes. In his eyes, Desdemona remains his property. Inviting her to the nuptial bed, he employs the lexicon of commerce, not of love:

> Come, my dear love,
> The purchase made, the fruits are to ensue;
> The profit's yet to come 'tween me and you. (2.3.9–11)

Later he laments in the language of the patriarchy:

> O curse of marriage,
> That we can call these delicate creatures ours,
> And not their appetites! (3.3.274–76)

Since Desdemona is his possession, Othello views her presumed unfaithfulness not only as a loss of love but also as a loss of male honor. Furthermore, Othello unquestioningly affirms his prerogative to chastise his wife and never questions that if Desdemona is unchaste, he has the right to kill her. He feels guilt only after discovering that she has committed no conjugal transgression. Lastly, Othello sees Desdemona not as a unique individual but as a reflection of himself—his "fair warrior," an image that Desdemona enthusiastically endorses, terming herself an "unhandsome" warrior (3.4.152) when she fears that she has failed to live up to her husband's marital ideal. As Carol McGinnis Kay expresses it:

> The basis for their love, then, is the grand romantic picture of Othello that they both admire and pity, the image of Othello that Desdemona reflects to him. He does not have a reciprocal concept of her as a human being. . . . Instead he projects onto Desdemona the image of himself he wants to see reflected there. (1983, 265)

I am here reminded of Virginia Woolf's famous observation that "women have served all these centuries as looking glasses possessing the magic and delicious power of reflecting the figure of man at twice its natural size" (1929, 35). For Othello, therefore, Desdemona's supposed perfidy becomes not only a loss of public honor, but a loss of his magnified identity. With his "fair warrior" a presumed deserter, Othello's martial occupation is lost (3.3.355–362).

Thus, all of the male characters I have discussed project onto Desdemona their individual fantasies concerning the opposite sex. She becomes their fetish or their scapegoat, and their perceptions of her tell us more about their own needs and fears than about Desdemona herself (Garner 1976).

Othello exemplifies not only society's negative myths about women, but also patterns of spouse abuse remarkably similar to those appearing in numerous statistical profiles of conjugal crime. Psychologist Terry Davidson identifies three familiar clinical profiles that I find graphically depicted in Shakespeare's play.

First there is the intractable wife abuser. Davidson quotes the following description of this type offered by Hal Steiger, a Minneapolis Gestalt therapist working on the problem of wife abuse: "The intractable type doesn't give a damn. Violence is part of his lifestyle, his repertoire of usual behavior." (1978, 23) According to Steiger, it makes good sense criminally to prosecute this universally abusive type (1978, 23).

Iago, I submit, embodies this type. The ensign functions as the ubiquitous source of disorder in *Othello* and the play is bracketed by the brawls that he incites: the abortive riot in Venice opens the drama, the midnight attacks on Cassio and Roderigo conclude it. In between, Iago foments the injurious fray between Cassio and Montano and, before the play is over, he effects not only the wounding of both Cassio and Montano but the death of four other persons, including two wives. Furthermore, although Iago is never shown physically abusing his wife Emilia before he murders her at the dénouement, he indulges in consistent psychological abuse, continually insulting and demeaning her. We learn that he has previously falsely accused her of unfaithfulness and, during the play, he publicly derides her as a shrew, while privately slighting her as a strumpet (3.3.308). Indeed, Iago cannot speak of women without a jeer. When Cassio makes bold to salute Emilia with a kiss, Iago baits his wife:

> Sir, would she give you so much of her lips
> As of her tongue she oft bestows on me,
> You would have enough. (2.1.101–102)

He later defames women generally:

> . . . you are pictures out of doors
> Bells in your parlors, wildcats in your kitchens,
> Saints in your injuries, devils being offended,
> Players in your huswifery, and huswives in your beds. (2.1.109–112)

Emilia's list to Desdemona in the "willow-scene" of the abuses chronically suffered by wives at the hands of tyrannical husbands may give the audience further insight into her life as Iago's spouse (4.3.89–106).

Far more interesting to our study is the second clinical type, the treatable abuser. Steiger characterizes this type as follows:

> The treatable wifebeater is heavily invested in control of all his emotional life—sadness, joy, anger. He must stay in charge. Much energy is invested in not letting go. When he does pop finally, it's with the socially approved "masculine" way of aggressive violence, versus the "feminine" way of being hysterical or falling apart. (Davidson 1978, 23–24)

Davidson further comments that the person conforming to this profile often displays the following additional characteristics:

1. He is frequently respected and successful.
2. He is often rigid and uncompromising, convinced that his wife deserves punishment for violating his moral standards.
3. He is a victim of low self-esteem.
4. He is unable to express his feelings openly.

5. He lacks self-awareness.
6. He has doubts about his masculinity and/or sexuality. (1978, 26–37)

Psychologist Lenore Walker adds: "Batterers tend to be less educated than their wives, from a lower socioeconomic class, and from a different ethnic, religious, or racial group" (1984, 11). Lastly, Roy describes the explosion into violence:

> Violence is the end product of pent-up frustration, denial of perceived legitimate rights over a period of time, and the constant erosion of self-esteem. It is an eruption similar to the explosive outpouring of volcanic lava following a period of dormancy. (1982, 3)

The above profile, I submit, offers a remarkably accurate portrait of Othello and of his behavior throughout the play. First, Othello is certainly successful and respected; he is the "valiant," "the noble Moor." Yet despite the esteem awarded him by the Duke and senators of Venice and the Governor and citizens of Cyprus—and despite also his boast that he fetches his being from men of "royal siege" (1.2.21–22)—almost everyone in the play also considers him of lower status than the patrician Desdemona. Like the typical abusive husband, therefore, Othello comes from a different racial group and social status than his wife. Moreover, Othello, like the clinical type I have just delineated, is dedicated to rigid self-control. Unlike his open and candid wife, who freely accepts her sexuality, stressing that she "did love the Moor to live with him" (1.3.251), Othello refuses to acknowledge his strong sexual attraction to Desdemona, insisting that he wishes to have his wife with him not to please his appetite, since the passions of youth are now in him "defunct," but only "to be free and bounteous to her mind" (2.264–268). He further protests his indifference to the "light-wing'd toys/Of feather'd Cupid" (2.1.271–277). Others share Othello's view of himself as a man of iron discipline, the man, according to Lodovico, "whom passion could not shake" (4.1.267). This inability to acknowledge and openly accept his sensuality and passion—this egregious lack of self-awareness (another salient characteristic of the wife abuser)—makes Othello more vulnerable when these long-suppressed emotions do erupt. Furthermore, rigid and uncompromising, like the typical abusive partner, Othello believes that his wife deserves the punishment that he inflicts upon her, rationalizing his murder into a sacrifice, performed to prevent the betrayal of more men (5.2.6, 68). Lastly, Othello's lack of self-esteem, revealed in his need for reflecting mirrors and for audiences, has been explored by a number of perceptive critics.[3] These feelings of inferiority concerning his race, age, and background, are further revealed in a series of Freudian slips, such as the poignant lines, "For she had eyes, and chose me" (3.3.195), or "Haply, for I am black/And have not those soft parts of conversation/That chamberers have, or for I am declin'd/Into the vale of years" (3.3.269–272). Thus, in the face of the enormous respect he evokes from almost everyone in the play, Othello doubts his own value and sexual attractiveness as well as the integrity of Desdemona. In short, he accepts the racism and sexism of his society, and this destroys him.

Desdemona is the classic battered wife. Davidson limns this profile as follows: "The victims may exemplify society's old image of ideal womanhood—submissive, religious, nonassertive, accepting of whatever the husband's life brings" (1978, 51). Moreover, although her background might indicate a measure of independence, the battered wife frequently looks up to the male as superior and looks down on herself as inferior (1978, 53). Davidson further points out that for many of these wives, the admired husband has become their closest relative and best friend, the center of their world. When this loved one is transformed from a Dr. Jekyll into a Mr. Hyde, from a beloved husband into a wife beater, the battered wife is catapulted into a state of ambivalence, becoming a kind of split personality, not knowing where to turn for help (1978, 8). The response of the battered wife tends to be withdrawal, silence, and denial (particularly in the case of the middle-class or upper-class abused wife). Retaliating would be contrary to this woman's conditioning and breeding; exposing her husband's behavior would be equally unthinkable (1978, 50). Many women in this situation seem determined to take the guilt upon themselves, assuming that they have somehow provoked their husbands and are thus responsible for their predicament. They will, therefore, lie about the cause of their obvious injuries, defending their husbands when anyone begins to suspect the truth, making excuses for their spouses' violence (1978, 52). The battered wife thereby falls into a state in which she feels that she has lost all control over her life, a condition termed by psychologists as "learned helplessness."

Although accepting the battered wife as an unwitting accomplice in her torture, Davidson is careful to avoid anything remotely suggesting "victim blaming." Rather, Davidson insists that the battered wife is victimized not only by her assailant but also by "the tolerating/denying society," which callously ignores her suffering and intimidates her into remaining with her abusive partner (1978, 10). Or, to quote Lenore Walker, the sociologist who first coined the term "learned helplessness":

> Inequality between men and women impacts on the perceptions of violent behavior for the women so that they are unable to develop adequate skills to escape from the relationship. Such sexism also pervades society's institutions so that women feel that they are unable to receive any assistance to help them or their batterers. (1984, 151)

Thus women become victims because society has socialized them to believe that they have no other choice but to be victims.

How does Desdemona fit this profile? Certainly, Othello becomes Desdemona's dearest friend, the extension of her being, the warrior who fulfills the romantic yearnings of her repressed and sequestered psyche. Desdemona's commitment to Othello is total and unequivocal. For him, she has defied convention and forsaken father, position, and friends. When he inexplicably turns on her, like the typical battered wife she withdraws, stunned into passivity, denial, and helplessness. Like this prototype, she never attempts to retaliate or expose Othello. Even after he has publicly humiliated her—striking her and demeaning her before Lodovico, vilifying her before Emilia, accusing her of whoredom—she takes no steps to escape or even to defend herself. Instead, she affirms her love for him:

> . . . Unkindness may do much;
> And his unkindness may defeat my life,
> But never taint my love. (4.2.161–163)

Like the typical battered wife, she also seeks excuses for her violent husband, blaming herself:

> Nay, we must think men are not gods,
> Nor of them look for such observancy
> As fits the bridal. Beshrew me much, Emilia,
> I was, unhandsome warrior as I am,
> Arraigning his unkindness with my soul;
> But now I find I had suborn'd the witness,
> And he's indicted falsely. (3.4.149–155)

Finally, she lies to protect her mate, with her dying words asserting his innocence and her own responsibility. When asked by Emilia, "O, who hath done this deed?" she replies "Nobody; I myself" (5.2.129).

Many critics would demur, however, that the early Desdemona does not display the conventionality associated with the battered wife. Indeed, many commentators have found unconvincing Desdemona's change from the courageous, self-confident, candid, young woman in the opening scenes to the dazed, helpless wife of the denouement. A close reading of the text, however, reveals that Desdemona is never all that self-confident. Furthermore, despite her daring defiance of her father and her poise in confronting the senators, she is, in many ways, thoroughly conventional. From the very beginning of the play, she defines herself in relation to men, either as a wife or a daughter, not as an independent individual:

> . . . My noble father,
> I do perceive here a divided duty;
> To you I am bound for life and education:
> My life and education both do learn me
> How to respect you. You are the lord of duty;
> I am hitherto your daughter. But here's my husband,
> And so much duty as my mother show'd
> To you, preferring you before her father,
> So much I challenge that I may profess
> Due to the Moor my lord. (1.3.182–191)

Her triple reiteration of the word duty accentuates her acceptance of the subordinate female role. Desdemona's description of her feeling toward Othello further "betray an almost holy dedication to the man she has married" (Dash 1981, 117):

> I saw Othello's visage in his mind,
> And to his honors and his valiant parts
> Did my soul and fortunes consecrate. (1.2.254–256)

Yet despite her initial conventionality, Desdemona undoubtedly does diminish as the self-confident, young single woman dissolves into the confused and helpless wife, desperately trying to discover her role (Dash 1981, 123). Diane Elizabeth Dreher argues that the change in Desdemona's character "demonstrates how the traditional feminine role reinforces masochism and neurotic self-effacement" (1986, 13). I agree that the patriarchal concept of marriage is the Procrustean bed to which Desdemona shrinks her vibrant personality.

On one level, therefore, this rich and complex play is centrally concerned with stereotypes and the way that this conventional thinking fixes and limits human growth and relationships. Trapped in a situation outside of their control, racked by a sense of powerlessness, both Desdemona and Othello enact the stereotypic roles in which they have been encased by society. Othello expresses his frustration in the acceptable "masculine" manner of aggression and violence; Desdemona withdraws into the acceptable "feminine" mode of passivity and guilt. Just as Desdemona's defenselessness becomes explicable in terms of the "feminine" ideal of submission in marriage, so too are Othello's aggressions traceable to the "manly" ideal of character and conduct involved in his dual roles as soldier and husband. Irene Dash sees the play as the tragedy of a woman "pummeled into shape by the conventions that bind" (1981, 104), marital conventions that demand more from a woman than from a man (103). I would expand her statement to include both Othello and Desdemona as victims of the distorted expectations of the patriarchal family. Viewed from this perspective, both Desdemona and Othello would arouse ambivalent responses from the audience. For although we cannot but condemn Othello's cruel and irrational actions, we must also pity him. And although we cannot but admire the purity and steadfastness of Desdemona's devotion, we must also deplore her docility, excessive altruism, and lack of healthy self-love, a lack that will ultimately contribute not only to her death but to that of the man she loves not wisely but too well.[4]

Fortunately, Shakespeare offers an alternative perspective—he offers us Emilia. Literary criticism of *Othello* has tended to divide into "Othello" and "Iago" critics; however, like Carol Thomas Neely, I see myself as an Emilia critic (Neely 1980, 213). I submit that from one perspective, at least—the perspective taken in this chapter—Emilia is dramatically and symbolically the play's fulcrum. Significantly, Shakespeare counterpoises two sets of marriages: one a fresh, young marriage, fecund with promise; the other a weary, sterile alliance, stuck in the groove of dissatisfaction and routine psychological abuse. In fact, there are actually three couples, if we include illicit ones—Desdemona and Othello, Emilia and Iago, Bianca and Cassio. In all three cases, the men mistreat their wives and lovers, whereas the women respond with unflinching affection. Emilia alone breaks the cycle of subservience and despite her earlier slavish obedience to her husband, and her "humiliating need to win his approval" by filching the fatal handkerchief (Grennan 1987, 283), she alone speaks for some dignity of equality between men and women, presenting women not as goddesses or temptresses but as human beings. Emilia's passionate indictment of the gender double standard echoes "Venetian Shylock's plea for human recognition of another victimized group" (Grennan 1987, 281). Later, Emilia defies her husband and delivers an unvarnished narration of events, even as her language acknowledges her subordination: "Tis proper I obey him, but not now" (5.2.203). Ultimately, female bonding gives Emilia the courage and strength to resist the bullying of her abusive mate, and although her valor and devotion end in death, she offers a positive standard for all women and the measure of value in the play. To quote Carole McKewin's eloquent tribute: "Emilia's loyalty to her friend, enlightened by her egalitarian view of man and woman in marriage, is what remains whole in the debacle of *Othello*" (1980, 129). Emilia thus provides an all-too-rare literary example of a wife who breaks the cycle of abuse.

In conclusion, I will comment again on the remarkable accuracy of Shakespeare's character portraits in light of clinical research on spouse abuse. To note this striking resemblance is not to suggest that Shakespeare intuited universal aspects of human personality, but rather to point out that Shakespeare was an astonishingly observant chronicler of both human behavior and society's stereotypes. And since the societal stereotypes and familial patterns producing spouse abuse have changed deplorably little since the Elizabethan period—at least, until the past 20 years—it is not surprising that Shakespeare's emblematic characters appear familiar to us. I further suggest that *Othello*, like all of Shakespeare's multivalent, complex plays, is composed of many different discourses, inviting interpretation on many diverse levels. But, from one perspective, at least, the play is a wrenching study of the institutionalized abuse of women by men in our society, and of the gender hierarchies, the patriarchal dominance, and the legitimation of violence that have trapped society for 5000 years in a vicious cycle of spouse abuse.

Notes

1. The kaleidoscope image and the idea of alternating perspectives in *Othello* was first suggested to me by Sally Bartlett (1989) in her paper, "Shakespeare's Kaleidoscopic Phantasmagoria: Oscillating Perspectives in *Othello*."

2. All quotations from Shakespeare's plays are taken from David Bevington's (1980) edition of Shakespeare's works.
3. Othello's lack of self-esteem has long been a commonplace of Shakespearean criticism. For the definitive presentation of this point of view, see Carol McGinnis Kay (1983), "Othello's Need for Mirrors."
4. The proper audience response to Desdemona has occasioned considerable critical debate. "Iago" critics, adopting the perspective of the cynical ensign, tend to censure Desdemona as either too forward, too domineering, or, less often, too passive. "Othello" critics assume the point of view of the early Othello, idealizing Desdemona into a disembodied divinity. More recently, however, a number of critics have tried to rehabilitate Desdemona's balanced humanity, treating her not as a saint, a strumpet, or a shrew, but as a normal, psychologically healthy, fallible, but admirable human being. For a lucid survey of the sentimental versus the censorious view of Desdemona, see Carol Thomas Neely (1980, 211–213). Critics depicting Desdemona as a sexually healthy human being include S. N. Garner (1976), Neely (1978), W. D. Adamson (1980), Ann Jennalie Cook (1980), and Grennan (1987).

References

Adamson, W. D. "Unpinned or Undone?: Desdemona's Critics and the Problem of Sexual Innocence." *Shakespeare Studies* 13: 169–186, 1980.

Bartlett, Sally. "Shakespeare's Kaleidoscopic Phantasmagoria: Oscillating Perceptions in *Othello*." Unpublished paper, presented at the International Association for the Fantastic in the Arts, Tenth Anniversary Conference, Ft. Lauderdale, 1989.

Bevington, David, ed. *The Complete Works of Shakespeare*, 3d ed. Glenview, IL: University of Chicago Press, 1980.

Calderwood, James L. "Speech and Self in *Othello*." *Shakespeare Quarterly* 38(3) (Autumn): 293–303, 1987.

Chesler, Phyllis. *Women and Madness*. Garden City, NY: Doubleday, 1972.

Cook, Ann Jennalie. "The Design of Desdemona: Doubt Raised and Resolved." *Shakespeare Studies* 13: 187–196, 1980.

Dash, Irene. *Wedding, Wooing, and Power*. New York: Columbia University Press, 1981.

Davidson, Terry. *Conjugal Crime: Understanding and Changing the Wifebeating Pattern*. New York: Hawthorne Books, 1978.

Dobash, R. Emerson, and Russell Dobash. *Violence Against Wives: A Case Against the Patriarchy*. New York: The Free Press, 1979.

Dreher, Diane Elizabeth. *Dominion and Defiance: Fathers and Daughters in Shakespeare*. Lexington: The University of Kentucky Press, 1986.

Furman, Nellie. "The Politics of Language: Beyond the Gender Principle?" In Gayle Greene and Coppelia Kahan, eds., *Making a Difference; Feminist Literary Criticism*, pp. 59–80. New York and London: Methuen, 1985.

Garner, S. N. "Shakespeare's Desdemona." *Shakespeare Studies* 9: 233–252, 1976.

Grennan, Eamon. "The Women's Voices in Othello: Speech, Song, Silence." *Shakespeare Quarterly* 38(3): 275–292, 1987.

Kay, Carol McGinnis. "Othello's Need for Mirrors." *Shakespeare Quarterly* 34(3) (Autumn): 261–270, 1983.

Levi-Strauss, Claude. *The Elementary Structures of Kinship*. Trans. James Harle Bell, Richard Von Strumer, and Rodney Needham. Boston, MA: Beacon Press, 1969.

McKewin, Carole. "Chronicles of Gall and Grace: Intimate Conversations Between Women in Shakespeare's Plays." In C. R. Lenz, G. Greene, and C. T. Neely, eds., *The Woman's Part: Feminist Criticism of Shakespeare*, pp. 117–132. Urbana: University of Illinois Press, 1980.

Neely, Carol Thomas. "Women and Men in *Othello*: 'What should such a fool/Do with so good a woman?' " In C. R. Lenz, G. Greene, and C. T. Neely, eds., *The Woman's Part: Feminist Criticism of Shakespeare*, pp. 211–239. Urbana: University of Illinois Press, 1980.

Roy, Maria, ed. *Battered Women: A Psychosociological Study of Domestic Violence*. New York: Van Nostrand Reinhold, 1977.

Roy, Maria, ed. *The Abusive Partner: An Analysis of Domestic Battering*. New York: Van Nostrand Reinhold, 1982.

Stone, Lawrence. *The Family, Sex, and Marriage in England 1500–1800*. New York: Harper & Row, 1977.

Stone, Lawrence. "Honor, Morals, and Adultery in Eighteenth-Century England: The Action for Criminal Conversation." Unpublished paper delivered at the Third Annual De Bartolo Conference on Eighteenth-Century Studies, March, 1989.

Walker, Lenore E. *The Battered Woman Syndrome*. New York: Springer, 1984.

Woolf, Virginia. *A Room of One's Own*. New York: Harcourt Brace, 1929.

7

Altars to Attics

The State of Matrimony in Brontë's Jane Eyre

NANCY JANE TYSON

There is a central paradox in *Jane Eyre* between the rights of the individual and the need for social order. The romantic side of the issue gives Brontë's novel its Gothic and Byronic elements, and the rational side supports its essential morality. Specifically, the novel asks what becomes of the individual in the institution of marriage. Must marriage— or love—be sacrificial? Must union involve the compromise or annihilation of individuality and, particularly, of woman's individuality? The implied answer, I believe, is that because Victorian courtship and marriage demeaned and dehumanized women, they invited abusive situations, several of which threaten Brontë's heroine. Jane escapes the usual entrapment partly by accident and partly because of her healthily aggressive personality.

While there are some violent moments in *Jane Eyre*, what relevance the novel has to the theme of conjugal abuse is purely psychological rather than physical. The violence at its heart, of course, is personified in Bertha Mason Rochester, the "Madwoman in the Attic." But Fairfax Rochester's titular marriage to her is not a traditional spouse abuse situation. On a symbolic level, "mad Bertha" may well represent the degradation of women in a society that denies and represses her passionate instincts (Gilbert and Gubar 1979, 359–362).

On a literal level, however, Rochester does his wife a kindness by locking her in the attic under the care of Grace Poole, when the alternative is an early-nineteenth-century insane asylum. "'It is cruel,'" Jane charges; "'—she cannot help being mad'" (384). Still, Rochester may have saved the madwoman's life by treating her as he did. He tells Jane:

> "I possess an old house, Ferndean Manor, even more retired than this where I could have lodged her safely enough, had not a scruple about the unhealthiness of the situation, in the heart of a wood, made my conscience recoil from the arrangement. Probably those damp walls would soon have eased me of her charge. . . ." (383)

Compelled to restrain the woman, Rochester is still as gentle as he can be. After his bigamous near-wedding to Jane, when the madwoman's existence is revealed, she attacks him before the assembled company:

> The lunatic sprang and grappled his throat viciously, and laid her teeth to his cheek: they struggled. She was a big woman, in stature almost equalling her husband, and corpulent besides: she showed virile force in the contest—more than once she almost throttled him, athletic as he was. He could have settled her with a well-planted blow; but he would not strike: he would only wrestle. (371)

In the end, Rochester is maimed and blinded attempting to save her from a fire she has set.

Despite her propensity to violence, Bertha Mason, utterly deranged, can even less be accused of abusing her husband. The only instance in the novel of genuine physical victimization is the very early memorable scene from Jane Eyre's childhood, involving the young John Reed, 14-year-old scion of Gateshead, where Jane is raised as a kind of second-class charity child. John takes habitual pleasure in tormenting the little 10-year-old, both spiritually and physically: "He bullied and punished me," Jane recalls,

> not two or three times in the week, nor once or twice in the day, but continually: every nerve I had feared him, and every morsel of flesh on my bones shrank when he came near. There were moments when I was bewildered by the terror he inspired. (7)

On one such occasion, he calls the little girl to him:

> Habitually obedient to John, I came up to his chair: he spent some
> three minutes in thrusting out his tongue at me as far as he could
> without damaging the roots: I knew he would soon strike, and
> while dreading the blow, I mused on the disgusting and ugly
> appearance of him who would presently deal it. I wonder if he
> read that notion in my face; for all at once, without speaking, he
> struck suddenly and strongly. I tottered, and on regaining my
> equilibrium retired back a step or two from his chair. (7)

In the ensuing moments, John hurls a book at Jane with such force
that it throws her against a door and draws blood from a cut on her
head. When Jane is finally driven to retaliate, more from self-defense
than returned aggression, adult authority is quick to condemn *her*:
"'For shame! for shame!' cried the lady's maid. 'What shocking conduct, Miss Eyre, to strike a young gentleman, your benefactress's son!
Your young master!'" (9). This episode lays the groundwork for a
pervading subtheme in Brontë's novel: the victimization of women by
men, condoned by the system. With the exception of this childhood
trauma, the theme occurs principally in the context of marriage or
intended marriage.

Even in the romantic fantasy that constitutes the central plot of
Jane Eyre—her courtship with Rochester—there are many sinister
notes. From the outset of their acquaintance, he dominates the young
governess in conversation, demanding that she entertain and divert
him. He spies on her and orders her from room to room with a
personal interest more intense than that of employer for employee.
When she begins to love him, and he perceives it, he flaunts his
liaison with the cold socialite, Blanche Ingram, and forces Jane to
occupy the very chambers where this other, overt courtship is going
forward. "'I feigned courtship of Miss Ingram,'" he confesses later,
"'because I wished to render you as madly in love with me as I was
with you; and I knew jealousy would be the best ally I could call in for
the furtherance of that end'" (331). Jane's response is grief, rather
than jealousy, but in all their dialogues, though Jane refers more than
once to her "bitter pain" (331), Rochester expresses no regret for
having caused it.

Instead, during the period of their sham engagement, he treats
her like one of his continental mistresses, showering her with cavalier
attentions, buying her clothing and jewels, though he should know,
and she assures him, that such tokens only offend her. Rochester

speaks and acts in these scenes in terms of conquest, evoking imagery of master and slave suggestive of potential abuse. His eye, Jane says,

> most pertinaciously sought mine, though I averted both face and gaze. He smiled; and I thought his smile was such as a sultan might, in a blissful and fond moment, bestow on a slave his gold and gems had enriched: I crushed his hand, which was forever hunting mine, vigorously, and thrust it back to him red with the passionate pressure. . . .
>
> He chuckled; he rubbed his hands: "Oh, it is rich to see and hear her!" he exclaimed. "Is she original? Is she piquant? I would not exchange this one little English girl for the grand Turk's whole seraglio; gazelle-eyes, houri forms and all!" (339)

For Jane, anxiety overtakes joy at Rochester's continued allusions to bondage and servitude. He speaks of the time approaching when convention will grant him mastery as it now permits her freedom:

> "It is your time now, little tyrant, but it will be mine presently; and when once I have fairly seized you, to have and to hold, I'll just—figuratively speaking—attach you to a chain like this (touching his watch-guard)." (341)

But the real domestic tyrant in *Jane Eyre*—and fortunately for Jane he is only a potential spouse—is St. John Rivers, who nearly wins Jane by default after her abortive trip to the altar with Rochester. St. John is a fanatic, driven and loveless, who covets Jane only for her strength, which he would subdue and sacrifice to his missionary purpose. Even her friendship with him is chillingly oppressive:

> I could no longer talk or laugh freely when he was by; because a tiresomely importunate instinct reminded me that vivacity (at least in me) was distasteful to him. I was so fully aware that only serious moods and occupations were acceptable, that in his presence . . . I fell under a freezing spell. When he said "go," I went; "come," I came; "do this," I did it. But I did not love my servitude; I wished, many a time, he had continued to neglect me. (508)

It is not much of a surprise to the reader when one day St. John takes Jane out into the wasteland moors and, in the name of the Highest, makes one of the most offensive marriage proposals in all of fiction: "'God and nature intended you for a missionary's wife,' " he intones:

"It is not personal, but mental endowments they have given you:
you are formed for labour, not for love. A missionary's wife you
must—shall be. You shall be mine: I claim you—not for my pleasure, but for my Sovereign's service." (514)

Here is the potential for abuse—not the blood-letting knockabout
kind of abuse that the adolescent John Reed represented, but a total,
life-draining, soulless, mental and spiritual thralldom that seems, by
comparison, much worse. Jane remarks, in response to one cold re-
joinder, "I would much rather he had knocked me down" (523).
"Alas," she muses, "If I join St. John, I abandon half myself: if I go to
India, I go to premature death" (516).

The terrible irony is that in an age which referred to unmarried
women as "redundant females," St. John would have been the husband of choice. Martin Day observes:

He was a Greek god in appearance; he was impeccable in manners and morals; he was strongly intellectual; he was decently
provided with this world's goods (largely through Jane's generosity) and super-abundantly provided (we are assured) with oth-
erworldly blessings. . . . They are to unite in self-sacrificial Christian service without the low taint of passion. . . . a pious
Victorian mother would probably urge such a suitor upon a de-
vout daughter. (1960, 497)

St. John himself repeatedly invokes the weight of institutions—the
church and the law—as he attempts to win Jane to his purpose.
Denouncing her obsession with Rochester, he calls it, in an unusually
heated moment, "lawless and unconsecrated" (529).

Rochester, by contrast with St. John, is a most socially unacceptable suitor. He is not handsome, he has led a licentious life, and,
worst of all, he is already married. St. John and Rochester thus illustrate in divergent ways how society's dictates may be at variance with
the deeper needs of the individual. Though *Jane Eyre* (1847) is by no
means an anarchist document, in its time it was a revolutionary cele-
bration of individualism, especially for women. Particularly, its protagonist exemplified female passion, which was not supposed to
exist.

Jane's strong, passionate spirit is her most engaging feature from
childhood. Counteracting her orphan status, independence makes a
survivor of her and pits her against the establishment at an early age.

Much of her youth is spent in isolation—ostracized first by the Reeds and then, for a time, at Lowood School. At Lowood she pairs with one friend, Helen Burns, who dies of consumption. Helen is a model of submission, the very opposite of Jane, enduring with Christian humility all the degradation that Mr. Brocklehurst and his minions can heap upon her. In effect, the whole Lowood mission is to teach these charity-school girls to appreciate their lowly role in life. Jane's speech to Helen, upbraiding her for her passivity, can be read in the context of female subjugation:

> "If people were always kind and obedient to those who are cruel and unjust, the wicked people would have it all their own way: they would never feel afraid, and so they would never alter, but would grow worse and worse. . . . I must dislike those who, whatever I do to please them, persist in disliking me; I must resist those who punish me unjustly."

"'Heathens and savage tribes hold that doctrine,'" Helen quietly replies, "'but Christians and civilised nations disown it'" (65). In its ironic context, this last speech institutionalizes the blame. Oppression is inherent in the social order. The obedient Helen reflects the self-repression that supposedly inferior individuals are expected to cultivate under the powerful onus of gender and class.

When her protector, Miss Temple, marries and leaves the school, Jane has no girlish dream of following in her steps. Instead she leaves Lowood, alone. Above all things, Jane cherishes her own precious selfhood, and whatever threatens it she instinctively mistrusts. A supreme impediment to individual sovereignty in any age, of course, is romance. Love is a wonderful, sought-after thing, but it can have its price. If we give up autonomy in love or marriage, what becomes of us? The same self-reliance makes Jane apprehensive of Rochester in his first incarnation and, in turn, of St. John. For her own peace of mind in marriage as in love, Jane must remain psychically aloof.

Rochester's marriage with Bertha Mason is the novel's central instance of the mutual prison that is wedlock. Both parties are caged, one literally, one figuratively. But other situations arise as well from the unnatural subordination of one person's will to another's. In fact, the very origin of Jane's mistreatment as a child is in matrimonial obligation. Mrs. Reed, who hates Jane with all the intensity of a constitutional dislike, is compelled to care for her because of her husband's dying wish. "It must have been most irksome," Jane observes, "to find herself bound by a hard-wrung pledge to stand in the stead of a parent to a strange child she could not love, and to see an uncongenial alien permanently intruded on her own family group" (14). Mrs. Reed's reaction is to keep her promise minimally, by sending Jane to a charity school at fifteen pounds a year.

Rochester feels a comparable responsibility for his ward, Adèle, because of a former liaison with Adèle's mother, a French opera star. Although Adèle is not Rochester's own daughter, nor was he ever married to her mother, this odd triangle forms a parody of family commitment in the context of the novel. Rochester's empty infatuation with Céline Varens and her infidelity to him are a mockery of ideal union. His sustained indifference to Adèle despite her attempts to please echoes the contempt Mrs. Reed felt for Jane in the face of that necessity. Surely the similarity is part of what draws Jane toward the little French girl.

One thing is very clear from *Jane Eyre*. If society or social pressures dictate the union of two people, that union is doomed. When Jane almost marries St. John, she narrowly escapes a life of loveless abuse in the name of religion. The arranged marriage between Rochester and Bertha Mason is hardly more hellish than theirs would have been. In the same way, the contemplated marriage between Rochester and Blanche Ingram would have been a mere social contract for the sake of fortune. Early in her tenure at Thornfield, Jane comments: "I saw he was going to marry her, for family, perhaps political reasons; because her rank and connexions suited him; I felt he had not given her his love, and that her qualifications were ill adapted to win from him that treasure" (232).

In this instance as elsewhere throughout *Jane Eyre*, human institutions are to blame for most of the misery: "I had thought him a man unlikely to be influenced by motives so commonplace in his choice of a wife," Jane continues,

> but the longer I considered the position, education, &c., of the parties, the less I felt justified in judging and blaming either him or Miss Ingram, for acting in conformity to ideas and principles instilled into them, doubtless, from their childhood. All their class held these principles; I supposed, then, they had reasons for holding them such as I could not fathom. (234)

Marriage in the bonds of social compulsion is stultifying. Rochester feels this keenly, after a prominent scene when he and Jane

have been up all night in the wake of a violent outbreak by the
madwoman. Life's ultimate choice is seen here in terms of domestic
imprisonment versus natural freedom:

> "Come where there is some freshness, for a few moments," he
> said; "that house is a mere dungeon: don't you feel it so?"
> "It seems to me a splendid mansion, sir."
> "The glamour of inexperience is over your eyes," he an-
> swered; "and you see it through a charmed medium: you cannot
> discern that the gilding is slime and the silk draperies cobwebs;
> that the marble is sordid slate, and the polished woods mere
> refuse chips and scaly bark. Now *here* (he pointed to the leafy
> enclosure we had entered) all is real, sweet, and pure." (270)

There are moments in the novel when Brontë seems to reject the
institution of marriage altogether. *Jane Eyre* is a condemnation of marriage inasmuch as most marriages occur for all the wrong reasons.
Only marriage from the heart is worth having, and in Brontë's world
that is not often possible. Even when realized, such a marriage will
likely be dashed by convention. Witness the pathetic circumstances of
Jane's own parents who married for love across class boundaries and
died for it. As much as Jane loves Rochester, she still taunts him with
a vision of what their love could become, fettered by custom: "'What
do you anticipate of me?'" asks Rochester. "'For a little while,'" Jane
rejoins,

> "you will perhaps be as you are now,—a very little while; and
> then you will turn cool; and then you will be capricious; and then
> you will be stern, and I shall have much ado to please you; but
> when you get well used to me, you will perhaps like me again,—
> *like* me, I say, not *love* me. I suppose your love will effervesce in
> six months, or less. I have observed in books written by men, that
> period assigned as the farthest to which a husband's ardor ex-
> tends." (327)

Still, Jane insists on marriage before she will give herself up to
love. Although she has nothing else to live for, she refuses to live in
luxury with Rochester on the continent, where there would be no one
to censure or condemn. The reason is the sanctity of self, the one
thing needful for love to prevail. Rochester importunes, and she responds, "'I care for myself. The more solitary, the more friendless,
the more unsustained I am, the more I will respect myself. I will keep
the law given by God; sanctioned by man'" (404).

Jane's self-discipline and integrity serve her well in the novel's conclusion, but it is an improbable outcome. Given the repression of women in Victorian society, an equal marriage was unlikely if some drastic occurrence did not alter the roles of husband and wife. In *Jane Eyre* there are two such occurrences: the sudden discovery that Jane is an heiress, and the accidental blinding and maiming of Rochester. Her new property makes Jane a fitting mate for Rochester, under no debt of gratitude for being raised from her station. At the final reconciliation, the gratitude is all Rochester's, expressed in a feminine response with which Jane can sympathize:

> Again, as he kissed me, painful thoughts darkened his aspect. "My seared vision! My crippled strength!" He murmured regretfully.
>
> I caressed, in order to sooth him. I knew of what he was thinking, and wanted to speak for him; but dared not. As he turned aside his face a minute, I saw a tear slide from under the sealed eyelid, and trickle down the manly cheek. (568)

"'I love you better now,' " Jane declares, "'than I did in your state of proud independence, when you disdained every part but that of the giver and protector' " (570). Ironically, a woman's insane vengeance has made of him a "sightless Samson" (552), stripping him of power, and Rochester perceives the justice of the reversal: "'Of late, Jane—only of late—I began to see and acknowledge the hand of God in my doom' " (571). The specific sin implied by his atonement is, of course, the bigamous duplicity of his earlier courtship. But also gone, lost with his left hand in the searing, purifying flames, are his former arrogance, his possessive "houri" visions, his materialistic ardor: "'The third day from this must be our wedding-day, Jane. Never mind fine clothes, and jewels, now: all that is not worth a fillip' " (570). When Brontë restores his sight in the epilogue, it is only a partial restoration but a clear metaphor, nonetheless, for *in*sight.

Because of his often noted symbolic "emasculation," Rochester at least temporarily experiences the otherness, the dependency, the victimization, that was woman's common lot in the Victorian period, and even—regrettably—today. The extraordinary empathy that results is what makes this so memorable a love story. Jane and Rochester are not a typical couple for their time, or for ours. In Victorian fiction, the inevitable fate of the independent heroine is submission in marriage, or death. The social order would permit her no other end. Only Jane Eyre, winning against impossible odds, attains both marriage and emancipation.

References

Adams, Maurianne. *"Jane Eyre:* Woman's Estate." In Arlyn Diamond and Lee R. Edwards, eds., *The Authority of Experience,* pp. 137–159. Amherst: University of Massachusetts Press, 1977.

Benvenuto, Richard. "The Child of Nature, the Child of Grace, and the Unresolved Conflict of *Jane Eyre." English Literary History* 39: 620–638, 1972.

Berg, Maggie. *Jane Eyre: Portrait of a Life.* Boston: Twayne, 1987.

Brontë, Charlotte. *Jane Eyre.* Jane Jack and Margaret Smith, eds. London: Oxford University Press, 1969.

Day, Martin S. "Central Concepts of *Jane Eyre." The Personalist* 41: 494–505, 1960.

Deming, Barbara. "Two Perspectives on Women's Struggle." *Liberation* (June): 30–37, 1973.

Gilbert, Sandra M., and Susan Gubar. "A Dialogue of Self and Soul: Plain Jane's Progress." In *The Madwoman in the Attic: The Woman Writer and the Nineteenth-Century Literary Imagination,* pp. 336–371. New Haven: Yale University Press, 1979.

Grudin, Peter. "Jane and the Other Mrs. Rochester: Excess and Restraint in *Jane Eyre." Novel* 10: 145–157, 1977.

Moglen, Helene. "The End of *Jane Eyre* and the Creation of a Feminist Myth." In Harold Bloom, ed., *Charlotte Brontë's* Jane Eyre, pp. 47–61. New York: Chelsea, 1987.

Showalter, Elaine. *A Literature of Their Own: British Women Novelists from Bronte to Lessing.* Princeton: Princeton University Press, 1977.

Wagner, Geoffrey. *"Jane Eyre.* With A Commencement on Catherine Earnshaw: Beyond Biology." In *Five for Freedom: A Study of Feminism in Fiction,* pp. 103–137. London: Allen and Unwin, 1972.

8

Altars to Attics
The Madwoman's Point of View

LISA S. STARKS

As Sandra M. Gilbert and Susan Gubar (1979) have observed, the figure of the "madwoman in the attic" permeates nineteenth-century gothic fiction. Depicted as a creature of unbridled passion, the madwoman represents the "dangerous" side in the dual image of woman inherent in the history of Western philosophy, literature, and religion: she is the whore rather than the Madonna, the devil instead of the angel. Her nature is mysterious, uncontrollable, unfathomable; therefore, she must be controlled—restrained, silenced, incarcerated. Although our attitudes toward women and mental illness may have changed since the Victorian era, the legacy of our heritage continues to haunt us. The madwoman's screams still echo down the lofty corridors of the gothic mansions in our literary imagination, her cries ignored, misunderstood, muffled.

It is from such a literary masterpiece—Charlotte Brontë's *Jane Eyre*—that Jean Rhys derives the subject for her 1966 novel, *Wide Sargasso Sea*, in which she liberates the madwoman, Bertha Mason, from the attic of Thornfield Hall. Rhys's "prenovel" narrative of *Jane Eyre* probes the inner lives of Bertha (Antoinette) and Rochester (her husband) to reveal the underlying sources of Bertha's "madness": patriarchal oppression and mental spouse abuse. Through the narrative perspectives of both husband and wife, Rhys examines the destructive effect of English Victorian sexism (and racism) on the female psyche and the marital relationship. Interestingly, Rhys's insightful portraits mirror situations that confront many women today. Antoinette can be viewed not only as a victim of Victorian ideology, but also as a case study of contemporary attitudes and problems. Interpreted in this light, *Wide Sargasso Sea* can be seen to comment on current research on the relationship between spouse abuse and mental illness, its possible causes and effects.

The novel has a tripartite structure: part one relates Antoinette's memories of her childhood in the West Indies; part two focuses on Rochester's account of their marriage; and part three reconstructs the events of *Jane Eyre* through Antoinette's eyes. In the initial section we are introduced to Antoinette Cosway, a young Creole girl, who suffers from poverty and isolation. Her mother Annette, a young and beautiful widow of an infamous plantation owner, has been left to care for her daughter and mentally handicapped son Pierre, with the help of Christophine, a Martinique woman of uncanny perception and fortitude. Hated by the blacks of the island since the Emancipation Act of 1834, the Cosways face bitter hostility and violent threats that escalate after Annette marries Mr. Mason, a wealthy Englishman. Annette, apprehensive of impending danger, begs her husband to allow the family to flee the island, but he rebukes her pleas, belittling her fear. As Annette predicts, the island people burn down the plantation, resulting in the destruction of their marriage, the death of Pierre, and the mental collapse of Annette.

Meanwhile, her daughter Antoinette attends a convent school until she is betrothed to a young Englishman, Edward Rochester (unnamed in Rhys's text). Richard Mason, Antoinette's stepbrother, offers the young man Antoinette's inheritance, giving him complete financial power over his future wife. Although Rochester is indifferent to Antoinette, he plays the role of suitor and convinces her to marry him despite her reservations. The couple then travels to the West Indies for a honeymoon, where Antoinette is reunited with Christophine.

Soon Antoinette yields to Rochester, giving him complete power over her emotional and physical well-being. Rochester, on the other hand, merely "thirsts" for but does not love Antoinette, resenting her connection with the island itself—its vitality, beauty, and mysteriousness. His indignation heightens when he receives letters from Daniel Cosway, Antoinette's half-brother, her father's illegitimate son. Cosway insists that Antoinette inherited "bad blood": like her mother, Antoinette is "damaged merchandise," a madwoman. Determined not to be made a fool of by "that Creole girl," Rochester rejects Antoinette, treating her with coldness and cruelty, renaming her "Bertha" and rejecting her affection.

Distraught over her failing marriage, Antoinette desperately seeks the help of Christophine, who has practiced *obeah*, or island magic. Christophine advises Antoinette to leave Rochester immediately, but Antoinette refuses, begging Christophine to give her a love potion to revive her husband's love. Christophine reluctantly agrees on the condition that Antoinette discuss the situation with her husband. Antoinette grants Christophine's wish, but her efforts to communicate with Rochester fail. That night, Rochester becomes ill from the "love potion" in his wine and assumes that he has been poisoned. In retaliation, he has a sexual encounter with the maid Amelie in the room next to his wife's, and plots to turn Christophine over to the authorities for her dabbling in *obeah*. Antoinette reacts strongly to this emotional abuse and explodes with indignation and anger. When Rochester threatens his wife with physical violence, she desperately defends herself with a broken wine bottle. Christophine comforts Antoinette and sedates her with drugs, but Antoinette's fate is beyond her friend's control.

Determined to retain his "possession" despite his lack of emotional commitment, Rochester drags his wife to England and imprisons her in the attic of his home under the care of Grace Poole, an abrasive old woman. In England, Antoinette suffers from a distorted sense of time and place, driven to a state of extreme despair and distress. Living a nightmarish existence, she strikes out in violent outbursts, attacking her stepbrother Richard Mason and, eventually, setting fire to Thornfield Hall. Thus, she completes her "mission" and brings her life full circle by destroying the walls that have imprisoned her as well as by annihilating herself.

Of course, this summary greatly reduces Rhys's text, for within the framework of this plot Rhys develops a multifaceted, psychologically complex novel that explores the problem of emotional abuse from both female and male perspectives. Through the character of Rochester, she probes the possible alternative causes of such abusive behavior—family role modeling as well as cultural inheritance. Similarly, in her characterizations of both Annette and Antoinette, Rhys emphasizes the roles of both personal experience and ideological transmission in the make-up of the potential victim of mental abuse.

Rochester has derived expectations of himself, Antoinette, and their marriage from personal and social experience. His apparent misogyny, racism, and lack of compassion or emotion stem not only from his strained relationship with his father, as evidenced in his thoughts and letters, but also from his socialization as a nineteenth-century Englishman. In fact, at one point in the text Rochester asks himself, "How old was I when I learned to hide what I felt? A very small boy. Six, five, even earlier. It was necessary, I was told, and that view I have always accepted" (Rhys 1985, 519). Rochester has learned how to be "masculine"; his gender identity has been constructed by external forces. Unfortunately, Rochester's rigidly defined gender identity leaves little room for adaptation to that of his mate. As Suzanne Prescott and Carolyn Letko argue, contrasting male–female gender roles acquired "through social learning and . . . personal histories" are forced together in the act of marriage. Consequently, "individuals learn not only what is appropriate to their own roles, but adopt expectations about appropriate behavior of the opposite sex" (1977, 76). Unfortunately, Antoinette fails to adhere to Rochester's expectations of what the ideal woman—a "pure" Englishwoman—should be and how she should behave. Emblematic of English imperialism, the character of Rochester sets out to "colonialize" the other, Antoinette, in a struggle for domination and supremacy. Since he views Antoinette as foreign and unknowable, Rochester refuses to adapt himself to his wife, and is thus unable to break out of the rigidly traditional role in which he has been cast.

On a personal level, Rochester's ambivalent relationship with his father appears to be the single most important influence on his attitude toward himself, women, and marriage. Like the scurrilous Daniel Cosway, Rochester hates his father's lack of compassion and love for him, yet, as noted by Teresa O'Connor, both he and Daniel "have become the things they hate in their fathers." In fact, they "translate their bitterness and hurt, their feeling of love denied, into a preoccupation" (1986, 162–163) which, in turn, becomes the most dominant factor in their relationships with others, dictating many of their actions. Finally, in Rochester this obsession with "anger and hate degenerate into an overt desire to bully, to possess, and to destroy" (O'Connor 1986, 167). Rochester, like Daniel, becomes a literal embodiment of his father's insensitivity and greed.

Like her husband, Antoinette's behavior is clearly related to her personal experience, specifically her relationship with her mother. As a child, Antoinette suffers from feelings of estrangement, insecurity, and rejection. Alienated from the blacks of the island and spurned by her friend Tia, Antoinette spends a solitary childhood filled with fear. She has no identity to which she can cling: she is neither a white European nor a black native of the island. This lack of cultural identity coupled with intense financial hardship cause the child to adopt an attitude of "learned helplessness," or complete resignation. Finally, Antoinette's rejection by her mother adds to her sense of isolation and alienation. Annette, suffering from severe depression, channels her parental love into affection for the disabled Pierre to the exclusion of her daughter. Similarly, after her "breakdown," Annette—incarcerated and sexually abused by caretakers—fails to recognize her daughter when she visits, thus reinforcing the cycle of Antoinette's rejection. Therefore, as O'Connor points out, it is no surprise to find Antoinette in a situation similar to her mother's, becoming her mother to fill the void left by the absence of parental affection and security:

> That Antoinette suffers not only from this rejection by her mother but also from her mother's inability to protect her is never overtly stated, but that it occurred is a theme throughout *Wide Sargasso Sea*; it insures that Antoinette inevitably follows in her mother's footsteps. That is, in some sense, Antoinette finally retrieves her mother by becoming her. (1986, 172)

Like her misunderstood and mistreated mother, Antoinette also becomes a victim—exploited, labeled as "mad," and imprisoned. In her final act, the burning of Thornfield Hall, Antoinette completely seals her mother's fate with hers; she thus reenacts the burning of the plantation that figuratively killed her mother.

The causes of Rochester's and Antoinette's abusive relationship, however, cannot be completely attributed to their family experience, for their attitudes and behaviors also result from inherited belief systems. Therefore, Rochester's fear of intimacy and his deeply rooted misogyny and racism can be traced back much further than his father's influence; for both Rochester and his father are products of their culture, having learned certain ideas about gender roles and sexual relationships from a tradition that has sustained Western culture since its origin. Rhys's novel explores these characters' actions against the backdrop of their historical legacy. In fact, as Sue Roe notes, *Wide Sargasso Sea* is a novel "which powerfully reveals the effects upon the mind of the kinds of exploitation historically inherent in gender difference" (1987, 253).

It is within this context of Western European history that we need to locate the roots of spouse abuse as depicted in this novel and as reported in today's newspapers. Susan Schechter, in *Women and Male Violence*, states:

> Woman abuse is viewed here as an historical expression of male domination manifested within the family and currently reinforced by the institutions, economic arrangements, and sexist division of labor within capitalist society. (1982, 209)

She adds that "The historical context within which battering has developed is that of male domination within and outside the family" (1982, 216), and that context is one that has been validated by religious ideology and legal practice. Thus, wife beating—whether physical or, as in the case of *Wide Sargasso Sea*, emotional—is a logical outcome of a patriarchal society in which women are legally "owned" by men and sworn into subjection to men by their wedding vows. Indeed, as R. Emerson Dobash and Russell Dobash argue in *Violence Against Wives*, the traditional family itself—along with its religious, economic, and political justifications—legitimates both mental and physical violence against wives:

> The seeds of wife beating lie in the subordination of females and in their subjection to male authority and control. This relationship between women and men has been institutionalized in the structure of the patriarchal family and is supported by the economic and political institutions and by a belief system, including a religious one, that makes such relationships seem natural, morally just, and sacred. (1979, 33–34)

This belief system, upholding the patriarchal structure as well as the actions and attitudes of Rochester and Cosway and all that they represent, lies at the foundation of the Western culture.

The patriarchal justification of wife abuse stems from misogynist concepts of the nature of woman that have developed from antiquity through Judeo-Christian history to the present. Although Western misogyny has a complex history, we can find its primary location in the figures of Eve in Judeo-Christian mythology and Pandora in classical. Because Eve—a secondary creature inferior to God's primary creation in intellect and spiritual strength—tempted Adam to sin and thus to fall from God's grace, she is the source of all human misfortune. This view of woman, further supported by images of a myriad of temptresses recurring throughout biblical and literary texts, represents woman as a dangerous, libidinal creature of uncontrollable passions and desires. Juxtaposed with this image of woman is that of the "non"-woman, the Virgin Mary, hailed as the purest of women because she, unlike every mortal woman, is not tainted with Eve's sin— not only because she is a virgin but also because she immaculately conceived. The worship of the Virgin and of chastity, which reached its height in medieval Catholicism, complements rather than contradicts the idea of woman as a figure of sin. The idealization of Mary valorizes the spirit and demeans the flesh, giving further justification for misogyny since, because women give birth, society has traditionally associated the female with body or matter and the male with spirit. Mary's perfection stresses the imperfection of all women who, unlike Mary, are unchaste and therefore impure. Both of these representations—Eve and Mary—idealize and hence dehumanize woman. Objectified as either a Madonna or a whore, woman is anything but a thinking self, an individual human being.

Trapped within this cultural heritage, Rochester can only view Antoinette through this dichotomy. He desires a "pure," chaste Englishwoman, and so when he conceptualizes Antoinette as a sweet, silent woman, he "thirsts" for her. Ironically, however, by quenching that thirst or consummating his desire for her, he makes her unpure and therefore unfit as a love object. From this perspective, argues Helen Nebeker, Rochester functions as an emblem of the Victorian concept of woman inherited from this tradition:

> For having awakened in Antoinette all the passionate abandon of which she is capable—the consuming passion which is the essence of man's fantasies concerning woman—Rochester is caught in the dichotomy of that masculine myth which is epitomized in the Victorian morality. If woman is "pure," a "lady," she cannot know "evil" (sexual abandonment); if she is sexually abandoned, she must be "devilish" and a whore. (1981, 153)

This Madonna–whore complex acts as an underlying motif in *Wide Sargasso Sea*, woven in the text through images and references to the dual concept of woman. Throughout the novel are descriptions of the Edenic nature of the island, and in Part One Antoinette pictures the Cosways' garden as once "large and beautiful as that garden in the Bible" where "the tree of life grew" but now "gone wild" (Rhys 1985, 466). At the convent, Antoinette is taught the complementary image of the Virgin Mary and the worship of chastity; the nuns tell her that "chastity" is a "flawless crystal that, once broken, can never be mended" (489). From the nuns Antoinette learns to think in terms of binary oppositions, the logic that predetermines the dichotomized image of woman: "Everything was brightness, or dark. . . . That was how it was, light and dark, sun and shadow, Heaven and Hell" (491).

As a young woman, Antoinette's emerging sexuality is sublimated into recurring dreams filled with fear and anxiety. When Antoinette finally expresses such desire with her husband, however, she becomes completely vulnerable to him. She gives herself to him so completely that she equates her surrender with death. In bed she whispers to him, "'If I could die. Now, when I am happy. Would you do that? You wouldn't have to kill me. Say die and I will die. You don't believe me? Then try, try, say die and watch me die'" (513). Following Rochester's rejection and abuse, however, the nun's words return to haunt her. Locked away at Thornfield Hall, Antoinette anxiously worries about her appearance in a red dress, thinking, "'Does it make me look intemperate and unchaste?'" (571). In this state of confusion, Antoinette reveals the frustration of forcing her own sexual identity into the rigid confines of Victorian morality.

Like Antoinette, Rochester also thinks in binary oppositions. Trapped within a misogynist ideology, Rochester is unable to realize Antoinette as a human being outside of the Madonna–whore conception of woman and is therefore predisposed to accept Daniel Cosway's slanderous remarks against his wife. Moreover, Cosway's letters emphasize not only his own misogyny, racism, and greed, but also Rochester's. Cosway's rhetoric is transparent; unlike Rochester, his motives are obvious. In his letter, Cosway writes that it is his "Christian duty to warn the gentlemen that she is no girl to marry with the bad blood she have from both sides" (Rhys 1985, 516). His appeal to Rochester's sense of racial as well as sexual supremacy is successful because Rochester's inherited racism makes him especially vulnerable to Cosway's implications. As his attraction for his wife wanes, Rochester becomes increasingly more repulsed by Antoinette's Creole heritage and her black relatives. As a white Englishman, he will not be fooled by a Creole woman who pretends to be without blemish but in reality is "tainted with a diseased mind."

Rochester's evidence for Antoinette's so-called madness, however, lies only in her free expression of passion, her sexual abandon. In Rochester's mind, a pure, good, sane woman would not harbor such desires, or know something as "evil" as sexual pleasure. Therefore, Antoinette becomes for Rochester the whore, a "beast," a "drunken lying lunatic" who "thirsts for *anyone*," who "loves no one, anyone" (Rhys 1985, 560). Emblematic of the patriarchy itself, Rochester must crush, stamp out the likes of Antoinette, for feminine sexuality—dangerous, excessive, uncontrollable—cannot be allowed to exist. The power of female sexuality, symbolized by the island and by Antoinette herself, therefore poses a threat to patriarchal control and dominance.

Rochester abuses Antoinette because of his inability to accept her sexuality or "femininity." His reactions to her openness move from shock to anger and disgust, as he treats Antoinette with indifference and finally destructive possessiveness. Initially, he sees the island as analogous with Antoinette and femininity itself; he dislikes the "excess" of the place, its lack of British restraint. He thinks, "Everything is too much. . . . Too much blue, too much purple, too much green. The flowers too red, the mountains too high, the hills too near. And the woman is a stranger. Her pleading expression annoys me" (Rhys 1985, 498). His early observations of Antoinette who, now in familiar surroundings, is no longer taciturn and docile, show his "shock" at this vivacity: "one afternoon when I was watching her," he thinks he was "hardly able to believe she was the pale silent creature I had married" (510). Constantly placing his wife under his scrutinous gaze, Rochester "watched her critically," noticing her "long, sad, dark alien eyes" which did not reflect the image of himself, of England, or of the pure Englishwoman. Thus, Rochester begins to see Antoinette and the island as something beyond his reach, something which deliberately makes itself secret and separate from him, and this resentment builds into hatred:

> I hated the mountains and the hills, the rivers and the rain. I
> hated the sunsets of whatever colour, I hated its beauty and its

magic and the secret I would never know. . . . Above all I hated
her. For she belonged to the magic and the loveliness. She had
left me thirsty and all my life would be thirst and longing for what
I had lost before I found it. (Rhys 1985, 565)

Rochester's abhorrence of the femininity that he desires but cannot
accept soon finds expression in violent anger.

Rochester's ire surfaces early in the novel in emblematic scenes
that prefigure his later emotional torture of Antoinette. When he first
arrives at the honeymoon house, he finds two wreaths of flowers,
frangipani, lying on the bed. Irritated with their "uselessness," he
mindlessly steps on them, crushing the flowers. Similarly, after reading Cosway's letter he passes an orchid that reminds him of Antoinette and immediately destroys it: "'They are like you,' I told her.
Now I stopped, broke a spray off and trampled it into the mud" (517).
Soon, however, his desire to destroy Antoinette transforms into an
obsessive wish to own and torment her. He decides that since she
loves the island, she must never see it again, and that even though he
no longer wants her, she must never belong to anyone else, for "She's
mad but *mine, mine*" (561). As Rochester observes in himself, "Desire,
Hatred, Life, Death came very close in the darkness" (514), and by the
end of the novel Rochester is unable to distinguish between these
emotions and desires.

Rochester, like the patriarchal culture that he represents, deals
with Antoinette by stripping her of any identity and by forcing her
into a state of mental distress that he can label as madness. First, he
isolates her from those she loves and needs, such as Christophine,
with whom she shares a close bond. This behavior—as observed by
Marjorie Homer, Anne Leonard, and Pat Taylor—seems to be common in abusive husbands, for "the husband's control within the marriage was often manifested and reinforced by his ability to forbid
his wife contact with family and friends" (Homer *et al.* 1985, 94).
Rochester can reclaim his power over Antoinette by isolating her from
her home and Christophine, and then attempting to silence her
altogether.

Rochester also regains his sovereignty by redefining the situation
and Antoinette in his own terms. Despite the clearheaded observations of Christophine, who fights to alter Rochester's behavior,
Rochester persists in inventing a reality that suits his view of the

world. This behavior is also evident in many wife batterers, as Prescott and Letko argue in "Battered Women: A Social Psychological Perspective." According to their research, men often interpret female actions and qualities differently from women, as in this one example: ". . . what men automatically see as masculinity in females, women sense as their own competence" (1977, 73). Rochester rationalizes his treatment of Antoinette and transforms guilt into self-pity. He thinks, "Pity. Is there none for me? Tied to a lunatic for life . . ." (Rhys 1985, 560). Thus he writes his own narrative with himself as victim.

Moreover, Rochester tries to redefine and recreate Antoinette herself. Consumed with obsessive hatred, he visualizes his wife as an inanimate object, a dehumanized puppet or "marionette" (553). Similarly, earlier in the text he renames her Bertha so that her name will not resemble that of her mother. In this action Rochester strips Antoinette of any identity or "subjecthood," as well as any tie with her mother or her past. He will not allow her to live as an autonomous subject; she must exist only as an object defined and controlled by him.

Antoinette, like many battered women today, reacts to her husband's abuse with rebellion, frustration, anger, and finally learned helplessness and mental illness. Early in the novel she finds comfort in her relationship with Christophine and in laughing at Rochester's inability to understand their discourse. She also lets out a "crazy laugh" when she confronts him about his affair with Amelie (549). Her laughter, like that described by French feminist theorist Helene Cixous (1976) in "The Laugh of the Medusa," is a subversive act directed against patriarchal oppression. She also lashes out at Rochester's claim to "justice," which she calls "a cold word" (Rhys 1985, 548). Finally, she attacks Richard Mason in Thornfield Hall when he utters the word "legally" (570), rebelling against "justice," the patriarchal structure that legitimates the behavior of the Rochesters in this world. She also reacts violently to Rochester when he threatens to harm her physically (549). Unfortunately, her rebellion is futile; the patriarchy is too strong to overcome, and its power finally drives her to her only escape: learned helplessness and "madness." As noted by Lenore E. Walker, Antoinette's behavior is not unique. Many battered women, after experiencing powerlessness and depression, lapse into a state of learned helplessness (1984, 75–87) in which they give up any resistance to abuse, retreating into silence and passivity. In *Wide*

Sargasso Sea, as in many of today's situations, Antoinette turns to sedatives for relief, drugs to numb her consciousness.

Thus, Antoinette can only resign herself to abuse or retaliate through subversive behavior, which then supports Rochester's claim that she is mad. As Phyllis Chesler (1972) discusses in *Women and Madness,* it is the patriarchy and its institutionalization of "madness" that perpetuates the myth of the hysterical madwoman. Unfortunately, the line between true mental illness and imposed "madness" is thin; redefined and treated as a deranged, inhuman beast, the woman may either act or actually become "mad," thus reinscribing the patriarchy's assumptions underlying mental illness and the nature of woman. This subversive madness becomes Antoinette's final refuge and, ironically, her final source of strength. From this perspective, Antoinette's last act is one of rebellion rather than resignation.

In Jean Rhys's *Wide Sargasso Sea,* therefore, we see the full effect of mental spouse abuse, which is every bit as violent and destructive as physical abuse. And, in viewing the "madwoman in the attic" from her own point of view on the margin of "sane" civilization, we hear her "hysterical" laughter and cries as frustrated attempts to subvert an oppressive, abusive patriarchy that has tried to silence them. Rhys's revisionist text does just that; it explores what those mad screams possibly signify, finally emancipating the "madwoman" from *Jane Eyre's* Thornfield Hall and from our own imaginations as well.

References

Cixous, Helene. "The Laugh of the Medusa." Trans. Keith Cohen and Paula Cohen. *Signs* 1(4): 875–893, 1976.

Chesler, Phyllis. *Women and Madness.* New York: Doubleday, 1972.

Dobash, R. Emerson, and Russell Dobash. *Violence Against Wives: A Case Against the Patriarchy.* New York: Macmillan, 1979.

Gilbert, Sandra M., and Susan Gubar. *The Madwoman Writer and the Nineteenth-Century Literary Imagination.* New Haven: Yale University Press, 1979.

Homer, Marjorie, Anne Leonard, and Pat Taylor. "Personal Relationships: Help and Hindrance." In Norman Johnson, ed., *Marital Violence.* Boston: Routledge, 1985.

Nebeker, Helen. *Jean Rhys, Woman in Passage: A Critical Study of the Novels of Jean Rhys.* Montreal: Eden Press, 1981.

O'Connor, Teresa. *Jean Rhys: The West Indian Novels*. New York: New York University Press, 1986.

Prescott, Suzanne, and Carolyn Letko. "Battered Women: A Social Psychological Perspective." In Maria Roy, ed., *Battered Women: A Psychosociological Study of Domestic Violence*. New York: Reinhold, 1977.

Rhys, Jean. *Jean Rhys: The Complete Novels*. New York: Norton, 1985.

Roe, Sue. "'The Shadow of Light': The Symbolic Underworld of Jean Rhys." In Sue Roe, ed., *Women Reading Women's Writing*. New York: St. Martin's, 1987.

Schechter, Susan. *Women and Male Violence: The Visions and Struggles of the Battered Women's Movement*. Boston: South End, 1982.

Walker, Lenore E. *The Battered Woman Syndrome*. New York: Springer, 1984.

9

Soul Murder and Other Crimes of the Heart

Familial Abuse in Nathaniel Hawthorne's Fictional Psychodramas

MARYHELEN C. HARMON

In the middle of the nineteenth century, when Nathaniel Hawthorne was writing the romances and short stories that would secure his position in the first rank of American authors, enjoyment was not the exclusive goal of readers. Any imprimatur of a literary work depended on its moral or tropological meaning, a mode of medieval critical response that stressed the lesson of the work as applied to individual behavior, that is, a depiction of what people ought to do.

Much in the body of Hawthorne's work can be seen, in fact, as a collection of didactic object lessons in the aberrant behavior of those who abuse others, what one critic sees as Hawthorne's "fascination with malice and humiliation" (Leverenz 1989, 227). Hawthorne's fiction thereby dramatizes both nineteenth-century attitudes toward such physical and psychological violence as well as the mores of the historical period chosen for the particular story's setting. While most literary critics judge this moralistic element as the least original thing about his work, it should be recognized that "it is what he shared with nearly all his lesser contemporaries in the sentimental vein"

(Crews 1966, 7), for Hawthorne was ever one to be aware of and respond to the *zeitgeist*.

One of the assumptions underlying this volume is that insights revealing uncharted territory can be gained by considering incisive references to the problem of familial crime in major literary works. Developing this assumption, I argue that by looking closely at certain of Hawthorne's fictions that dramatize the trauma resulting from family violence, we might frame our relationships to avoid such abuse, as well as effect societal and judicial change in this all too prevalent classless crime. Morton Schatzman in *Soul Murder: Persecution in the Family* agrees:

> There are benefits in studying written words. Unlike people, they are uninfluenced by the fact of being observed (1973, 12) . . . for we cannot experience directly events occurring in other people's minds. (1973, 141)

It is toward this goal of sensitizing us to the suffering of others that we look at some of Hawthorne's fictions—to learn what people ought to do.

Repeatedly, Hawthorne responded to readers' demands for instruction: In his preface to *The House of the Seven Gables*, for example, he is particularly insistent as he observes, "Many writers lay very great stress upon some definite moral purpose, at which they profess to aim their works. Not to be deficient, in this particular, the Author has provided himself with a moral" (1965). In his characteristic self-deprecatory manner, he here refuses "to flatter himself with the slightest hope" that his work "might effectively convince mankind" to alter its behavior; yet he displays an acute insight into human conduct when he observes that when books "do really teach anything, or produce any effective operation, it is usually through a far more subtle process than the ostensible one" (1965).

Hawthorne was caught in a personal bind; he was by all accounts an exceedingly private person, describing himself in the 1851 edition of his *Twice-Told Tales* as "a mild, shy, gentle, melancholic, exceedingly sensitive, not very forcible man." He was obviously in accord with the genteel tradition of his times, an American conformation of Victorian taste and behavior that anticipated an era when correctness and conventionality (especially among New England writers) would be challenged by the more vital concurrent literary movements of realism and naturalism. Yet, despite his propriety, he nevertheless was obviously aware of the pragmatic and utilitarian aspects of literature— the dramatization of moral didacticism, albeit by a "subtle process."

D. H. Lawrence observed about Hawthorne that "that blue-eyed darling Nathaniel knew disagreeable things" but "he was careful to send them out in disguise" (1923, 89). Another critic observed that despite nineteenth-century conventions, Hawthorne's fictions portray "manliness as aggressive, insensitive, and murderously dominant . . . as strong men collectively try to shame weaker, yet nobler individuals" (Leverenz 1989, 231)—these victims being their wives, lovers, and daughters.

Recalling Hawthorne's intention of providing a moral in *The House of the Seven Gables,* the specific moral that he wished to communicate was "that the wrongdoing of one generation lives into the succeeding ones," a succinct approximation of one of the clinical models contemporary therapists follow in dealing with problems in human relationships—the "social learning" model, which stresses that behavior is acquired by imitation. This pattern of passing on "the sins of the fathers" Hawthorne characteristically understates as one that "becomes a pure and uncontrollable mischief" (1965).

Familial abuse, whether physical or psychological, is indeed the ultimate "pure and uncontrollable mischief." As an intelligent, inquiring New Englander, Hawthorne must certainly have known of many incidents of such violence in the small towns where he lived and wrote, the residents of most of these communities still persisting in the Puritan belief that the public must be concerned with private acts, that there was a civic duty to regulate family life. Also, his years of reading annals of New England history provided the author with graphic, documented cases of such conflict. Hawthorne's best-known work, *The Scarlet Letter,* can be seen as an extended case study of Hester Prynne as an example of what R. Emerson and Russell Dobash describe as "women who did not know their place and were seen to be outside their husbands' control," and, as such, Hester was "subjected to public ridicule and degradation" (1979, 59). Evidently Hester's sufferings were too much for the hypersensitive Mrs. Hawthorne: When her husband read the story's conclusion to her, it "broke her heart and sent her to bed with a grievous headache," a reaction, the author exulted, "which I look on as a triumphant success!"[1] A critic observed that "ostensibly his 'triumphant' sense of professional satisfaction depends on breaking a woman's heart and mind" (Leverenz 1989, 259).

In tracing the various punishments such transgressors as Hester Prynne suffered, the Dobashes cite that during the Reformation (the time setting of Hawthorne's Puritan drama) such women were "sentenced to placarding" (1979, 59). Whether such "placarding" was a symbol of opprobrium pinned to a bonnet or, as in Hester's case, embroidered on the bodice, such public shaming was a visible extension of Puritan society's concern with private behavior, further dramatized in *The Scarlet Letter* by Hester's forced display on the town scaffold ("a portion of a penal machine") as an object lesson to others: in effect, a living sermon against sin.

For some in the Puritan community, of course, the scarlet letter A on Hester's breast never meant anything more or less than the brand of "adulteress." Yet as her good works and sympathetic powers extended into that community through long years, "many people refused to interpret the scarlet A by its original signification. They said it meant 'Able!'" Hawthorne also describes Hester's stigmatized bosom as the "pillow of Affection." In the novel's conclusion he suggests additional meanings for the letter A: Hester as "the angel and apostle of the coming revelation," one which would "establish the whole relation between man and woman on a surer ground of mutual happiness." Here Hawthorne specifically recognizes the plight of wretched women who came to Hester for counsel—bringing to her for comfort or remedy their "continually recurring trials of wounded, wasted, wronged, misplaced, or erring and sinful passion" (1962). Although these suffering women wore no A ostensibly on their bosoms as did Hester Prynne, they shared her sad burden of the scarlet letter as signifying "Abused."

Concealment of behavior within a Puritan family was obviously an impossibility, as contrasted with nineteenth- and twentieth-century societal and judicial attitudes revealed graphically in a North Carolina court opinion of 1874:

> If no permanent injury has been inflicted, nor malice nor dangerous violence shown by the husband, it is better to draw the curtain, shut out the public gaze, and leave the parties to forgive and forget. (Davidson 1978, 103)

In her recent book *Domestic Tyranny*, Elizabeth Pleck, in describing the period in which Hawthorne was growing up and forming the attitudes toward family life that would be reflected in his work, notes that "in the early nineteenth century the curtain was drawn on family life, closing off private troubles from public view" (1987, 6).

In several of his fictions, Hawthorne employs this technique of "drawing the curtain," veiling the behavior of the characters from public scrutiny. Probably the most vivid example is the tale of psychological abuse, "The Minister's Black Veil," which relates the saga of a young cleric who dons a cloth over his face, perhaps because of guilt for a sexual sin broadly hinted at in the narrative, thereby alienating the affection of Elizabeth, "his plighted wife." She responds to his baffling refusal ever to remove the symbolic barrier between them by tearfully bidding him farewell, although she dutifully returns to nurse him in his final illness. Although not using an actual veil, Hawthorne often employs devices of equally effective obfuscation: A character climbs high in a church steeple to observe and ponder "all heeding and unheeded" on those passing below; another hides beneath an umbrella in order to observe with impunity the private lives of others; still another confesses "I love to spend (all day Sunday) behind the curtain of my open window" admiring such as the white-stockinged legs of young girls climbing the steps into church.[2]

These random instances, while seemingly innocuous, suggest the predilection of the author for veiling and concealment. Using third person, when the subject of his character is broached, he observes about himself: "You must . . . look through the whole range of his fictitious characters, good and evil, in order to detect any of his essential traits." Thus it is not surprising that despite the complex familial relations that Hawthorne analyzes in his fiction, there is no overt depiction of violence such as physical battering. As Murray A. Straus and Suzanne K. Steinmetz observe, in such novels no material is found on "fights, slappings, or throwing things between husband and wife"—although there is murder. "We think that says something about the extent to which husband–wife violence is unconsciously repressed by novelists" (1974, preface). Rather, the abusive situations of which Hawthorne writes are almost universally psychological, which, of course, makes them no less destructive. In her discussion of such "mental harm," Maria Roy considers incidents of violence "not confined to the physical kind," and in comparing it with physical abuse, argues that such "injury is far more significant, for it touches the human psyche. The wounds are deep. The spirit is defiled. The damage is insidious" (1982, 10). Lenore E. Walker in her study, *The Battered Woman Syndrome*, reinforces Roy's observation: "psychological abuse created longer-lasting pain than did many . . . physically induced injuries" (1984, 202).

Characters suffering "mental harm" constitute one of Hawthorne's favorite and ubiquitous themes, what he termed "The Unpardonable Sin"—wherein a violating intellect invades the sanctity of another's heart and soul—"soul murder," in effect. Leonard Shengold in his 1989 study, *Soul Murder*, defines his topic as "neither a diagnosis nor a condition. It is a dramatic term for circumstances that eventuate in crime—the deliberate attempt to eradicate or compromise the separate identity of another person" (1989, 2). Just as portrayed by Hawthorne, Shengold observes, "Victims of soul murder remain in large part possessed by another, their souls in bondage to someone else" (2). Lionel Trilling also saw soul murder as violation of the essence of morality: ". . . making a willing suspension of disbelief in the selfhood of somebody else" (1955, 94).

Hawthorne would qualify his theory of the unpardonable sin to include both acts of commission and omission. He wrote in his journal in 1842, "The Unpardonable Sin might consist of a *want* of love and reverence for the Human Soul; in consequence of which, the investigator pried into its dark depths, not with a hope or purpose of making it better, but from a cold philosophic curiosity" (*American Notebooks* 1972, 251). This causing of pain or injury as an end in itself Steinmetz and Straus, in their *Violence in the Family*, term "expressive violence" (as opposed to "instrumental violence"), which is "the use of pain or injury or physical restraint as a punishment or to induce the other person to carry out some act" (1974, 4).

To Hawthorne, any act of violence evinces intellectual pride carried to such an extreme that it permits one to manipulate the souls of others in order to gratify cold curiosity and thirst for power. Examples of such psychic damage abound in his fiction. In "My Kinsman, Major Molineux," set in the time of the American Revolution, he portrays the suffering of Major Molineux, an old man whose heart is trampled on by a violent mob, a participant in which is young Robin, his kinsman.

Robin is his adolescent nephew who, having left his family behind in the country, comes to the city only to be seized by the crowd's fury: as his tarred and feathered uncle passes in agony, "Robin's shout (of laughter) was the loudest there." Another abusive character is Ethan Brand, who, "looking on mankind as the subject of his experiment," specifically converts a woman, Esther, "to be his puppet"; for "with such cold and remorseless purpose, Ethan Brand had made [her] the subject of psychological experiment, and thereby wasted, absorbed, and perhaps annihilated her soul, in the process" (1974). Hawthorne characteristically offers no specific reason for Brand's "soul murder" abuse.

Elsewhere in his fiction there continues a veritable cavalcade of the detailed acts of such "mad scientists" as object lessons of experimenters and exploiters who, by one means or another, also relentlessly abuse and destroy their mates or children. Whereas his focus is on the popular interest in science in nineteenth-century America, especially in the pseudosciences of mesmerism and homeopathy, Hawthorne's fascination with the mysterious and evil practitioners of science provides a wealth of examples of those who, in perpetrating the unpardonable sin, each in his own way, plot to subjugate helpless innocent victims. Taylor Stoehr's *Hawthorne's Mad Scientists*, in providing details of this concern, notes that "Hawthorne wrote at a time when one popular movement was replacing another, as pseudoscience made way for social science, and also at a turning point in literary history, the overlap of gothic and utopian fictions" (1978, 11).

We have seen that exertion of power lies at the core of Hawthorne's unpardonable sin. As Roy emphasizes, the exploitive and manipulative facets of power "are very definitely rooted in varying degrees of destruction," what she terms "violent coercion" of helpless female victims. Such "woman battering objectifies women by reducing them to objects of possession" (1982, 93). The Dobashes reinforce this argument:

> Almost all of the writings about women discuss them in only one type of relationship, their personal relationships with men. The only roles truly allowed women in the real or the imaginary world have been those of wife, mother, daughter, lover, whore, or saint [all terms of possession]. (1979, 32)

In Hawthorne's "imaginary world" that we are here examining for possible tropological meaning, the proprietary title of one of his most powerful tales, "Rappaccini's Daughter," is obvious. We learn that Beatrice Rappaccini, kept isolated in a high-walled garden filled with fantastic flowering plants, is locked in a medieval pattern of conflict with her father. Portentously, we hear their first words: he calls her name; she responds "Here am I, my father. What would you?" He is, in psychoanalytic terminology, obviously "master of his child forever," able to rule "with only a glance, a word, a single threatening gesture," his victim resembling "a person in a trance" (Schatzman 1973, 66).

Beatrice attracts the love of the shallow young Giovanni, who schemes to visit her in the garden. He is warned that Rappaccini's science has led him beyond moral or humane constraints, and that Beatrice's very nature is a product of his sinister art. Evidence accretes to support the awful truth: her breath is indeed deadly, her body steeped in exotic poisons by her father's experiments, just as the garden flowers are. Dr. Rappaccini exults in defending his ghastly experiment, asking rhetorically if she would "have preferred the condition of a weak woman, exposed to all evil and capable of none?" Of course Beatrice was not allowed to make the choice.

A nineteenth-century German teacher and writer, Dr. D. G. M. Schreber, echoes Dr. Rappaccini's goal in child raising, regardless of the radical repressive methods, as he writes of the "victory of spiritual nature over body-nature," exulting that the new generation would therefore be better, "nobler, and more perfect," and that necessary constraints toward this goal include control of the child's sex life (quoted in Schatzman 1973, 81). The paranoid fictional doctor Rappaccini, of course, silently masterminds the seduction of Giovanni to be Beatrice's mate: his patriarchal benediction to the now equally poisoned young man and his intended bride: "Pass on, then, through the world, most dear to one another and dreadful to all besides!"

Misdirected enthusiasm for perfection of the race at whatever personal cost (often Hawthorne's thematic material) leads to the deadly combination of paranoia and power, a totalitarianism that at the family level he dramatizes as despotism, a microsocial situation of familial abuse. By extension such zealotry would lead to Nazi greed for purity and perfection of the race, a macrosocial situation that produced the Holocaust. The key word is "control" by power, whether in a family situation or extended globally. In *Mein Kampf*, Hitler describes

> the woman whose inner sensibilities are not so much under the sway of abstract reasoning but are always subject to the influence of a vague emotional longing for the struggle that completes her being, and who would rather bow to the strong man. (1927, 42)

Comparing the female personality to the psyche of the masses who prefer to be ruled and not make choices, he sees them both as feeling

> very little shame at being terrorized intellectually . . . scarcely conscious of the fact that their freedom as human beings is impudently abused. (42)

In a more recent analysis of the abuser and the abused, the behaviorist B. F. Skinner in *Walden Two* observes that "the controlled . . . feel free. The curious thing is that . . . the question of freedom never arises" (1962, 262).

Such a victim is the unquestioning and unprotesting Beatrice Rappaccini. Critics suggest that her father may have even raped her, as his name suggests; "in any case, he has abused her body to give her power," as well as to assert his own to all rivals (Leverenz 1989, 240).

We saw that Giovanni becomes toxic himself as his relationship with Beatrice continues, and, when he recognizes his own fate, he erupts at Beatrice, now the scapegoat of both men: "Let us join our lips in one kiss of unutterable hatred, and so die!" Beatrice's death ultimately is the result of a failed homeopathic treatment; in a classic pattern of manipulation, Giovanni reaches out with hope to his beloved in a psychologically abusive ploy: "Dear Beatrice . . . dearest Beatrice, our fate is not yet so desperate," he croons as he produces the vial that supposedly contains an antidote, and she responds, "Give it to me! I will drink!" As Stoehr describes her, she is herself "a poisoned vessel devilishly prepared by her father" (1978, 129), and she dies from drinking the contents of a deadly vessel that purports to neutralize her toxicity.

Beatrice Rappaccini, the "poor victim of man's ingenuity," is not the only Hawthornian female character who accepts a supposed remedy for some bodily condition only to have it fail. Georgiana (in "The Birthmark") willingly drinks a fatal potion for the sake of her "mad scientist" husband Aylmer, an obsessed alchemist with a history of failed experiments, and Sybil Dacy in *Septimius Felton* also unquestioningly quaffs the cup that kills to satisfy the delusions of her mate.

We will return to examples of these and other victims of violence in Hawthorne's procession of family member abusers—as already observed in "Rappaccini's Daughter"—especially as they remarkably profile sufferers of a psychologically abusive situation outlined in Walker's study of the battered woman: (1) isolation of victim, (2) induced disability, (3) monopolization of perception including possessiveness, (4) threats, (5) degradation, (6) drug administration, (7) altered states of consciousness produced through hypnotic states, and (8) occasional indulgences "to . . . keep hope alive" (her outline appears on pages 27 and 28). Walker observes that "battered women tend to be very suggestible and want others to think well of them," and are "easily frightened" (1984, 206). Their abusers, she argues, are "men who are insecure," and "who often need a great amount of nurturance and are very possessive of a woman's time," often paying victims "extra attention and flattery" (1984, 12).

We can now consider Hawthorne's "The Birthmark" as a classic case study in spouse abuse, an uncannily precise counterpart in fictional character delineation of Walker's psychologically battered woman syndrome.

The tale of Aylmer the scientist and his wife Georgiana is set "in the latter part of the last century," which would be the end of the 1700s. The narrator tells readers that the union of Aylmer and the beautiful Georgiana "was attended with truly remarkable consequences and a deeply impressive moral," a typically Hawthornian scheme. The consequence is Aylmer's obsession with removing a tiny birthmark on his wife's face. Although he flatters her as "so nearly perfect," eradication of the blemish increasingly becomes "the central point" of his existence. Wanting to be thought well of, in desperation Georgiana, although very frightened, agrees to its removal: She declares, betraying her lack of self-esteem, "let the attempt be made at whatever risk." Her life with her husband now "wretched," she sees the mark as "a burden which I would fling down with joy." In rapture, her husband praises her excessively and kisses her, murmuring "Noblest, dearest, tenderest wife." "Persecutors may persuade or force their victims to see their persecution as love, especially if the persecutors are the victim's parents or spouses" (1973, 149), observed the psychoanalyst Schatzman.

Aylmer isolates Georgiana in apartments previously "occupied by Aylmer as a laboratory." Georgiana faints as she enters her lavishly decorated and elegant boudoir prison, recovering to inhale a "penetrating fragrance from perfumed lamps," and in this drugged seclusion Georgiana is progressively prepared for her fate. Her husband rejoices now about her tiny birthmark, what "a rapture to remove it." She begins to hallucinate as a result of the narcotizing atmosphere, as Aylmer boasts of all his scientific ambitions, including concocting incredibly powerful poisons and discovering the elixir of life (a potion that appears with disastrous results in several of Hawthorne's works, particularly in "Dr. Heidegger's Experiment")—all of this filling Georgiana "with amazement and fear." Despite increasing evidence of his many scientific failures, Georgiana's altered consciousness cannot react normally: she says of his dismal record as a scientist, "It has made me worship you more than ever" (1974).

The insecure Aylmer now senses that the triumph of his abusive power over his wife is at hand and, for proof, cruelly orders her like a bird in his cage to "sing to me, dearest." Immediately after her song he rushes to his laboratory to prepare the eradicating potion, where Georgiana follows him. His mood at her intrusion is outrage: he physically abuses her as he "seized her arm with a grip that left the print of his fingers upon it" and verbally assaults and degrades her: "Go, prying woman, go!" The drugged wife calmly reassures him of her resolve to submit to his treatment of her birthmark: "Remove it, whatever the cost; I shall quaff whatever draught you bring me." Aylmer then flatteringly addresses her as "my noble wife" (1974).

Georgiana departs to muse on her "imperfection" which, by now, she is convinced is a monstrous disfigurement; "and with her whole spirit she prayed that, for a single moment, she might satisfy his highest and deepest conception." When Aylmer brings the draught that he has concocted to perfect her, she is now totally his victim. She assures her "dearest Aylmer" that "being what I find myself, methinks I am of all mortals the most fit to die." Eagerly she tells him "Give me the goblet. I joyfully stake all upon your word." She speaks her dying words—"My poor Aylmer!"—as the tiny birthmark seems to fade with a gentle reluctance (1974).

We recall that Hawthorne promises his readers not only a recounting of the "truly remarkable consequences" of Aylmer's physical and psychological violence against his wife, but, as well, "a deeply impressive moral," namely, that by Aylmer's manic pursuit of ideal
perfection, even to the sacrifice of a trusting, suggestible wife who
only wanted to please her husband, he failed "to find the perfect
future in the present."

Homeopathy was not the only nineteenth-century pseudoscience
that Hawthorne exploited to dramatize the limitless power a male
"man of science" can exert over a helpless female victim. We recall that
Walker's profile of the psychologically abused victim included isolation
and "induced disability" as well as "altered states of consciousness
produced through hypnotic states," in which the individual loses
critical powers and becomes consequently open to suggestion and
domination. In the nineteenth century, Franz Anton Mesmer, an Aus-
trian physician, developed a theory and method of mental treatment,
called by him "animal magnetism" because he saw it as analogous with
the electric phenomenon then in contemporary public interest. His
fantastic ideas included the possibility of magnetized trees, mirrors,
water, and animals, and the "magnetic" influence of one person over
another.

Hawthorne was especially alarmed by mesmerism, in the stern-
est of language warning his wife, a psychosomatical invalid from
chronic headaches, not to fall under its influence ("I beseech thee to
take no part"). As an author he borrowed heavily from Mesmer's
theories in *The House of the Seven Gables* and also in *The Blithedale
Romance*, in both of which the power of diabolic characters intent on
sexual bondage and enslavement is exercised by mesmerism (by
Maule over Alice Pyncheon in *Gables* and by Westervelt over the passive "veiled lady" Pricilla as well as the assertive Zenobia in
Blithedale). Such hypnotic control as dramatized in these works "becomes the narrator's recurrent symbol for the dangers of enslavement
lurking in any entangling domestic alliances" (Leverenz 1989, 248).
The German Dr. Schreber, earlier noted as a popular educator of child
rearing, evoked the term "soul murder" as analogous with hypnosis—asserting on a number of occasions that in such "treatment" a
person's nervous system is influenced by another's to the extent of
imprisoning his (or her) willpower (another variation of Hawthorne's
concept of "the unpardonable sin").

In dilating upon such exploitation of another, Hawthorne saw hypnosis as resulting in psychological abuse: ". . . the sacredness of an individual being violated by it" (in a letter of October 18, 1841). He describes the suicide of Zenobia, with her "miserable, bruised, and battered heart," as a result of the mesmeric power plays she suffered and could suffer no longer. Following the familiar pattern remarked by Walker, "the violence between man and woman escalates out of control and someone dies" (1984, 38), usually the woman as a suicide. Over the body of the fated Beatrice Rappaccini three men stood, each or all of them possibly her killer—certainly all exploiters of a dominating power over the female victim. As Schatzman observes, "A feature of 'soul murder' . . . was forbidding the victim to identify his or her murderer correctly" (1973, 38).

In an early key scene in *Blithedale*, the massive blacksmith Hollingsworth, when provoked by the feminist Zenobia's challenge for "woman's wider liberty" against the power of "the vast bulk of society that throttles us, and with two gigantic hands at our throats!" responds with fiercely glowing eyes that woman's only place is at man's side, "unquestioning." A woman without a "man as her acknowledged principal" he sees as a "monster." Further revealing the prevailing attitude of mid-nineteenth-century society, he is cheered by the fact that since few such women exist, he thanks Heaven that any would be "an almost impossible and hitherto imaginary monster." Continuing his fulmination, he swears that if "these petticoated monstrosities," these poor, miserable, abortive creatures, had a chance of attaining their goals, he "would call upon my own sex to use its physical force, that unmistakable evidence of sovereignty, to scourge them back within their proper bounds!" Consoling himself again, he sees such violence as unnecessary: "The heart of true womanhood knows where its own sphere is, and never seeks to stray beyond it!" Zenobia bitterly responds "Did you ever see a happy woman in your life?" (1964)

Another intrapsychic abuser in Hawthorne's cavalcade of characters appears in "Wakefield," where the eponymous husband, after ten years of marriage, for no reason whatever, "absented himself for a long time from his wife"—20 years, in fact. Before his departure he had taken "lodgings in the next street to his own house," and during two decades, perversely and by means of disguise, selfishly observes his wife's "widowhood." Hawthorne describes him as "never violent," of course, but cold of heart. Yet, his pathological abuse provokes him at first not to return "until she be frightened half to death." Wakefield ponders excitedly, "Dear Woman! Will she die?" as a result of his monstrous scheme for her entrapment. All the while, he consoles himself that should he "deem it time to re-enter his parlor, his wife would clap her hands for joy." Yet Mrs. Wakefield, despite her husband's abuse, now has "the placid mien of settled widowhood," possessing the strength of character to survive her dominating husband's cruel and "unmerciful" treatment of her (1974).

As expected, Hawthorne promises the reader of "Wakefield" that "there will be a pervading spirit and a moral," part of which he interjects during the narrative: "It is perilous to make a chasm in human affections." He concludes with the truth that when a breach is made in a familial relationship, "a man exposes himself to a fearful risk of losing his place forever. Like Wakefield, he may become . . . the Outcast of the Universe" (1974).

With our contemporary recognition of psychological spouse abuse, we might insist that Wakefield warranted punishment more severe than being a cosmic pariah; certainly he did not deserve to cross his threshold again after 20 years of absence, to "become a loving spouse till death." Hawthorne does temper this "happy event" with the observation that Wakefield "has left us much food for thought" (1974). Perhaps such thought should direct us to recall the sad chronicles of history in which "to become a wife . . . placed her in the same category as children and servants, demanded surrender and obedience, and elevated her husband to the position" of being one in which his abusive treatment "in any other setting would clearly not be considered offenses" (Dobash and Dobash 1979, 59).

In a recent column by the syndicated writer Ann Landers (April 15, 1990), the heading heralded the obvious advice that the "abused must tear away from web of abuse." Landers informs her readers that the thousands of letters she has received from abused women "all sound as if they were written by the same person," recognizing, as do clinicians and therapists, that "patterns of abuse are similar." My analysis of the victims of abuse dramatized in Hawthorne's fiction supports yet a further truth: that fictional victims suffer in the same ways as their counterparts in reality, yet there is a crucial advantage of an aesthetic distancing between the reader and those dramatizations of violence to which he or she is responding.

Such psychological detachment permits balancing the initial

emotional impact of horror and outrage which feels pain emphatically, against later, more objective judgment, which not only reinforces the enormity of the abused victim's sufferings, but also encourages rational evaluation and analysis of the mode of familial abuse. More significantly, aesthetic detachment can suggest resources for survival available to "real life" victims locked in analogous destructive relationships. After one is murdered—whether psychically ("soul murder") or physically—it is too late.

Art should not, of course, be confused with reality; but if art that vividly portrays the agonies of tragic victims of familial abuse does not move the reader to a greater sensitivity for the welfare of the individual, that art has failed. I argue that the fiction of Nathaniel Hawthorne, on this score, does not miscarry.

Notes

1. Stewart cites the quotation, which is included in a letter to Hawthorne's friend, Horatio Bridge, February 4, 1850 (95).
2. These nameless voyeuristic first-person narrators appear in "Sights from a Steeple," "Night Sketches Under an Umbrella," and "Sunday at Home."

References

All references to the works of Nathaniel Hawthorne are to the Centenary Edition, edited by William Charvat, Roy Harvey Pearce, and Claude Simpson, 20 volumes to the present (Columbus: Ohio State University Press, 1962). Works cited (with or without brief quotation) include the following volumes: vol. I, *The Scarlet Letter* (1962); vol. II, *The House of the Seven Gables* (1965); vol. III, *The Blithedale Romance* (1964); vol. VIII, *The American Notebooks* (1972); vol. IX, *Twice-Told Tales* (1974) ("The Minister's Black Veil," "Wakefield," "Night Sketches Under an Umbrella," "Sights from a Steeple," "Sunday at Home," "Dr. Heidegger's Experiment"); vol. X, *Mosses from an Old Manse* (1974) ("Rappaccini's Daughter," "The Birthmark"); vol. XI, *The Snow Image and Uncollected Tales* (1974) ("Preface," "My Kinsman, Major Molineux," "Ethan Brand"); vol. XIII, *Elixir of Life Manuscripts* (1977) (*Septimius Felton*)

Crews, Frederick. *The Sins of the Fathers.* Berkeley: University of California Press, 1966.

Davidson, Terry. *Conjugal Crime: Understanding and Changing the Wifebeating Pattern*. New York: Hawthorn Books, 1978.

Dobash, R. Emerson, and Russell Dobash. *Violence Against Wives: A Case Against the Patriarchy*. New York: The Free Press, 1979.

Hitler, Adolf. *Mein Kampf*. Trans. Ralph Manheim. Boston: Houghton Mifflin, 1927.

Landers, Ann. "Abused Must Tear Away From Web of Abuse." *St. Petersburg Times*, 15 April, 1990, 9F.

Lawrence, D. H. *Studies in Classic American Literature*. New York: Penguin Books, 1923.

Leverenz, David. *Manhood and the American Renaissance*. Ithaca, NY: Cornell University Press, 1989.

Pleck, Elizabeth. *Domestic Tyranny: The Making of Social Policy Against Family Violence from Colonial Times to the Present*. New York: Oxford University Press, 1987.

Roy, Maria, Ed. *The Abusive Partner: An Analysis of Domestic Battering*. New York: Van Nostrand Reinhold, 1982.

Schatzman, Morton. *Soul Murder: Persecution in the Family*. New York: Random House, 1973.

Shengold, Leonard. *Soul Murder*. New Haven: Yale University Press, 1989.

Skinner, B. F. *Walden Two*. New York: Macmillan, 1962.

Stoehr, Taylor. *Hawthorne's Mad Scientists*. Hamden, CT: Archon Books, 1978.

Straus, Murray A., and Suzanne K. Steinmetz, eds. *Violence in the Family*. New York: Harper & Row, 1974.

Trilling, Lionel. *Beyond Culture*. New York: Viking Press, 1955.

Walker, Lenore E. *The Battered Woman Syndrome*. New York: Springer, 1984.

10

Family Portraits

Ominous Images in High School Literature

RALPH M. CLINE

"American Literature" is one of the most universal experiences of United States citizens. Sometime in each American's high school career—usually in the junior year—he or she takes "American Lit." On the first day of this course, the teacher issues an anthology containing representative selections from America's most famous authors. These anthologies, as it turns out, are nearly as universal as the "American Lit" experience itself. Their tables of contents are remarkably similar, both in the authors and in the selections chosen. In fact, virtually all American students use an anthology published by a mere handful of publishers—Macmillan, Harcourt Brace, Scott, Foresman, Ginn and Company.

Just as homogenous, probably, are the choices that American literature teachers make in supplementary works. The list of works used in addition to the adopted literature anthologies is very nearly as predictable as the contents of the anthologies themselves—Fitzgerald, Twain, Faulkner, Hemingway. Of course, one of the most striking similarities in these American literature anthologies and supplemental texts is the fact that most are written by men. The reason for such male preponderance has doubtless caused hot and vituperative debate. But the fact remains: "American Lit" is written by men.

Another of the curricular similarities is the remarkable number of works concerned with family violence in one form or another. As we will see, the spouse abuse to which virtually all Americans are vicariously exposed takes many forms. This violence is not, perhaps, as dramatic and obvious as such violence in British and Continental literature, but cruelty of one spouse to another permeates the literature to which American school children are exposed.

A police officer, a family counselor, a shelter volunteer—all of these people deal with Americans who are victims and witnesses of spouse abuse. But odds are good that the public school teacher is—knowingly or unknowingly—the first to broach the subject of family violence. Awareness of the varied forms of spouse abuse presented in the literature typically covered in American literature courses is, therefore, highly desirable—if not absolutely necessary—if spouse abuse is to be confronted in our country.

* * * * *

> They were careless people . . . they smashed up things and crea-
> tures and then retreated . . . and let other people clean up the
> mess they had made.
>
> F. Scott Fitzgerald, *The Great Gatsby*

The research makes some characteristics of spouse abuse abundantly clear. First, spouse abuse is not merely the abuse between legally married men and women; abuse between those living together or just immersed in an intimate and long-lasting relationship falls into this category. Second, spouse abuse can be both physical and nonphysical. Third, nonphysical (called "psychological" or "verbal") abuse is often more threatening, demeaning, and memorable than physical abuse (Siegel, Plesser, and Foster 1987, 54). Fourth, no matter what the type of abuse, in the vast majority of cases it is aimed *at* females *by* males.[1] And, fifth, the

> disproportionate frequency with which wives are the victims (of
> abuse) reflects the structure of contemporary Euro-American so-
> cieties in the form of cultural norms which implicitly make the
> marriage license a hitting license in the sexist organization of both
> society and the family system. (Siegel *et al.* 1987, 67)

A survey of nonhumorous American literature most often taught in high schools affirms these characteristics. As is often the case, fine authors know by intuition what researchers must discover by experimentation. American authors have given us many portraits of men and women leveling both physical and psychological abuse at one another. In nonhumorous literature, at least, the abuse is congruent with the research: the abuse is male initiated. When women are abusive, they act in self-defense or in aggression that could be called preemptive self-defense. And, in most serious American literature studied in high schools, women are abused largely because of the submissive roles that they have been taught to play by their society.[2]

Nathanial Hawthorne's (1804–1864) "Young Goodman Brown," included in many high school literature courses, is a good example. In this story, Brown does not abuse his wife physically. He merely uses the traditional Puritan role as a superior male; he applies the double standard in a devastating manner. As the story begins, Brown is embarking, at twilight, upon a mysterious journey into the dark forest. Many readers take the dark forest to be symbolic of Brown's (and mankind's) libidinous psyche. In other words, *Mr.* Brown may venture into the world of libidinous desire, but *Mrs.* Brown must stay at home. The young husband insists upon going on the journey as energetically as his wife Faith urges him to stay. The man tells the woman to go to bed and to cover herself safely and chastely in her blankets while he goes on his journey of experience—of course, for this one night only! Interpreted from a literal point of view, Brown, at the climax of the story, discovers that all of the village's citizens— prostitute and preacher alike—are attending a witches' Sabbath with him in the forest. Their presence there surprises him, but he is able to accept it. What devastates him is the sound of his *wife's* voice. That *she* is human in the same way that he and the other citizens of Salem are human is more than he can stand. At that point, Brown shouts to Faith to resist the devil (the same devil which Brown has so dramatically *failed* to resist) and to look heavenward. He never knows whether or not she has taken his hypocritical advice.

Upon his return to Salem village, Young Goodman Brown is a changed man. For the rest of his life, he treats Faith with utter disdain. He uses his discovery about her as a weapon to hurt her, thus participating in cruel psychological abuse. Brown and his wife live long and unhappily; he "shrinks from the bosom of Faith" (Hawthorne 1962, 708) for the rest of their married life.

Of course, the misery possible in marriage is shown unforgettably in Hawthorne's *The Scarlet Letter* (which, along with *Huck Finn* and *Moby-Dick*, is one of America's "big three" in high school English courses). Roger Chillingworth—like Goodman Brown—has seen his wife's "weakness," and he dedicates his life to scourging Hester and Rev. Arthur Dimmesdale, his cuckolder, using his knowledge to ruin them. He delights when Hester is exposed to public ridicule; he relishes the promise of her being brought low; he dances satanically when he sees (or thinks he sees) Dimmesdale's A-scarred chest. In other words, the woman Hester is held to a standard of truth, loyalty, and goodness that is far above the man Chillingworth's ability to attain. In one of the great ironic triumphs of American literature, Hester defeats her abuser. The cost, however, has been everything.

The same pattern is seen in "The Birthmark," another widely anthologized Hawthorne story taking place in male-dominated Puritan New England. Aylmer, a scientist far from perfect himself, becomes fixated upon his beautiful wife's one physical flaw, a birthmark. Georgiana dies—willingly, obediently, one almost adds "wifely"—as a result of Aylmer's experiments to remove the birthmark. Aylmer rejects "the best the world has to offer" (1962, 738) in an attempt to make his wife perfect—something that no human can be. Yet he never applies the same scrutiny to his own person.

In all three works, therefore, Hawthorne has painted portraits of men who feel that they deserve the right to control their women completely—women who must be perfect or must suffer horribly for their imperfections. In all three works, the abuse is aimed by men toward women. The men use their traditional societal roles of power—husband, divine, scientist—to subjugate their women. The abuse is both psychological and physical.

Much the same syndrome is obvious in F. Scott Fitzgerald's *The Great Gatsby*, certainly the most widely read twentieth-century American novel in high schools. Daisy Buchanan is hardly a corporeal human in the novel; her body is never described. She merely floats as a disembodied voice through the chapters, dressing always in white. She is merely a possession both to her husband Tom and to Jay Gatsby. Tom is having an affair with another woman and is interested in Daisy only insofar as she remains his chattel and out of the clutches of Gatsby. Gatsby himself is interested in Daisy as a kind of antique, an object for collection, for Gatsby is attempting to recreate his past in nostalgic splendor. Gatsby is interested in a Daisy who lived many years before. The desires of the Daisy of the novel are immaterial to this materialistic man. Both Tom and Gatsby, in other words, subject Daisy to psychological spouse abuse since neither is in the least interested in her as a person. They are interested only in their uses for her, and only when these uses are threatened does Daisy become important.

Daisy, of course, realizes the female's role in Jazz Age society. In one of the novel's most touching scenes, Daisy discusses the birth of her baby:

> Well, she was less than an hour old and Tom was God knows where. I woke up out of the ether with an utterly abandoned feeling; [the nurse] . . . told me it was a girl, and so I turned my head away and wept. "All right," I said, "I'm glad it's a girl. And I hope she'll be a fool . . . that's the best thing a girl can be in this world, a beautiful little fool. (Fitzgerald 1953, 17)

That Tom Buchanan is an abusive male is made all the more obvious in one of his scenes with Myrtle Wilson, his lover, whom he uses as he uses Daisy—but for another reason. In the apartment he keeps in New York for Myrtle, Tom argues with his mistress over her right to say Daisy's name. When Myrtle asserts her right to say "Daisy" whenever she pleases, Tom, with "a short deft movement," breaks "her nose with his open hand" (1953, 37).

The Great Gatsby is a complex novel treating the decline of American morals, the evils of both cupidity and concupiscence. But it is also a novel about spouse abuse, about men who wish to possess women as if they were medals or cars.

The five characteristics of spouse abuse noted by Siegel (1987) are also apparent in many of the works of William Faulkner (1897–1962), whose "Barn Burning" is one of the most frequently studied short stories in American literature courses. Abner Snopes, sharecropper, horse thief, barn burner, and spouse abuser, demands complete obedience from his wife and family. In many cases, this obedience includes helping Abner to break the law. Whenever he has even a slight disagreement with a landlord, Snopes's revenge is to burn the landlord's barn and to leave the area. His wife and some of his children are horrified by this facet of the old man's personality, but they are equally terrified by his irascibility and his propensity to violence. When his wife tries to stop Abner from carrying kerosene to a landlord's barn, Abner "shifted the lamp to the other hand and flung her back . . . into the wall, her hands flung out against the wall for balance, her mouth open and in her face the same quality of hopeless despair as had been in her voice" (Faulkner 1959, 513). Abner hits the boy Sarty (Colonel Sartoris Snopes) so often and resorts so often to violence against the establishment of rural Mississippi that Sarty finally runs away—with such determination that he never again appears in a Faulkner work. Abner reappears, however, in the Snopes trilogy (*The Hamlet, The Village,* and *The Mansion*). In these novels, Abner's son Flem marries the lovely Eula Varner for all sorts of reasons—but certainly not for love. He insults her; he threatens her; and he blackmails her daughter. He even uses to his own benefit Eula's chaste affection for a kind man. In the end, she escapes through the only avenue open to a woman in the south in the 1930s: she commits suicide.

American students see, therefore, what we could call "typical" spouse abuse in much that they are assigned to read. These troubled male–female relationships span the history of American literature and are placed in historical settings from the seventeenth to the twentieth centuries. These nonhumorous depictions of domestic mistreatment would, no doubt, be interpreted by the experts as credible, true-to-life instances of spouse abuse.

Comic presentation of the same subject, however, offers a strangely different picture.

* * * * *

A quieting draught out of Rip Van Winkle's flagon.
WASHINGTON IRVING, "Rip Van Winkle"

An American student's familiarity with the comic presentation of spouse abuse probably begins with America's first truly literary figure, Washington Irving (1783–1859) (Leary 1973, 63). Irving treats the archetype of the abusive spouse with the same comic tone found in Aristophanes thousands of years earlier—a bleak, yet undeniably funny humor.

"The Devil and Tom Walker"—appearing in virtually all anthologies of American literature—is one of many stories about a man's bargain with the devil and the man's subsequent attempts to evade the consequences of the compact. "The Devil and Tom Walker" differs from most of these stories, however, in the inclusion of Tom Walker's wife—a character to whom Irving devotes several pages but whose presence does nothing to advance the plot. Walker's wife, "a tall termagant, fierce of temper, loud of tongue, and strong of arm" (Irving 1962, 265), is a more terrible foe than the devil himself. As a matter of fact, Irving points out that Tom was so accustomed to the horrors of married life "that he did not even fear the devil" (1962, 267). She and Tom live in a matrimonial hell. Strangers avoid their house because of the terrible screaming usually issuing from it. Mere screaming, however, is not the most painful manifestation of the misery resident in the Walker home. Tom's physiognomy sometimes gives witness "that their conflicts were not confined to words" (1962, 265). Ironically, Tom and his wife live at a time when men were given the legal right to "exercise moderate chastisement (of their wives) in cases of great emergency . . . without being subjected to vexatious prosecutions" (Siegel *et al.* 1987, 50). Presumably, therefore, what Irving's contemporary readers found unusual about the Walkers' situation was that the wife exercised the right of beating the husband rather than the fact that corporal "chastisement" was a component of the marriage.

In this early story, the husband and wife are equally to blame for the disharmony, which springs—not surprisingly—from financial conflicts "about what ought to have been common property" (Irving 1962, 265). The Walkers cannot share. They hide from each other anything of value. When Tom's wife has gone into the forbidding swamp to bargain with the devil, Tom's only concern is that she plans to bargain with the couple's silverware. Her safety interests him not at all.

Tom's wife is killed by the devil, but not without a terrifying fight. After all, muses Irving's tongue-in-cheek narrator, a "female scold is generally considered a match for the devil" (1962, 268). When Tom finds evidence of his wife's death, he is anxious to retrieve the silver teapot; however, he decides that he can easily live without his wife. He even feels "something like gratitude" (1962, 268) toward the devil for having rid him of his wife, and she is never considered again in the story.

"Rip van Winkle" is a better-known Irving tale. It is read by virtually every American student, often at several levels of schooling. Rip, whose temperament is rendered "pliant and malleable in the fiery furnace of domestic tribulation" (Irving 1962, 228), is beloved by every member of the village—every member, that is, except Dame van Winkle. Tom Walker was himself difficult and abusive and in some way "deserved" the beatings he took from his wife as recompense for the abuse that he heaped upon her. While Rip van Winkle is far from an effective husband (he finds it impossible to husband his own farm even as he helps all of his neighbors manage theirs), he is passive—dramatically passive. When set upon by his wife, Rip merely "shrugged his shoulders, shook his head, cast up his eyes," saying nothing (1962, 229). Finally Rip's only escape is retreat; he runs to the outside of the house ("the only side which . . . belongs to a henpecked husband" [1962, 229]).

During one of these retreats, Rip goes into the mountains, meets Hendrick Hudson's crew, and falls asleep while drinking from their magic cask. Sleep is, of course, a symptom of his depression—a common symptom. Rip is a fugitive from family violence. Like Tom Walker, Rip is unable to assume either the role he feels should be his or the role his wife thinks should be his. He is neither a proper man from his own perspective nor a proper husband from his wife's. So, he retreats.

When Rip awakes, of course, Dame van Winkle is long dead. Rip, via retreat, has declared his independence from domestic tyranny in the same way the United States, via aggression, has declared her independence from British tyranny. Yet, just as Americans in their new independence still labor under the old tyranny of political factionalism, Rip is never quite free from Dame van Winkle. Whenever her name is mentioned, Rip still involuntarily shakes his head, shrugs his shoulders, and casts up his eyes (1962, 234). To this day, says Diedrich Knickerbocker, Irving's fictitious narrator, all of the men in the neighborhood, when set upon by a shrewish wife, wish "that they might have a quieting draught out of Rip van Winkle's flagon" (1962, 234).

Thus students' introduction to American literary humor is an introduction to family violence. Both the Walkers and the van Winkles violently disagree over what one study calls the "most frequent conflict" in marriages: housekeeping (Straus, Gelles, and Steinmetz 1980, 157). Neither partner sees the other as fulfilling the proper role in the maintenance of the home. The van Winkles demonstrate the pattern of one abusive spouse and one passive spouse that is so often seen as a component of spouse abuse (Margolin, Sibner, and Gleberman 1988, 99). Conversely, the Walkers are both aggressive. In both families the batterer and the battered exhibit "negative personality characteristics" (Margolin *et al.* 1988, 98), making a simple diagnosis of right and wrong quite difficult. The abuse is comical, seemingly, primarily because the accepted sexual roles are reversed. Thus, we laugh—as Henri Bergson postulated—because both partners act an alien role as if they did not recognize its alien nature. We do not laugh because we think that spouse abuse is funny; spouse abuse *reversed* is funny. Perhaps females laugh from a sense of retribution; the male abuser—at least literarily—finally get his just deserts. Perhaps males laugh satanically because humor such as Irving's is itself abusive of females.

Whatever its source of humor, whatever its social implications, men dominated by their women are recurrent characters in American humor.[3] Between Irving and Mark Twain, most American humorists employed this motif. Few of these humorists are anthologized, but one of the most popular will serve as an example and will demonstrate the omnipresence of this source of humor in American literature. Sut Lovingood, a creation of humorist George Washington Harris (1814–1869), advises men what to do with strong-minded women:

> . . . just you fight her like she wore whiskers or run like hell, ef you dont, ef she dont turn you inter a kidney worm'd hog what cant raise bristiles in less nor a month, you are more or less ove a man than I takes you to be. Ove all the varmints I ever see'd I's feardest of them. (1858)

Even though he seems obscure today, Sut was one of America's favorite characters for many years. Harris's brand of humor (and the humor of his "school," usually called "Southwestern humor") was often more brutally misogynistic than Irving's, and this type of sketch had a great influence upon the work of Mark Twain. Twain is gentler, more accomplished than Harris, but Southwestern humor and its view of women are apparent in *Huckleberry Finn* and other Twain works.

Mark Twain's (1835–1910) fictional world is one in which women exert control, and males (men as well as boys) inexorably follow the women's directions—as much as they do not want to. Huck and Jim both flee the stern Miss Watson "Don't put your feet up there, Huckleberry"; "Don't scrunch up like that, Huckleberry—set up

straight"; and . . . "Don't gap and stretch like that, Huckleberry—
why don't you try to behave?" (Clemens 1981, 144). As has been
pointed out by so many readers of Twain, life is happy for the
fugitives when they are away from the influences of women. At the
end of their odyssey, however, they find that they have actually made
no progress. After all the miles and all the adventures, they are still
the captives of "aunts." Only the women's names are different: Aunt
Sally has replaced Aunt Polly and Miss Watson. Huck's final words
tell the tale of the endless and fruitless escape of the male from the
female: "I reckon I got to light out for the Territory ahead of the rest,
because Aunt Sally she's going to adopt me and civilize me, and I
can't stand it. I been there before" (Clemens 1981, 144).

In other words, in nineteenth-century American humor, happiness
between the sexes is lightheartedly presented as an improbability. *Huck
Finn* features an inordinate number of single parents and guardians:
Aunt Polly, Widow Douglas, Miss Watson, Jim's wife. Those married
(i.e., Sally and Silas Phelps) are able to remain married precisely because
of the husband's acceptance of the dictates of his wife.

While in Twain we have no fistfights such as those between Rip
and his wife or between Sut Lovingood and strong-minded women,
the disharmony of the male–female relationship survives from the
beginning of American humor in Washington Irving to its apogee in
Mark Twain. The most obvious characteristic of this disharmony is
the aggressive role of the woman vis à vis the submissive role of the
male—a role that clinical research tells us is contrary to most actual
marital situations (Siegel *et al.* 1987, 49).

The urbanity that the *New Yorker* magazine brought to American
humor in the 1920s might be expected to have risen above the frontier
humor of the nagging wife and the henpecked husband. But the
pattern continues into the twentieth century in the work of James
Thurber, especially in "The Secret Life of Walter Mitty," a short story
included in virtually every anthology of American literature used in
high schools. Mitty is every bit as controlled by his wife as Rip van
Winkle is by Dame van Winkle, or as Huck is by Miss Watson. And,
like Huck and Rip, Mitty's salvation is to escape, for he is no match for
an evil-tempered woman. Once, he tries to defy her, retorting, "'I
was thinking . . . Does it ever occur to you that I am sometimes
thinking?'" (Thurber 1945, 49). Rather than listen to him, she decides

to take his temperature when she gets him home. To be sure, Mitty is obsequious to the world in general (parking garage valets, car repairmen). Even inanimate objects mock him; the revolving door makes a "derisive whistle" (Thurber 1945, 51) as he walks through. But Mrs. Mitty holds special horror for him. Mitty's final escape is to imagine himself facing a firing squad as he waits for his wife to emerge from the drugstore. As he stands against the drugstore wall in the sleet, Walter Mitty escapes into fantasy much as Huck Finn escapes to "the Territories" and much as Rip van Winkle escapes to the magic mountains of New Amsterdam.

* * * * *

> The end of writing is to instruct; the end of poetry is to instruct by pleasing. That the mingled drama [humorous as well as serious presentations] may convey all the instruction of tragedy and comedy cannot be denied, because it includes both in its alternations of exhibition and approaches nearer than either to the appearance of life.
>
> SAMUEL JOHNSON, "Preface to Shakespeare"

Although Johnson is here speaking of Shakespeare's insertion of comic scenes into his tragic plays, his remarks are relevant to this consideration of spouse abuse in American literature. High school students, in their junior year, are presented with two types of hateful violence between men and women: the serious and the comic. In the former, they experience—albeit vicariously—remarkably accurate depictions of abuse; they learn that one criterion of literary greatness is the extent to which a writer's art imitates life. In the latter, they see "things most disproportioned to ourselves and nature"; they learn that the reader "who seeth not the filthiness of evil wanteth a great foil to perceive the beauty of virtue" (Sidney 1970, 94).

The characters Sut Lovingood, Walter Mitty, Rip van Winkle, and others embody a clear message: The mistreatment of one spouse by another is ugly. That the students laugh is, perhaps, merely a "momentary anesthesia of the heart"[4] without which the horror of spouse abuse would inflict harm upon its witnesses, themselves. The characters Abner Snopes, Tom Buchanan, Roger Chillingworth, and others present the same message: The abuse of one spouse by another is still ugly. That the students are so often moved, so often angry is perhaps the genesis of the cure for this devastating national disease.

Whatever the method of delivery, the presence of family violence in American literature is unmistakable. Perhaps, in the combination of comic and serious presentations, American high school students see, as Johnson noted, an "alternation or exhibition" which "approaches nearer . . . to the appearance of life" than either presentation would have provided alone (p. 16).

Notes

1. Richard J. Gelles (1979) points out that husband abuse does, indeed, exist. Numerically, his research shows that about as many wives hit their husbands as husbands hit their wives. Gelles goes on to say, however, that much of the hitting done by women is in self-defense and that researchers must look at the potential for serious harm as a major component in evaluating physical abuse.
2. In their review of the history of family violence scholarship, Wini Breines and Linda Gordon (1983) repeatedly refer to two conflicting schools of thought. Some researchers, they say, concentrate upon a clinical approach: "narrow, intrafamily, gender-neutral," and nonideological. Others, they say, concentrate upon wife battering in a much larger context of "societal male supremacy." A survey of nonhumorous American literature clearly supports the ideological view of male dominance. The humorous literature presents a much more perplexing paradigm.
3. Indeed, critic Leslie Fiedler (1960) makes a telling case that all American literature (e.g., *Moby-Dick, Huckleberry Finn, The Last of the Mohicans*) involves males fleeing females.
4. Walter Jackson Bate's memorable metaphor describes Henri Bergson's theory concerning the audience's ability to laugh at horrible and pitiful occurrences (1970, 290).

References

Bate, Walter Jackson, ed. *Criticism: The Major Texts*. New York: Harcourt Brace Jovanovich, 1970.

Bergson, Henri. *Laughter: An Essay on the Meaning of the Comic* (Cloudesley Brereton and Fred Rothwell, trans.). New York: Macmillan, 1912.

Breines, Wini, and Linda Gordon. *Signs: Journal of Women in Culture and Society* 8: 3, 1983.

Clemens, Samuel L. *The Adventures of Huckleberry Finn*. In *Treasury of World Masterpieces*, pp. 141–318. London: Octopus Books, 1981.

Faulkner, William. "Barn Burning." In *The Faulkner Reader*, pp. 499–516. New York: Random House, 1959.

Fiedler, Leslie. *Love and Death in the American Novel*. New York: Criterion Books, 1960.

Fitzgerald, F. Scott. *The Great Gatsby*. New York: Scribner, 1953.

Freud, Sigmund. "Humour." In James Strachey, ed., *Collected Papers*, vol. 5, p. 220. London, 1952.

Gelles, Richard J. "The Truth About Husband Abuse." *MS*, 1979.

Harris, George Washington. *Nashville Union and American*, June 30, 1858.

Hawthorne, Nathaniel. "The Birthmark." In *Major Writers of America*, vol. I, pp. 730–737. New York: Harcourt, Brace and World, 1962.

Hawthorne, Nathaniel. *The Scarlet Letter*. New York: Rinehart, 1955.

Hawthorne, Nathaniel. "Young Goodman Brown." In *Major Writers of America*, vol. I, pp. 702–708. New York: Harcourt, Brace and World, 1962.

Irving, Washington. "Rip van Winkle." In *Major Writers of America*, vol. I, pp. 227–234. New York: Harcourt, Brace, and World, 1962.

Irving, Washington. "The Devil and Tom Walker." In *Major Writers of America*, vol. I, pp. 265–269. New York: Harcourt, Brace and World, 1962.

Johnson, Samuel. *Johnson on Shakespeare*, p. 16. London: Oxford University Press, 1959.

Leary, Lewis. "Washington Irving." In Louis D. Rubin, Jr., ed., *The Comic Imagination in American Literature*, pp. 63–76. New Brunswick, NJ: Rutgers University Press, 1973.

Margolin, Gayla, Linda Gorin Sibner, and Lisa Gleberman. "Wife Battering." In Vincent B. van Hasselt, Randall L. Morrison, Alan S. Bellack, and Michel Hersen, eds., *Handbook of Family Violence*, pp. 89–118. New York: Plenum Press, 1988.

Sidney, Sir Philip. "An Apologie for Poetrie." In Walter Jackson Bate, ed., *Criticism: The Major Texts*, pp. 82–106. New York: Harcourt Brace Jovanovich, 1970.

Siegel, Mark A., Donna R. Plesser, and Carol D. Foster, eds. *Domestic Violence: No Longer Behind the Curtains*. Plano, TX: Information Aids, 1987.

Straus, Murray A., Richard J. Gelles, and Suzanne K. Steinmetz. *Behind Closed Doors: Violence in the American Family*. New York: Anchor Press/ Doubleday, 1980.

Thurber, James. "The Secret Life of Walter Mitty." In *The Thurber Carnival*, pp. 47–52. New York: Harper & Row, 1945.

11

Cries of the Children in the Novels of Charles Dickens

WILLIAM H. SCHEUERLE

"Please, sir, I want some more" is Charles Dickens's most famous demand for the nineteenth-century society to recognize the needs of neglected and abused children. Oliver Twist's plaintive but urgent request is, of course, for more gruel; but it also signifies Oliver's insistence on his right to live and to be treated as a human being. Not only is he undernourished from lack of food but from the lack of loving parental care. Oliver is only the first in a long line of Dickensian fictional children who are abused by their real or surrogate parents or by society in general, are denied the security of a loving, compassionate family, are maltreated into submission, and are repressed by others' stern convictions, while struggling to maintain their worth and dignity. These struggles are more prominent in Dickens's novels than in many other nineteenth-century novelists' works because Dickens, a social critic, was one of the first English novelists to present social injustices through the eyes of the child victim (Spilka 1984, 169). His method in *Oliver Twist* (1837), and in most of his other novels with child victims, is to give the reader an innocent, appealing, and beguiling young person, craving love, attention, and approval, who is vulnerable in a world of social injustice, an adult world that is vicious or, at best, indifferent. To underscore

the presentation, the child victim is usually an orphan or has only one
parent who is either unsympathetic or too weak to protect the child.
Although all types of abuse assault these children and, in fact, many
of his minor characters die from physical abuse, his main child victims suffer from what Leonard Shengold dramatically calls "soul
murder."

"Soul murder" refers to the "abuse and neglect of children by
adults that is of sufficient intensity and frequency to be traumatic"
(Shengold 1988, 390). It can range from the most extreme conscious
acts (e.g., beatings and incest) to "parental affectless indifference"
(1988, 390). Margaret Jay and Sally Doganis also emphasize parental
neglect by calling it an "insidious form of abuse" (1987, 61). Parental
neglect, according to N. A. Polansky, occurs when "a caretaker responsible for a child deliberately or by extraordinary inattentiveness
permits a child to experience avoidable present suffering or fails to
provide one or more of the ingredients generally deemed essential for
developing a person's physical, intellectual and emotional capacities"
(Jay and Doganis 1987, 61–62). Jay and Doganis state that trauma
caused by physical or sexual assault may be more easily identified,
but a child can receive just as much long-term damage from parental
neglect as from more physical abuse: "lack of love and attention may
stunt a child's happy development and growth in ways that are as
important as lack of food and water" and can cause severe, maladaptive behavioral and emotional development (1987, 61–62). The term
"parental neglect" may lack specificity, but it certainly applies to
many of Dickens's fictional children as this chapter attempts to show.
Although most of Dickens's child heroes survive without serious
emotional scars, their backgrounds include an emotional undernourishment from lack of love and attention that could have caused
severe maladaptive behavioral and emotional development in real
children (Shengold 1979, 1988).

Dickens's concentration on child abuse and parental neglect may
be traced to two main sources: his own childhood and the plight of
children in the nineteenth century. On February 9, 1824, two days
after his twelfth birthday, Dickens became a child laborer in James
Lamert's blacking factory at a salary of six or seven shillings a week
and also became, at least in his mind, a victim of child abuse. His
parents, John and Elizabeth Dickens, had readily accepted this em-
ployment for Charles because of their ever-worsening impecuniosity.

Approximately two weeks later, John Dickens was imprisoned for debt in the Marshalsea, where the rest of the family, all except Charles and Fanny, the eldest daughter who was a boarder at the Royal Academy of Music, joined him. For four months, Charles, humiliated and feeling cruelly neglected by his parents, pasted labels on blacking bottles in a rat-infested, dirty, river-fronted warehouse. Weekdays he lived in a cheap boardinghouse near the prison; on weekends and for some of the weekday meals he joined the rest of his family in prison. Twenty-five years later, he confided to his friend and first biographer, John Forster, the trauma he suffered from that experience:

> It is wonderful to me how I could have been so easily cast away at such an age. It is wonderful to me, that, even after my descent into the poor little drudge I had been since we came to London, no one had compassion enough on me. . . . My father and mother were quite satisfied. They could hardly have been more so, if I had been twenty years of age, distinguished at a grammar school, and going to Cambridge. (Forster 1899, 1: 25)

His self-pity continues:

> No words can express the secret agony of my soul. . . . The deep remembrance of the sense I had of being utterly neglected and hopeless; of the shame I felt in my position; of the misery it was to my young heart to believe that day by day, what I had learned, and thought, and delighted in, and raised my fancy and my emulation up by, was passing away from me, never to be brought back any more; cannot be written. My whole nature was so penetrated with the grief and humiliation of such consideration, that even now, famous and caressed and happy, I often forget in my dreams that I have a dear wife and children; even that I am a man; and wander desolately back to that time of my life (Forster 1899, 1: 26–27).

Never understanding how his parents could have abandoned him in the first place, he was further traumatized when his mother wanted him to continue working in the warehouse even after an inheritance enabled John Dickens to be discharged from prison: "I never afterwards forgot. I never shall forget, I never can forget" (Forster 1899, 1: 38).

According to the majority of his biographers and critics, those four months of acute suffering—of being shunted aside—of feeling neglected haunted Dickens the rest of his life.[1] Unquestionably, Dickens felt abused, and his soul was damaged by his parents' insensitivity. This is one reason why his novels repeatedly depict scenes of parental neglect and of children drawn from middle class homes and placed into poverty situations—as he was himself (Spilka 1984, 166)—and why he relived his childhood experience by fictionalizing the warehouse nightmare in *David Copperfield* (1849–50). "Murder" may, however, be too strong a word in this case because Dickens, like his fictional heroes Oliver Twist and David Copperfield, was able to rise above his neglect, although it took him nearly 25 years to verbalize what he understates for Washington Irving as his "not-particularly-taken-care-of-boy-(hood)" (House, Storey, and Tillotson 1965, 2: 268).

His childhood experiences were, however, mild compared with those of many other children in the nineteenth century. The plight of children in that century was a second major influence on Dickens's novels. Pinchbeck and Hewitt remind us that "owing in a great deal to neglect and mismanagement, half the children [in England and Wales] born in 1831 died in five years. The chief part of this mortality occurred in the first two years" (1973, 2: 349). As historians and socialists have recorded, the Victorian household was an austere one. To the middle and upper classes, children were the "property" or appendages of their father in what seemed at the time to have been an earthly extension of a Father of Wrath (or, at least, Decorum) figure. The feelings of the child were not important. It was not until the first decades of the nineteenth century that children started to receive statutory protection. Blind obedience to the patriarch was the first rule, with religious faith, industry, thrift, and other Victorian virtues following closely after. Mary Martha Sherwood, a popular nineteenth-century writer of children books, relates approvingly in her *The History of the Fairchild Family* how the very pious Mr. Fairchild beats his children for any infraction and takes them to see the body of a murderer hanging in chains as a warning (quoted in Pinchbeck and Hewitt 1973, 2: 35). In *David Copperfield*, a *bildungsroman* based on Dickens's own life, the portrayal of Mr. Murdstone, David's stepfather, may reflect Dickens's personal rage against his own father, but this portrait is not an atypical image of the Victorian father. Children were to be molded and controlled. Dickens illustrates this Victorian maxim effectively when David returns home to find his silly and ineffectual mother married to Mr. Murdstone. Physical and psychological abuse are clearly threatened in Murdstone's warning to David: "'David,' he said, making his lips thin, by pressing them together, 'if I have an obstinate horse or dog to deal with, what do you think I do? . . . I beat him . . . I make him wince and smart. I say to myself, "I'll conquer that fellow," and if I were to cost him all the blood he had, I should do it' " (ch. 4: 43). Caning and then five days of solitary confinement for David soon follow. Dickens drew another such stern father in Thomas Gradgrind (*Hard Times*, 1854), who ruthlessly attempts to murder his children's imaginative souls. Mr. Dombey (*Dombey and Son*, 1847) dislikes his daughter, Florence, even repulsing her affection and abusing her physically; old John Harmon (*Our Mutual Friend*, 1869–65) throws out both his son and daughter because they disobey him; and Mrs. Clennam (*Little Dorrit*, 1855–57) seems to have only hatred toward her son, Arthur. In a speech to a fellow traveler on a cruise, Arthur describes the soul murdering of his childhood:

> "I'm the son . . . of a hard father and mother. I am the only child of parents who weighed, measured, and priced everything. . . . [T]heir very religion was a gloomy sacrifice of taste and sympathies that were never their own, offered up as a part of the bargain for the security of their possessions. Austere facts, inexorable discipline, penance in this world and terror in the next— nothing graceful or great anywhere, and the void in my cowed heart everywhere—this was my childhood. I may so misuse the word as to apply it to such a beginning of life."[2] (ch. 2: 19)

Other nineteenth-century novels project this same theme. The egoist Austin Feverel in George Meredith's *The Ordeal of Richard Feverel* (1859), for example, ruins his son Richard by attempting to raise (i.e., mold) him "scientifically," thus stultifying his natural impulses. Charlotte Brontë, in *Jane Eyre* (1847), sends her heroine to Lowood School, run by a parent substitute, Mr. Brockelhurst, who attempts to change all appearances and actions that "conform to nature." Anthony Trollope in *Orley Farm* (1861) flatly states "that children, as long as they are under the control of their parents, should be hindered and prevented in those things to which they are most inclined." Without a doubt, the most devastating attack on typical Victorian values, especially the father–son relationship, is Samuel Butler's savage presentation in *Ernest Pontifex: The Way of All Flesh* (1903).

For the children of the lower class, "chattel" may be a more appropriate synonym than "property." Many of Dickens's minor children characters are of this class (i.e., Jo in *Bleak House*, 1852–53, Fagin's child criminals in *Oliver Twist*). The enslavement or apprenticeship binding children to their masters for seven years lasted well into the second decade of the nineteenth century. With the emergence of the industrial revolution, which really did not grip England until after the battle of Waterloo, children as young as four worked picking up waste by creeping under dangerous machinery in cotton/wool mills. Conditions were inhuman, and these children were physically abused. Many worked 12 to 15 hours per day, including night shifts. A not unusual day was a shift from 5:00 AM to 8:00 PM with a break for breakfast at 7:00 AM and one for dinner at noon. On Sunday, they might clean the machinery from 6:00 AM to noon (Heywood 1978, 22). One can imagine the dirt and disease.[3]

Even worse were the lives of the children employed in coal mines. For 12 hours a day, children as young as six to eight opened and closed doors to control the air flow in the mines or filled and pushed coal carts. Workhouse children suffered the most: "these lads are made to go where other men will not let their children go. If they will not do it, they are taken to the magistrate who commits them to prison" (Pinchbeck and Hewitt, 1973, 354). A child's life was cheap, especially since the population was increasing and all members of a family unit were considered to be potential laborers almost as soon as they could walk. In fact, for fathers, many children became the breadwinners. For the mill owners, they became extensions of the machinery, and, if the children were orphans, they were expendable.

The Factory Act of 1833 brought the first relief; it prohibited children under the age of nine from working in factories and limited the hours that children could work. But still those hours ranged from 48 to 69 hours a week, depending on the age of the child. Later factory acts reduced the working hours for children. Children of these protected age groups were to attend school for at least two hours each day, but education was a luxury. It was estimated that in 1833 approximately half the children in England and Wales received no schooling at all, and the rest received only one or two years. Even in 1852, "out of 4,908,696 children in England and Wales, 2,861,848 receive[d] no instruction at all" (Brightfield 1971, 3: 351). Work, tiredness, and illness prevented many children from attending school as required by the Factory Act of 1833. But many of the schools, even those established for the middle-class children, were little better than no school at all. Dickens's novels graphically portray the ineffectiveness—even the dehumanizing effect—of the schools, for example, Mr. Wopsle's great-aunt's school in *Great Expectations* (1861), Miss Twinkleton's in *The Mystery of Edwin Drood* (1870), Bradley Headstone's in *Our Mutual Friend*, the notorious Yorkshire Dotheboys Hall in *Nicholas Nickleby* (1838–39),[4] Dr. Blimber's in *Dombey and Son*, and Mr. Creakle's Salem House in *David Copperfield*. The nine-year-old David writes:

> "I gazed upon the schoolroom . . . as the most forlorn and desolate place I had ever seen. . . . There is a strange unwholesome smell upon the room, like mildewed corduroys, sweet apples wanting air and rotten books." (ch. 5: 67)

Further days there attest that David's first impressions were correct. Dickens also implies through the characters of Noah Claypole (*Oliver Twist*), Robin Toodle (*Dombey and Son*), Uriah Heep (*David Copperfield*), and Charley Hexam (*Our Mutual Friend*) that the charity schools psychologically harmed their pupils by requiring them to wear conspicuous uniforms that set the boys off as recipients of charity.[5]

Oliver Twist skillfully dramatizes these personal and social influences on Dickens's novels, and a review of the first several incidences in Oliver's life may be used as the basis for a further discussion of Dickens's presentation of child abuse. On one level, *Oliver Twist* is certainly a nineteenth-century version of a morality play, or a *Pilgrim's Progress* (John Bunyan, 1678) in which a Parish boy progresses through a Slough of Depravity without getting soiled or tainted, because Dickens may have been fantasizing his own four-month progress through his slough; but even if Oliver is something of an allegorical figure, the novel is also a painfully realistic depiction of child abuse at its worse—both mental and physical, with children being oppressed by mainly surrogate parents who represent society and authority. The abused victim in the novel is not just Oliver, but all of the neglected children who die unloved like poor little Dick, or who are molded into thieves like Fagin's crew of young robbers or into prostitutes like Nancy and Betsy, or who are judged as property to be sold to the highest bidder like Oliver, who is put up for sale for five pounds (and then bargained down to three pounds ten shillings).[6] In her words to Rose Maylie, Nancy, another abandoned child, sums up the abuse that she and thousands like her suffered during childhood:

> "Thank heaven upon your knees, dear lady . . . that you had friends to care and keep you in your childhood, and that you were never in the midst of cold and hunger, and riot and drunkenness and—and—something worse than all—as I have been from my cradle. I may use the word, for the alley and the gutter were mine, as they will be my death-bed." (ch. 40: 358)

Dickens puts this same feeling of abandonment into the mouth of the convict Abel Magwitch (*Great Expectations*) when he describes to Pip his early parentless boyhood:

> "I've no notion where I was born. . . . I first become aware of myself, down in Essex, a thieving turnips for my living. Summun had run away from me—a man—a tinker—he'd took the fire with him and left me very cold." (ch. 42: 333)

Born a bastard (and almost immediately an orphan) into the faceless anonymity of the dehumanizing workhouse, Oliver at birth is classified as only a "thing," not as a child to be nurtured: he is an "item of mortality," "a new burden . . . upon the parish." He is "badged and ticketed," assigned his name "Twist" by his first indifferent surrogate parent, the bumbling Mr. Bumble, because it was the "t's" turn. With his cocked hat and cane, emblems of his authority, Bumble is representative of the ultimate authority, the indifferent and dehumanized Board. Until his escape to London, Oliver is beaten, sold, starved, and deprived both of love and physical comfort. Listen to his powerful cry of abandonment:

> "I am a very little boy, sir" Oliver cried to Mr. Bumble, "and it is so—so— . . . so lonely sir! So very lonely. . . . Everybody hates me. Oh! sir, don't, don't pray be cross to me." (ch. 4: 52)

After his birth as a parish child, Oliver, "for the next eight or ten months, was the victim of a systematic course of treachery and deception: He was brought up by hand" (ch. 3: 27). By that last expression, Dickens means that Oliver was kept alive but without being given compassion or love. That lack of compassion continues when Oliver is placed in a baby farm, run by his next surrogate parent, Mrs. Mann, the orphan's official parent. Dickens, of course, is playing with the name. Mrs. "Mann" possesses none of the loving, tender, maternal stereotypical characteristics that one wants to associate with a manager of a baby farm. Like many of Oliver's other surrogate fathers— Bumble, the Board, Gamfield, Sowerberry, and later Fagin—Mrs. Mann sees Oliver only as a source of money. At her establishment, babies (termed "culprits" and "juvenile offenders") fall into the fire from neglect or get "half-smothered by accident" or "inadvertently scalded to death when there happened to be a washing," extreme cases of child abuse that were, unfortunately, common in nineteenth-century baby farms. Although Oliver escapes death, he does not escape abuse in the form of hunger, beatings, and isolation. Oliver, in fact, suffers more from Mrs. Mann and others like her than from his real enemies, Fagin and Monks, who deliberately want to ruin him (Collins 1963, 184). Possibly remembering the darkness of the warehouse and his feeling of isolation there, Dickens continually depicts Oliver being pushed, stuffed, or shoved into dark coal cellars or basements, like a "thing" to be put out of sight; later at the Sowerberrys, Oliver's bed is located under the counter near the coffins. Symbolically, of course, these dark enclosures are associated with death and reflect the terror that the abandoned Oliver has to endure.

Probably one of the most terrifying scenes in Victorian novels depicting this cruel isolation of children is in Charlotte Brontë's *Jane Eyre*, when ten-year-old Jane is locked into a room that she had previously associated with death (ch. 2). Decorated totally in crimson with even its wall tinted pink, this bloodred room symbolizes for Jane a supernatural world of spirits and alien inhabitants. She feels totally alone—totally alienated from all other living persons. Abandoned by others, she also feels the loss of her own identity:

"My heart beat thick, my head grew hot; a sound filled my ears, which I deemed the rushing of wings; something seemed near me; I was oppressed, suffocated; endurance broke down; I rushed to the door and shook the lock in desperate effort." (ch. 2: 17)

Dickens does not detail Oliver's feelings as Brontë does Jane's, but Oliver's situations are just as suffocating. It is predicted, in fact, by the nameless "gentleman in the white waistcoat" that Oliver will be suffocated by hanging, and he probably would have been suffocated if he had been sold to Mr. Gamfield, the chimney sweep master.

No other child occupation was probably as dangerous and as

indicative of approved child abuse at that time as that of chimney sweeping. At the turn of the nineteenth century it has been estimated that England employed about 1000 boys as chimney sweeps serving 400 master sweeps (Heywood 1978, 24). Because of the dangers of the job, the boys were either unwanted or orphans—many sold from the workhouse. The unwanted Oliver who demands more food is an ideal candidate. Being underfed, he is small and thus suited to crawl through the dark, sooty, narrow passage that often turned at right angles. Suffocation was the death of these four- or five-year-old boys who would lose their way in the many turns and twistings. Dickens delineates seriocomically these dangers in the novel in the bargaining conversations between the "gentleman in the white waistcoat," who even brags that Oliver is underfed and is thus ideal for the apprenticeship, and Gamfield, who in the below quotation explains why boys are suffocated:

> "That's acause they damped the straw afore they lit it in the chimbley to make 'em come down again," said Gamfield; "that's all smoke, and no blaze vereas smoke ain't o'no use at all in making a boy come down, for it only sinds him to sleep, and that's wot he likes. Boys' is very obstinit, and very lazy, gen'lmen, and there's nothink like a good hot blaze to make 'em come down vith a 'run. It's humane too, gen'lmen, acause, even it they've stuck in the chimbley, roasting their feet makes 'em struggle to hextricate theirselves." (ch. 3: 40–41)

The bargaining regarding Oliver's price between Mr. Gamfield and members of the Board is inhuman, as there is no consideration of Oliver as a human being; he is only a commodity to be sold. It is only Oliver's tears before the magistrate that save him from being sold as a piece of property to Mr. Gamfield.

Dickens attacks these gentlemen of the Board caustically. Nameless, these "gentlemen" group together only to hand out punishments or to keep the operating cost of the workhouse at a minimum, not to protect the orphans. Oliver's first appearance at the Board is indicative of Dickens's intent, as he pits one frightened, starving child against the indifferent and even hostile adult world, here consisting of "eight or ten fat gentlemen," who certainly fail to provide for Oliver's "physical, intellectual and emotional capacities," needs that

Polansky insists are essential for all children (Jay and Doganis, 1987, 62). This scene is lengthy, but it should be quoted in its entirety so that the reader may clearly see both the physical and emotional abuse heaped upon Dickens's child victim by the very people who should be protecting him:

> Mr. Bumble gave him [Oliver] a tap on the head, with his cane, to wake him up, and another on the back to make him lively, and bidding him follow, conducted him into a large white-washed room, where eight or ten fat gentlemen were sitting round a table. At the top of the table, seated in an arm-chair rather higher than the rest, was a particularly fat gentleman with a very round, red face.
>
> "Bow to the board," said Bumble. Oliver brushed away two or three tears that were lingering in his eyes, and seeing no board but the table, fortunately bowed to that.
>
> "What's your name, boy?" said the gentleman in the high chair.
>
> Oliver was frightened at the sight of so many gentlemen, which made him tremble, and the beadle gave another tap behind, which made him cry. These two causes made him answer in a very low and hesitating voice, whereupon a gentleman in a white waistcoat said he was a fool. Which was a capital way of raising his spirits, and putting him quite at his ease.
>
> "Boy," said the gentleman in the high chair, "listen to me. You know you're an orphan, I suppose?"
>
> "What's that sir?" inquired poor Oliver.
>
> "The boy is a fool—I thought he was," said the gentleman in the white waistcoat.
>
> "Hush!" said the gentleman who had spoken first. "You know you've got no father or mother, and that you were brought up by the parish, don't you?"
>
> "Yes, sir," replied Oliver, weeping bitterly.
>
> "What are you crying for?" inquired the gentleman in the white waistcoat, and to be sure it was very extraordinary. What could the boy be crying for?
>
> "I hope you say your prayers every night," said another gentleman in a gruff voice, "and pray for the people who feed you, and take care of you—like a Christian."
>
> "Yes, sir," stammered the boy. The gentleman who spoke last was unconsciously right. It would have been very like a Christian and a marvelously good Christian, too, if Oliver had prayed for

the people who fed and took care of him. But he hadn't because nobody had taught him.

"Well! You have come here to be educated and taught a useful trade," said the red-faced gentleman in the high chair.

"So you'll begin to pick oakum tomorrow morning at six o'clock," added the surly one in the white waistcoat.

For the combination of both these blessings in the one simple process of picking oakum, Oliver bowed low by the direction of the beadle, and was then hurried away to a large ward, where, on a rough, hard bed, he sobbed himself to sleep. What a noble illustration of the tender laws of England! They let the paupers go to sleep! (ch. 2: 33–34)

Dickens seemingly gloried in giving a descriptive signature to some of his characters: a physical trait, speech mannerisms, or an item of dress, like Bumble's cocked hat and cane. These signatures become so prominent that when used they immediately identify and even substitute for the characters. Before the signature in the above scene is identified, it would be helpful to discuss a signature associated with child abuse in *Great Expectations* so that a comparison may be made. The child victim in that novel is Pip, whose acknowledged parent substitute is his older sister, Mrs. Joe, who brings Pip up with physical and verbal abuse. Her armor of respectability and her armor against hugging Pip and showing compassion to him are her signature: "A coarse apron fastened over her figure behind with two loops, and having a square impregnable bib in front, that was stuck full of pins and needles." The "white waistcoat" of the gentleman is another signature. The "white waistcoat" represents respectability, but, in reality, it becomes, like Mrs. Joe's apron, an inflexible and rigid armor against compassion. The white waistcoat and the whiteness of the room emphasize the coldness of the men to Oliver's needs. Oliver's bowing to the table may be humorous, but, underneath that humor, Dickens attacks: Little difference exists between the Board and the table; lacking any compassion and feeling, the Board has become as inflexible and as rigid as the wooden table. Oliver can expect to receive no assistance but only abuse from these surrogate parents. His only promised education is to learn how to pick oakum.

Mr. Sowerberry, the undertaker, who presides, it seems, over a never-ending funeral is Oliver's last master and surrogate parent before his flight to London. The undertaking profession reemphasizes the death image, and the funeral scene presented in this chapter is ugly and brutal. The reader knows that Oliver as hero will survive, but this section ends with the death of Oliver's friend Dick, another poorhouse inmate, who with Oliver "has been beaten and starved, and shut up together, many and many times." Death alone remains for child victims in later novels, such as Little Nellie Trent (*The Old Curiosity Shop,* 1840), who dies as the result of her many privations; poor Jo (*Bleak House*), who is totally neglected by society; and Smike (*Nicholas Nickleby*), who is "whipped, starved and caned." Again seen as a "thing," Oliver becomes only a piece of property, even being stripped of his own voice and whatever little identity he has when he is required to be a mute at children's funerals. The undernourishment theme is also restressed when Oliver is fed food left for the dog.

Later novels, especially *Dombey and Son, David Copperfield, Great Expectations,* and *Little Dorrit,* present child abuse by parents or parent substitutes more subtly and realistically than Dickens does in *Oliver Twist.* In those novels, Dickens also makes the reader more privy to the thoughts and feelings of the tormented child, but the same pattern that occurs in *Oliver Twist* exists in these later works. The involved child is thrust into an uncaring or hostile adult world that seemingly wants to victimize the child—to murder his/her soul. Although Dickens saves his child heroes from serious psychological damage, an uncaring world warps many of Dickens' children characters as Shengold and as Jay and Doganis state that it should. There is a streak of sadness in these characters: David Copperfield, as an adult, is still haunted by "shadows" that he has to dismiss; Pip and Estella suffer great sorrows, especially in the original ending of *Great Expectations.* This streak of sadness is expected because the instances of emotional deprivation in their lives affect them permanently, just as such childhood emotional deprivation affected their creator. These victimized children and the concomitant indictment of parents and of society in Dickens's novels reflect—sadly but naturally—his "grief and humiliation" that "I never shall forget, I never can forget."

Notes

1. See in particular John Forster (1899), Edgar Johnson (1952), and Edmund Wilson (1959). For a different interpretation of the childhood experience in Dickens's writings, see Welsh (1987).

2. For a further discussion of the Arthur's abusive childhood, see Leonard Shengold (1988).
3. A description of one Leeds's spinning mill in the 1830s reveals that more women–girls and children under the age of 14 were employed than men (Harrison 1979, 521):

Year	Men[a]	Women–Girls[a]	Children under 14[a]	Hours/week
1831	139/19s 10d	385/5s 3d	250/3s 23/4d	72
1836	144/21s 6d	442/5s 5 1/2d	307/2s 103/4d	66
1840	135/21s 8d	478/5s 11 1/1d	409/2s 53/4d	66

[a]Number employed/average weekly wages.

4. For an extended study of the infamous Yorkshire Schools on which Dotheboys Hall is based, see Michael Slater (1982).
5. For a further discussion of teachers and education in Dickens's novels see Philip Collins (1963).
6. Orphaned children were considered as part of the property in, for example, bankrupt sales, and some parish apprentices were murdered so that the master could get a fresh premium with fresh apprentices (Heywood 1978, 22).

References

Brightfield, Myron. *Victorian England in Its Novels 1840–70*, 4 vols. Los Angeles: University of California, 1971.

Brontë, Charlotte. *Jane Eyre*. 1847. Boston: Riverside, 1959.

Collins, Philip. *Dickens and Education*. London: Macmillan, 1963.

Dickens, Charles. *David Copperfield*. 1849–50. Boston: Riverside, 1958.

Dickens, Charles. *Great Expectations*. 1861. New York: Rinehart, 1972.

Dickens, Charles. *Little Dorrit*. 1855–57. New York: Odyssey Press, 1969.

Dickens, Charles, *Oliver Twist*. 1837. New York: Signet Classics.

Forster, John. *The Life of Charles Dickens*, 2 vols. London: Chapman & Hall, 1899.

Harrison, J. F. C. *Early Victorian England 1832–51*. Bungay, Suffolk: Fontana/Collins, 1979.

Heywood, Jean S. *Children in Care*. London: Routledge & Kegan Paul, 1978.

House, Madeline, Graham Storey, and Katherine Tillotson, eds. *The Pilgrim Edition of Charles Dickens*, 4 vols. Oxford: Oxford University Press, 1965.

Jay, Margaret, and Sally Doganis. *Battered*. New York: St. Martins Press, 1987.

Johnson, Edgar. *Charles Dickens*, 2 vols. New York: Simon & Schuster, 1952.

Pinchbeck, Ivy, and Margaret Hewitt. *Children in English Society,* 2 vols. London: Routledge & Kegan Paul, 1973.

Shengold, Leonard. "Child Abuse and Deprivation: Soul Murder." *Journal of the American Psychoanalytic Association* 27: 533–559, 1979.

Shengold, Leonard. "Dickens, *Little Dorrit,* and Soul Murder." *Psychoanalytic Quarterly* 52: 390–421, 1988.

Slater, Michael. "Essay." In *The Life and Adventures of Nicholas Nickleby,* 2 vols. Philadelphia: University of Pennsylvania Press, 1982.

Spilka, Mark. "On the Enrichment of Poor Monkeys by Myth and Dreams; or, How Dickens Rousseauisticized and Pre-Freudianized Victorian Views of Childhood." In Don Richard Cox, ed., *Sexuality and Victorian Literature.* Knoxville: University of Tennessee, 1984.

Welsh, Alexander. *From Copyright to Copperfield.* Cambridge: Harvard University Press, 1987.

Wilson, Edmund. *The Wound and the Bow.* New York: Oxford University Press, 1959 (reprint).

12

Victorian Fun and Games in Ibsen's *A Doll House*

FREDRICKA HOWIE

From the moment that Henrik Ibsen presented the first of his social plays on the Victorian stage, he stirred up controversy like a bear stirs up honeybees. In a portrait taken around 1890, his bearlike whirl of whiskers, impressive build, and unnerving quietude belied the daring artist who openly portrayed situations that offended Victorian sensibility. Storms of criticism raged against plays such as *Ghosts*, which deals with hereditary venereal disease, and *Hedda Gabler*, in which a neurotic woman is repelled by her possible pregnancy. These simplistic analyses cannot do justice to the individual plays, but illustrate the point that Ibsen consistently presents characters in conflict with traditional mores and beliefs.

Of all his plays, *A Doll House* represents most closely not only Ibsen's ideal of the supremacy of the individual over the group but also the disparity between the text and the expectations of the audience, particularly because of long-held beliefs in the play's sympathy for the emancipation of women from domination in marriage. From the play's first appearance, many interpretations have centered on the systematic degradation of the wife, Nora Helmer. According to this reading, her husband Torvald has effectively isolated her and destroyed her self-esteem, impairing her ability to see things in perspective. Nora has no family and her only friends are Dr. Rank, a close associate of her husband, and Kristine, a childhood companion whom she has not seen for many years. Torvald uses pet names for her—"my little lark," "sulky squirrel"—to which, in performance, Nora often responds with twittering sounds or squeaks.

But Torvald's humor is interspersed with other names and questions of a darker cast: "Has the little spendthrift been out throwing money around again?"; "Are your scatterbrains off again?"; ". . . how like a woman!" Nora's suggestion that the family borrow money is met with a scathing lecture, to which she meekly acquiesces. In one scene she is gratuitously wheedling. Torvald has given her money, and with sexual suggestiveness she coquettishly fumbles at his coat buttons to obtain even more cash. The following excerpt represents a typical interchange between the two:

> HELMER. (shaking an admonitory finger) Surely my sweet tooth
>   hasn't been running riot in town today, has she?
> NORA. No, I assure you, Torvald—
> HELMER. Hasn't nibbled some pastry?
> NORA. No, not at all.
> HELMER. Not even munched a macaroon or two?
> NORA. No, Torvald, I assure you, really—
> HELMER. There, there now. Of course I'm only joking. (Fjelde
>   1978, 128)

An emotional terrorist, Helmer uses the tactics of threats and ridicule, control over plans and finances, and sexual coercion to maintain his dominant role. Nora is Torvald's toy. She performs the role of perfect wife—acting the way Torvald directs. Ibsen illustrates the theory of genetic determinism, commonly accepted at the time, when Torvald compares Nora's aptitude with money to that of her father. He says that she is able to produce money when it is needed or wanted, but that money slips through her fingers. Despite these faults, he indulgently accepts in her the traits that he is unable to change.

Bernard Shaw claimed that at the end of the play, when Nora leaves her children and husband and walks out of the house to discover how to be an independent person, the slamming of the door was heard throughout Europe. Indeed, the echo of that slamming door was all too opportune for many supporters of women's rights. It certainly was not the first time that art had been appropriated to fit political rhetoric, and that is exactly what happened in the Britain of the 1880s. Henry Arthur Jones prepared an adaptation of the play entitled *Breaking a Butterfly,* but it was so saccharine that it was described as an original English play, "not an adaptation from Ibsen" (Henderson 1956, 404). Believing that Ibsen was undermining the sanctity of the marriage bond, religious and academic factions attempted to prevent the Unitarian minister, Philip Wicksteed, from lecturing on Ibsen. And almost everywhere *A Doll House* was performed, appeals were made for a different and happier ending.

But in addition to this astounding amount of hostility, the play also generated approval and discussion. The sensational and provocative lectures of Bernard Shaw, which eventually became *The Quintessence of Ibsenism* (1913) treated Ibsen "not primarily as poet and dramatist, but as a moralist, philosophic thinker, and ethical teacher" (Henderson 1956, 407). And so, for better or worse, and although he claimed to be neither, Ibsen was appropriated to feminist and socialist causes, and was designated their chief prophet.

The political reading of the play interprets Nora as both victim and heroine. And while Nora may be both, this position tends to take a one-sided view of the dramatic action, for to view the play solely in terms of Nora's taking a gigantic step toward personal independence denies the essential reality of family dynamics. Real people do not step from the shadows into the light quite so suddenly or so dramatically. To interpret the play as saying that women's emancipation can be achieved by the overthrow of traditional societal structures is too neat and too simple. Unfortunately, however, this reading has prevailed for nearly 100 years. Unchanging ideas and interpretations should set off warning bells. We should be suspicious because truly significant literature resists the temptation to remain static. For example, literary critics of every decade, considering Shakespeare's *Hamlet* or Jane Austen's *Pride and Prejudice* or Joseph Conrad's *Heart of Darkness,* find new approaches, new ways of interpreting words, and new small details that influence how we "read" the work as a whole.

Much of this neglect in reexamining Ibsen can be traced to literary critics who have simply failed to apply innovative analysis techniques to his works. But there is also the problem of translation. Most critics are necessarily forced to accept someone else's "interpretation through translation" of the original material. Because of this, much of Ibsen's wry Norwegian humor and delicate wordplay are not ade-

quately noted. Subtle shades of meaning are often carelessly overlooked. For example, it was not until 1965 that the play's title was
correctly translated as *A Doll House*—no possessive—rather than the
singular possessive, *A Doll's House* (Fjelde 1978, 121). This is no fine
line, however. The mistaken translation emphasizes Nora as the one
doll, the one plaything. The corrected version stresses the manipulative relationship among characters.

Jean Giles-Sims has established a general systems model of wife
abuse that furnishes the tools to analyze the social processes that lead
to violence. These six stages "form a temporal/logical hierarchy" with
which to assess the strengths and weaknesses of the system and
"how the different levels of feedback affect the ongoing processes
within the system" (Giles-Sims 1983, 120). These techniques can also
be useful in analyzing psychological instead of physical violence—the
kind of psychological violence occurring in *A Doll House*.

The first stage is the establishment of the family system. This is
the initial step for the evolution of patterns of interaction, boundaries,
and rules. Attention is given to factors that the couple bring to the
relationship—the established expectations, values, and strategies for
dealing with conflict. In *A Doll House*, when Helmer refers to Nora's
father's inability to control money and his fanciful speeches, he
focuses on patterns of behavior that are transferred from one generation to another. Helmer is implying that Nora really cannot help her
behavior; she cannot escape a destiny that she has inherited. Nothing
is mentioned in the text about Helmer's background, but he epitomizes those repressive attitudes and values that have become popu-
larly associated with the Victorian temper. Very often in this initial
stage, the couple is so enamored, so blinded by the expectations of
love, that aggressive behavior is overlooked. From a systems perspective, once an initial step has been made in the direction of commitment, it represents "a positive feedback loop." In general, society
encourages pair-bonding and this, too, reinforces and maintains the
system.

The second stage is the first incident of violence. The typical
response to initial aggressive behavior is to accept it as an isolated
incident and to forgive and forget. This response, however, appears
to the aggressor as compliance and thus provides positive feedback.
Helmer has become adept at biting reproaches that are presented in a
joking and teasing fashion; however, his "violence" is verbal and

psychological rather than physical. He knows that the way to acquire affection and sexual attention is to wave money under Nora's nose. Nora, in turn, reciprocates with behavior that both stimulates Helmer's initial (and expected) criticism and provides Nora with a reaction that allows her to appease Helmer and assume the role of victim. Each has developed behavior that will elicit an expected and manageable response.

The third step is a stabilization of violence. Giles-Sims asserts that "behavior which receives positive feedback will increase . . . and that once escalation occurred, corrective action within the system often does not work" (Giles-Sims 1983, 130). Neither Nora nor Helmer would be likely to change her or his pattern of behavior— even if she or he recognized the need for change—without a change in the boundaries, as when Nora shares Helmer's behavior with Kristine, or without the threat of outside intervention, as when Nora's reputation is threatened by the exposure of her forgery. Part of the system includes periods of "normal" family patterns between incidents of violence. These periods of normalcy reinforce the societal and personal goals of keeping the family unit together.

The next step is the moment of choice. Usually this point is reached when some new input is introduced into the system, some special crisis that becomes a critical factor that causes "the pattern of interaction within the system" to branch in different directions (Giles-Sims 1983, 134). For Nora, her husband's failure to offer to protect her from notoriety in connection with her forgery precipitates the change.

Leaving the system, or making a psychological move in the direction of leaving the system, takes place over a prolonged period. This fifth stage usually involves the development of "a bridging relationship" or confidante. For Nora, this relationship is supplied by the supportive presence of Kristine. Before the end of the play, Nora has already explored some of the avenues open to her because she has decided that the children will stay with their father and that she will return to her hometown. She tells Helmer that she will not accept financial help from him nor allow him to write to her. The slamming door indicates the completion of this step.

Stage six is resolution. Over time, the decision will be made either to return to the system, be it the same or altered, or to separate from the system altogether. Women who decide to create a new system "must reorient their goals, reestablish new patterns of interaction" that eliminate both aggressive behavior against them and their structuring of situations that lead to that aggression (Giles-Sims 1983, 139). Ibsen has left this stage open to conjecture. If Nora is using this step as a lever in the game of power, she will probably be successful for a time—at least until the pattern of mutually aggressive behavior draws both back into its web. Given contemporary statistics, however, return to the system outweighs other alternatives. In a 1980 study of 31 women, within six months of entering a women's shelter, 58% of those interviewed "had returned to the system, at least temporarily . . . sixteen percent had reconciled and later left. Forty-two percent were married to and/or living with the man . . ." (Giles-Sims 1983, 137).

Rolfe Fjelde asserts that "as Ibsen's retrospective emphasis insists, details throughout *A Doll House* release their richer meanings only when freed from the compulsions of propaganda" (1978, 120):

> It is the entire house (hjem, home) which is on trial, the total complex of relationships, including husband, wife, children, servants, upstairs and downstairs, that is tested by the visitors that come and go, embodying aspects of the inescapable reality outside (1978, 121).

And it is only when the critic is freed from the restrictions of traditional interpretations that Ibsen can be viewed in his most renowned role, that of realist. Upon careful reading, Ibsen has created through the character of Nora neither a feminist nor a victim totally at the mercy of her husband. He is exploring relationships of a marriage in which the inner workings have gone out of synchronization like the internal parts of a watch that keeps ticking but cannot keep time. Far from being her husband's "legal infant" or the pathetic plaything that some critics see, Nora is less a nineteenth-century model for women's rights in society than an anticipation of Edward Albee—a *Who's Afraid of Virginia Wolff* in Victorian drag. Albee's 1962 play exposes the virulent verbal and emotional lacerations between George, the college professor, and his wife Martha, the college president's daughter. George temporarily wins when he denies the carefully constructed existence of an imaginary son. He wins because he has changed the rules in the middle of the game. From this new perspective, we can see that in Ibsen's drama Torvald and Nora Helmer have created an equally elaborate network of mutual manipulation. When at the end of the play Nora confronts Helmer with the fact that she has never been allowed by the men in her family or society to develop independently, she is merely shifting the ground rules, changing the conditions of acting and reacting that they have established. The final slamming door is not necessarily symbolic of a new beginning, but more probably of a resounding "checkmate."

Ibsen was never very secretive about his motives. He claimed that his primary purpose in the play was to explore "the different ethical codes by which men and women live" (Ibsen 1957, xv). He clearly demonstrates how problems in intimate relationships are heightened by the rigid expectations of sex roles, but he also shows how both the marital partners are agents as well as victims in this game of gender stereotyping.

Basically, Ibsen uses the conventional three-step dramatic structure: exposition, presentation of a problem, resolution of the problem. The exposition is intriguing because Helmer's domination of Nora is continuously contrasted against her incredibly childish insensitivity. Ibsen does this by incorporating a game motif into the drama—the pet names, the teasing, the questions, the "hide and seek" game with the children. Torvald questions his "little lark" about her sweet tooth and she deliberately blames a friend for the forbidden macaroons that Nora herself brought into the house. Torvald scolds his "spendthrift" for squandering money, then attracts her sexual favors with money. Nora complains that she must scrimp and cut corners, and yet tips the delivery boy extravagantly and insists to Kristine that they must appear to live in the manner of a bank president. Nora is particularly insensitive when Kristine comes for the first visit in years. Throughout the visit, Nora draws attention to herself and the Helmer family's good fortune; meanwhile, Kristine, a penniless widow, has heard of Torvald's new position and has come to ask Nora to intercede with Torvald for a job at the bank. In response to Kristine's pitiful financial condition, Nora suggests that she should "go off to a bathing resort."

During the same visit, Torvald's petty jibes over Nora's lack of concern for money are revealed to be more true than even he suspects. Nora confides to Kristine that it was she who saved Torvald's life early in their marriage by borrowing money and telling Torvald that the money was an inheritance from her father. But Nora also confesses that she forged her dead father's signature as guarantor of the loan. Nora tells Kristine that the doctors said Torvald's life was in danger and that nothing could save him except a stay in a warmer climate. But she also admits that the "terrible illness" from which she saved her husband was only "overwork." In persuading Torvald to take a vacation, she tried various strategies: She mentioned how lovely it would be to travel abroad like other young wives; she begged and cried; she reminded him that since she was pregnant, he must be kind and indulge her.

Ultimately, we must conclude that Nora is in little danger of becoming an emancipated woman. She is too involved in the games people play to give up the sport that easily. She is not the kind of woman to take her chance with the unknown, not with all that she has invested in her relationship with Torvald, even when the relationship enforces inappropriate roles.

One of the obstacles that the reader must overcome, then, is the tendency to blame one of the partners exclusively. Ibsen's play describes not the violence of a drunken and angry husband against a shrewish or neglectful wife; rather it dramatizes the lives of two basically nice young people that have gone so terribly awry that change must come to the entire relationship.

But perhaps an even greater challenge is to acknowledge that psychological abuse can be as dangerous as physical violence. Most of us want easy answers and clear-cut positions. Bruises and scars help separate the "good guys" from the "bad guys." Unfortunately, in any kind of abuse there are no easy or absolute answers, and while emotional abuse is more subtle, it is no less painful. Society must understand that, like physical violence, psychological mistreatment requires the collusion of both parties and involves an intricate matrix of social conditioning and interpersonal need. We must understand that in most marriages, there is, or was at one time, a relationship of love and caring, of expectations, and of shared history. Emotional abuse strikes at the heart of the relationship while binding the participants in a recursive tangle of mind games and isolation: even abusive relationships provide essential buffers against what is often seen as a hostile and unsupportive world outside the immediate family.

One way of interpreting not only life but literature is by studying behaviors and relationships to discover familiar systems. Examination of the pattern or system of character interaction shifts the focus from isolated behaviors "to the effects of the individual's behavior on others, the reactions of others to that behavior, and the context in which behaviors take place . . . which adds a dynamic perspective to the study of the context" (Giles-Sims 1983, 4). By looking at the "concepts of boundaries, positive and negative feedback processes, open versus closed systems, and thresholds of viability within the systems," the analyst's conceptual tools are increased and improved (Giles-Sims 1983, 5).

In *A Doll House*, for example, boundaries are created through system rules. No social system is entirely closed, but the Helmer household is particularly nonadaptive. Patterns of behavior are stable, and thus resist change. There is a high degree of negative feedback to new behavior; for example, Torvald discourages Nora's friendship with Kristine and any involvement in the bank business. And the long-term stability of the relationship is changed with the appearance of Kristine, the impending death of the family's only close friend, Dr. Rank, and the possibility of Nora's forgery being made public. Giles-Sims again defines the situation: "When crises occur, or when there is a change in the environment in which the system exists, the internal regulation of the system may be disrupted" (1983, 11). For Nora, the failure of her husband to protect her from notoriety in connection with her forgery causes this change.

Nora and Torvald express aspects of life that only some experience. Of course, characters in literature are not "real," but sometimes in their "unreality" they reveal more about social and personal interaction than most of us discover in actual experience. They give us insight. They show us direction. And however we view the characters or interpret Ibsen's play, it is clear that he created a verisimilitude that bridges the division of generations. Joan Templeton has said that "Ibsen was as deeply anchored in his time as any writer has been before or since" (1989, 36). Perhaps it is his superb artistry that makes his play enjoyable, but it is also his firm grasp of people and their motives that makes the work rewarding and timeless.

References

Fjelde, Rolfe. *Ibsen: The Complete Major Prose Plays* (1965). New York: Plume, 1978.

Giles-Sims, Jean. *Wife Battering: A Systems Theory Approach*. New York: Guilford, 1983.

Henderson, Archibald. *George Bernard Shaw: Man of the Century*. New York: Appleton-Century-Crofts, 1956.

Ibsen, Henrik. *Six Plays by Henrik Ibsen*. Trans. Eva Le Gallienne. New York: The Modern Library, 1957.

Shaw, G. Bernard. *The Quintessence of Ibsenism* (1913). In *Major Critical Essays*. New York: Penguin Books, 1986 (reprint).

Templeton, Joan. "The *Doll House* Backlash: Criticism, Feminism, and Ibsen." *PMLA* 104(1): 28–40, 1989.

13

Husbands and Wives, Sons and Lovers
Intimate Conflict in the Fiction of D. H. Lawrence

CARLOS A. PEREZ

Sons and Lovers, the third novel written by D. H. Lawrence, is considered by many critics to be one of the most significant works of the twentieth century, not so much for its revolutionary style, as for its complex psychological portrayals. Lawrence's artistry is responsible for the studied depth of his characters, but the intense rendering of their interrelationships may in part be due to the novel's autobiographical origins, since the life of the Morels, particularly Paul's childhood and early adulthood, is so painfully patterned after Lawrence's own family life experiences. The story centers on a working-class family in England during the industrial revolution, and on the social and interpersonal forces that unite and divide the Morels and shape the development of the protagonist Paul. Focusing as it does on spouse abuse, this essay will concentrate on the first 20 years of the Morels' evolution, as depicted by Lawrence in part I of the novel.

As Dennis Poupard and James Peterson discuss, *Sons and Lovers* is a detailed portrait of the obsessive love and symbiotic bond that is formed when an empty and abusive relationship provides a barren soil from which grows the mother's quasi-incestuous substitution of each son for her husband. The Freudian connotations are rife, and not surprisingly, the "most prominent critical method used to examine the novel has been a psychoanalytic approach" (1985, 275). According to Geoffrey Harvey, Lawrence's novel came to be regarded as "the most profound examination in literature of the workings of the Oedipus Complex, and as an artistic corroboration of the scientific truths revealed by Freud's method of analysis" (1987, 20).

A different approach to examining the phenomenon of wife battering in the context of this novel is that of a family systems theory perspective, one in which the actions of the individual members are interpreted as having their roots in the interplay of forces working within the family, rather than the intrapsychic makeup of any given individual. Systems theory attempts to explain any family dynamic, in this case spouse abuse, in terms of what purpose it serves in the family, as opposed to establishing a linear cause–effect relationship. Rather than pointing to, for example, the innate aggressiveness of a husband or the dependent tendencies of a wife as causing such behaviors as battering, the interpersonal violence is viewed as a compensating symptom of a more fundamental process operating within the dynamics of a particular family system.

In order to understand the systems view more clearly, it is helpful briefly to review established theories on the causes of spouse abuse, roughly divided into three models: intrapsychic, behavior response, and social learning. The intrapsychic model concentrates on the individual personality traits of the batterers and the battered, and attempts to explain the spouse abuse in terms of how the pathological character makeup of individuals are manifested in physical or psychological violence. N. Shainess (1977) examines the personality traits of wife batterers and considers them to be passive–aggressive, obsessive–compulsive, paranoid, and/or sadistic. Abused women are described by Snell, Rosenwald, and Robey (1964) as aggressive, masculine, dominating, sexually frigid, and masochistic. Maria Roy (1982) describes male batterers as pathologically jealous, insecure, unexpressive, and possessive.

Behaviorists discount intrapsychic processes and focus instead on stimulus–response reactions. This is best exemplified by the frustration–aggression hypothesis of Dollard and co-workers (1939), which states that violent behavior is preceded by environmental frustration. The anger–control approach to the treatment of batterers is primarily based on changing the typical response patterns of the batterer to stressful and potentially anger-provoking stimuli in their environment.

Social learning theorists like Albert Bandura (1973) reject both of these views in favor of the theory that violence is strictly learned behavior, and that spouse abuse is acquired by learning from role models and reinforced through social approval: a man beats his wife because of his exposure to violence in his family of origin, or because he has been socially conditioned to exert control through the use of physical force. A variation of this model is referred to as profeminist, since it emphasizes social norms that reinforce the authoritative control males exert over females in the power structure of our society.

A systems theory view, while not discounting the validity of these perspectives, accentuates the family system as a complex, organic whole in which any individual's deviant behavior is a result of the interplay of forces operating to maintain that system. Jean Giles-Sims (1983), in *Wife Battering: A Systems Theory Approach*, posits that asking "how" wife battering occurs rather than "why" reflects a different way of thinking about social behavior:

> This approach is based on the assumption that linear cause–effect analyses cannot capture the complexity of mutually causal relationships. The question of how violence develops over time to the level of wife battering, and how the wife battering becomes an ongoing pattern resistant to change requires a process approach. (1983, 32)

M. A. Straus (1973) proposes two relevant factors in a systems theory of family violence. First, the victim may inadvertently be reinforcing the violent behavior, therefore stabilizing the pattern of violence in a relationship. Second, the person labeled as violent may be encouraged to play out the role through the development of a self-concept as "violent," and similarly the person labeled as victim may be encouraged to play out that role.

Lenore Walker (1984) describes a three-stage model, in which the first stage is characterized by mounting tension, leading to the second stage of the battering episode, followed by the third stage of reconciliation, with the husband expressing contriteness and the wife's return. Walker believes that the third stage provides the woman with the reinforcement to stay in the relationship: she is needed, she is a noble forgiver, and she is reconvinced that he loves her and will change. The battering discharges tension in the marriage and balances unequal forces that have built up over time; however, the cycle will tend to repeat itself because the forces are never directly addressed or modified. Walker also discusses the concept of "learned helplessness" in which women learn that all their attempts to change the situation have no effect, so that over time the motivation to respond in an active way decreases, and they "accept" the situation by default, because they have no control over it.

Central to a systems approach is the notion of the power–control issue underlying spouse abuse. If a male is generally powerless in his world, he may come to view his family as the one "domain" to be controlled and possessed. Physical as well as psychological violence becomes a way of controlling and establishing superiority in at least this one realm—an idea expressed in the familiar maxim, "A man's home is his castle, and in it he is king." When there is an imbalance of power, as when the man is unemployed or when the wife has a higher education level or higher-status jobs, increased risk of violence exists. As concluded by Susan Schecter (1982) and by Edward Gondolf and David Russell (1986), spouse abuse is not necessarily anger driven, but is more the consequence of a psychosocially imposed "need" to control women.

The conflicts, emotional as well as physical, between Gertrude and Walter Morel suggest multiple alternative perspectives concerning the causes of this interminable struggle. Early critics of the novel portray Mrs. Morel as a brave and enduring heroine and treat Paul's relationship with his mother "as representing the normal loving support given by a son, who is forced by circumstances to assume his shiftless father's domestic role" (Harvey 1987, 9). A majority of critics, however, like Judith Ruderman (1984), view Gertrude Morel as a dominating and smothering woman who drives her husband to his excesses, and is therefore primarily responsible for her own bitterness. Of course, it is the abnormal and obsessive love for her son that creates the fundamental self-destructive conflict in Paul Morel.

Lawrence himself varies in portraying the "victims" and "villains" of this family drama. While the overt story line portrays Walter Morel as a crude, unloving, and drunken figure and Gertrude as the long-suffering, sacrificing, high-minded wife, his narrative also conveys Gertrude's coldness and her grim determination to exclude her husband from his place in the family structure. As stated by H. M. Daleski:

> The weight of hostile comment which Lawrence directs against Morel is balanced by the unconscious sympathy with which he is presented dramatically, while the overt celebration of Mrs. Morel is challenged by the harshness of the character in action. The artist, it would seem, penetrated to the truth which the son subsequently thought he had not seen, for the impression which Mr. and Mrs. Morel make is not notably different from that which Lawrence had of his father and mother in later life. (1988, 24)

Lawrence's ambivalence toward the parents is revealed in the following passage:

> Morel made the meal alone, brutally. He ate and drank more noisily than he had need. No one spoke to him. The family life withdrew, shrank away, and became hushed as he entered. But he cared no longer about his alienation.
> Immediately he had finished tea he arose with alacrity to go out. The children waited in restraint during his preparations. When he had gone, they sighed with relief.
> He closed the door behind him, and was glad. . . . The Palmerston would be the cosier. . . . The men made a seat for him, and took him in warmly. He was glad. (1984, 45–46)

A strict interpretation of these and similar passages paints Morel as a harsh and rejecting scoundrel. Taking a systems perspective and examining the process rather than the content, however, the interpretation emerges that Morel indeed does care about his alienation, and his actions are an effort to repudiate this distance. He is vulgar only in comparison to "the reserved, watchful rest of the family," who have excluded him. He runs away not only from himself but from his wife's disgust and his children's shrinking. The company of his friends and his escape to the pub "thaws" not only responsibility and shame, but also the "icy disdain" of his family.

Rather than fixing blame or establishing cause and effect relationships, a systems view examines the functions being served by such behaviors: the "how" as opposed to the "why." By ostracizing her husband from the family, Mrs. Morel is able to engage the support and sympathy of the children, perpetuate her victimhood, and thereby reassert her control over the situation. Morel doles out shillings as well as blows, and his wife must perpetuate the means to balance that "power." Conversely, by condemning the wife as a puritanical shrew, Morel can justify his escape from the hostile environment of his home, and assert his "manly" privileges.

If the system contained only these two polarities, it would finally prove unstable; however, a homeostasis is established through the supersession of the sons. This replacement provides Gertrude an available surrogate as well as a vicarious attainment of meaning through their achievements. The father's retreat and the mother's unappeased love are continually regenerated, serving the needs of this family system to maintain an awkward but workable balance and thus preventing further unraveling.

A systems view avoids oversimplifying the fixing of blame for intrafamily violence and instead identifies it as a symptom, a kind of outgrowth of the processes that serve to maintain equilibrium. If one abstains from asking a chicken-or-egg question concerning which came first, Walter Morel's neglect and hostile aloofness or Gertrude Morel's belittlement and emasculation, and instead asks what purpose such behaviors accomplish, a case can be made that the physical battering that Morel dispenses is a counterbalancing force to the emotional battering generated by Gertrude. This does not excuse Morel or blame Gertrude for the violence; it places it in context. Morel's physical power and his escapism are the only "resources" he wields, but they are quasi-futile attempts to establish his dominance. Similarly, Gertrude's tongue-lashings and haughty reproach are her tools of sustenance.

For example, the Morel family would probably not change were Walter Morel to stop drinking, because this habit serves a purpose in maintaining this system. If his vice were removed, another behavior would replace it that would accomplish the same end: to give Gertrude Morel reason for her disgust. Rather than accepting her error of choice of a mate and confronting her frustration over unmet expectations, she can clearly point to his neglect and lack of ambition as justification for her misery and disaffection. He acts out the self-fulfilling prophecy of negligent boor, so that Gertrude can assume her role of suffering victim. In fact, each unconsciously conspires to reinforce this abusive pattern in the other, for it has become habitual and serves as the rationale for their pain and unhappiness.

Once the "glue" that holds the system together is identified, the question arises as to why the system maintains itself at all. In a literary work, it may serve as a plot device. In life, as Giles-Sims maintains, once patterns have been established and operate for long periods of time, they are extremely resistant to change: ". . . either partner may get more violent to establish or maintain his/her power position, and in turn a higher level of violence becomes a part of the family system" (1983, 15). Also, if it were not for her husband's failings, the substitution and subsequent "possession" of first William, the elder son, and then Paul could not be justified.

Ironically, it is the very factors that attracted Morel and Gertrude to each to the other in the beginning of their relationship that helps doom them to a marriage of incompatibility. Walter is fascinated with her fine bearing, quick mind, and sophistication, and Gertrude is intrigued with his physicality and natural earthiness. After a time, as Julian Moynahan writes:

> She tries to adapt herself, but is soon put off by the uncouth slackness of her husband . . . . The warm physical nature which had attracted Gertrude to him is soon ruined by hard work, by serious accidents occurring in the pit at regular intervals, and by drink. The rupture between husband and wife, although inevitable, is never total. In the midst of her contempt she respects what he once was; and Morel's drunken tirades hide an inarticulate admiration for her real refinement and intellectual superiority. (1963, 303)

Although cultural customs and economic necessities provide some of the impetus that keeps the system intact, at least in the early married life of the Morels, unspoken affection also provided part of the bond. A time arrives, however, when their dissimilarities divide them forevermore. This split is symbolized by an incident in which Morel shears from their son's head the long, beautiful curls cultivated by his mother:

> This act of masculine clumsiness was the spear through the side of her love for Morel. Before, while she had striven against him bitterly, she had fretted after him, as if he had gone astray from her. Now she ceased to fret for his love: he was an outsider to her. This made life much more bearable.
>
> Nevertheless, she still continued to strive with him . . . because she loved him, or had loved him. If he sinned, she tortured

> him. If he drank, and lied, was often a poltroon, sometimes a
> knave, she wielded the lash unmercifully. (1984, 21)

Daleski maintains that while the story depicts the Morels as equally
responsible for the failure of their marriage, it is Mrs. Morel who has
the most to answer for: "Morel is of course factually responsible for
the attack on his wife, but it is forcefully suggested that moral responsibility for the clash is Mrs. Morel's; it is she who goads him into fury"
(1988, 28).

The divergent backgrounds and temperaments that originally
fueled the attraction between these opposites later comes to stoke the
fires of their conflict. Gertrude cannot accept the loss of what that
earlier attraction had promised, therefore her survival is based on the
replacement of the husband with the sons. Through this supplanting,
she can sustain a measure of life:

> The pity was, she was too much his opposite. She could not be
> content with the little he might be; she would have him the much
> that he ought to be. So, in seeking to make him nobler than he
> could be, she destroyed him. She injured and hurt and scarred
> herself, but she lost none of her worth. She also had the children.
> (Lawrence 1984, 21)

As previously mentioned, various researchers have noted that
when there is a difference in social or economic status, there exists a
higher risk potential for battering. Walker finds that batterers tend to
be less well educated and lower in socioeconomic class than their
wives:

> It is probable that these issues are often measures of the funda-
> mental sexist biases in these men that indicates their inability to
> tolerate a disparity in status between themselves and their wives.
> Perhaps they used violence as a way to lower the perceived status
> difference. (1984, 11)

A concept from systems theory developed by Murray Bowen
(1978) is the triangle theory, which defines every relationship that
exists in terms of a three-way interaction. Bowen maintains that in all
family relationships there are never simply interactions between two
people, but always among three individuals. In this family drama, the
processes would evolve between Morel, Gertrude, and each of the
boys, in order to sustain the precariously balanced infrastructure of

the family system. Ross Murfin details the significant three-way interactions among the major characters in the story:

> What, then, happens to a soft, receptive, musical, and humorous father who cannot be appreciated—or fully appreciated— by his wife? He is likely to come to resent not only the son whose talents are more properly "male" but also his wife, who comes to appreciate her son more than she does her husband in spite of those natural, untaught instincts that initially drew her toward the man she married. If resentment leads a husband to hurt his wife, then the son through whom she is living her life is bound to protect the mother he so resembles." (1987, 60)

The Morel family can best be understood as a set of powerful forces of attractions and repulsions that sustain the structure of this system. Rather than looking at Paul's revulsion toward his father as an unresolved Oedipal fixation or at Morel's chauvinistic treatment of his wife as a sociocultural derivative, these characteristics may be considered as the necessary connective elements by which each character's respective position is fixed and affirmed in the constellation of the family system, thereby maintaining its integrity. Morel's "knavery" and neglect serve to produce Mrs. Morel's great dissatisfaction, and Gertrude's puritanism and condescension in turn propel Morel's need for escapism. In the third corner of the triangle, the sons successively play out the *raison d'etre* for their existence: to provide what the mother so desperately hungers for and will never have through her husband. This assigned role, supplanting the father as lover and partner, eventually consumes each son, as Moynahan explains:

> The older son is taken over completely. He [William] wears himself out in ambitious pursuits reflecting an intensity of frustration that is more his mother's than his own. Denied its legitimate satisfactions, Mrs. Morel's will has become inhuman. Paul, with some of the traditional slipperiness of the artist type, evades the full force of his mother's will, but is severely injured by the erotic concomitants of her drive for self-realization through a son's life. (1963, 21)

As William becomes an adult, his mother's implacable determination drives him until he eventually sickens and dies. Paul is substituted as surrogate lover and husband, though he too is ultimately unable to break free of the encompassing shackles:

> Sometimes he hated her, and pulled at her bondage. His life
> wanted to free itself of her. It was like a circle where life turned
> back on itself, and got no further. . . . He could not be free to go
> forward with his own life. (1984, 334)

The fundamental conflict in *Sons and Lovers* is not only between temperament and society, but also between love and power. Mrs. Morel is clearly the more powerful of the two spouses; in fact, she is by far the most formidable character in the story. Since the British working-class culture the Morels inhabit assigns the husband authority and overt control, Gertrude compensates by sheer strength of will, dominating and establishing the atmosphere in the Morel home. Morel may control the shillings and blows, but those serve as his sole means of asserting his "bestowed authority." It is his wife who wields actual control. Outwardly, he physically threatens; inwardly, he emotionally retreats:

> "No!" she cried loudly, "you shan't do all you like. I've got those
> children to see to . . . I should look well to leave them with you."
> "Go," he cried thickly, lifting his fist. He was afraid of her. "Go."
> (1984, 27)

From a systems perspective, when an imbalance of power exists and threatens the intactness of the family system, one or more members will manifest behaviors that serve to redistribute the control and balance the power. They do so, however, at the risk of losing their individual identity by becoming enmeshed in each other and the system. Daniel Schneider writes about this capitulation that threatens their individual being: "Paul's surrender to his mother cripples him and afflicts him with that 'ontological insecurity,' that fear of engulfment . . ." (1988, 144).

Individually, these people emerge as vigorous; however, as components in the family configuration their hopes and vibrancy fade. Early in the story, Morel is described as having a "proud, noble, selfhood," as "full of color and animation," with a "warm, a kind of gamboling humor," and "the sensuous flame of life" flowing "off his flesh like the flame from a candle" (15–16). Gertrude's life is also vivid: "She had a curious, receptive mind, which found pleasure and amusement in listening to other folk. She was clever in leading folk to talk. . . . In her person she was small and delicate" (15), and she is "one of those people who can walk in mud without dirtying their shoes" (123). Individually, these two personalities are richly alive; however, together they suffocate each other and their vitality is sucked dry. Although the mine pits scar and cripple Morel, the deepest wounding occurs in his marriage:

> The pity was, she was too much his opposite. She could not be content with the little he might be; she would have him the much that he ought to be. So, in seeking to make him nobler than he could be, she destroyed him. She injured and hurt and scarred herself, but she lost none of her worth. She also had the children. (21)

There will be no sundering of this system, and so the volatility of the power struggle grows, erupting at intervals with vicious verbal battles and physical conflicts:

> He came up to her, his red face, with its bloodshot eyes, thrust forward, and gripped her arms. She cried in fear of him, struggled to be free. Coming slightly to himself, panting, he pushed her roughly to the outer door, and thrust her forth, slotting the bolt behind her with a bang. (1984, 28)

The major question that arises in the application of systems theory to the issue of wife battering concerns responsibility. As Giles-Sims proposes, an analysis of spouse abuse that focuses on family processes may seem to imply that these system processes are responsible for the violence. It would be more accurate to say that these processes explain the violence, from a new, different perspective—one that augments other views rather than supplanting them. From the standpoint of changing these patterns of family violence, a systems perspective offers hope and flexibility, since a system may be altered by changing any of its component parts. As a marriage or family therapist, one may be able to do very little about social forces, past conditioning, or personality disorders, but strategic intervention with a system holds the promise of bringing about substantive changes in destructive family situations.

A final caveat, however, is that such a view does not remove individuals from the moral responsibility for their destructive acts. Physical violence, whatever the motivation or provocation, is an unacceptable and inappropriate act. Yet a systems view ultimately regards each character as alternatively a victim and a villain, and defines a new way of looking at the motivations and interactions of characters, in literature and in reality.

References

Bandura, Albert. *Aggression—A Social Learning Analysis.* Englewood Cliffs, NJ: Prentice-Hall, 1973.

Bowen, Murray. *Family Therapy in Clinical Practice.* New York: Jason Aronson, 1978.

Daleski, H. M. "The Son and the Artist." In Harold Bloom, ed., *Sons and Lovers: Modern Critical Interpretations.* New York: Chelsea House, 1988.

Dollard, J. L. W. Doob, N. E. Miller, O. H. Mowrer, and R. R. Sears. *Frustration and Aggression.* New Haven: Yale University Press, 1939.

Giles-Sims, Jean. *Wife Battering: A Systems Theory Approach.* New York: Guilford Press, 1983.

Gondolf, Edward, and David Russell. "The Case Against Anger Control Treatment Programs for Batterers." *Response* 9 (3): 2–5, 1986.

Harvey, Geoffrey. *Sons and Lovers.* Atlantic Highlands, NJ: Humanities Press International, 1987.

Lawrence, D. H. *Sons and Lovers.* New York: New American Library, 1984.

Moynahan, Julian. *The Deed of Life.* Princeton, NJ: Princeton University Press, 1963.

Murfin, Ross C. *Sons and Lovers: A Novel of Division and Desire.* Boston: Twayne Publishers, 1987.

Poupard, Dennis, and James Peterson. *Twentieth Century Literary Criticism.* Detroit: Gale Research, 1985.

Roy, Maria. *The Abusive Partner: An Analysis of Domestic Battering.* New York: Van Nostrand, 1982.

Ruderman, Judith. *D. H. Lawrence and the Devouring Mother.* Durham, NC: Duke University Press, 1984.

Schecter, Susan. *Women and Male Violence: The Visions and Struggle of the Battered Women's Movement.* Boston: South End Press, 1982.

Schneider, Daniel J. "The Artist as Psychologist." In Harold Bloom, ed., *Sons and Lovers: Modern Critical Interpretations.* New York: Chelsea House, 1988.

Shainess, N. "Psychological Aspects of Wifebattering." In Maria Roy, ed., *Battered Women—A Psychosociological Study of Domestic Violence*, pp. 111–119. New York: Van Nostrand Reinhold, 1977.

Snell, J. E., R. J., Rosenwald, and A. Robey. "The Wifebeater's Wife: A Study of Family Interaction." *Archives of General Psychiatry* 11:107–113, 1964.

Straus, M. A. "A General Systems Theory Approach to a Theory of Violence between Family Members." *Social Science Information* 12: 105–125, 1973.

Straus, M. A., R. Gelles, and S. K. Steinmentz. *Behind Closed Doors: Violence in the American Family.* Garden City, NY: Doubleday/Anchor, 1980.

Walker, Lenore. *The Battered Women's Syndrome.* New York: Springer, 1984.

14

Desire and Strife
The Violent Families of Eugene O'Neill

HELEN HOUSER POPOVICH AND
JAMES ROLAND KELLER

Horrifying portrayals of spouse abuse appear repeatedly in the plays of Eugene O'Neill, from his earliest writings through his mature tragedies and late autobiographical family histories. This abuse may be either psychological or physical and may be inflicted by either the husband or the wife or by each upon the other. When it is the central action of the main plot or an important subplot, the abuse usually results in the insanity, suicide, or murder of the victim; and the ensuing guilt leads to the literal or figurative destruction of the abuser.

In these attempts to portray marital violence, O'Neill anticipates the conclusions of contemporary spouse abuse theory. His incidents of violence reveal a more enlightened understanding of the causes of the phenomenon than was common for his day. Spouse abuse is a crime whose history has not been fully documented until recently (Davidson 1977, 3). It has been traditionally regarded as acceptable, provided the bodily injury to the partner was not permanent (Davidson 1977, 2), and this view has been reinforced by the almost universal, yet fallacious belief that the battered woman must have provoked her husband. Thus she was regarded as largely responsible for her own injury (Schechter 1982, 20). These theories, however, have been exploded by the recent intensive studies into the causes of marital violence. Researchers now understand that poverty (Schlesinger, Benson, and Zornitzer 1982, 162), alcohol abuse (152), and stress (161) are often contributing factors in abusive behavior. Occasionally, "ethnic, religious, or racial" differences play a role as well (Walker 1984, 11). Often, the batterer is less educated than the abused partner, and his violence is a "way to lower the perceived status difference." Maria Roy, a leading advocate of services for abused women, describes the psychological profile of the violent spouse in her classic study of family abuse:

> Violence is the end product of pent-up frustration, denial of perceived legitimate rights over a period of time, and the constant erosion of self-esteem. . . . It is related to power because it is a consequence of the absence of power—conceived and born of impotence. (1982, 3)

O'Neill's abusive spouses consistently display their impotence as they wallow in self-pity and are alternately frightened and enraged by feelings of powerlessness. They are so devoid of self-esteem that they are incapable of love; instead, they develop a life-sapping codependency with the abused partner, which prevents either of them from simply walking away from the destructive relationship. Infidelity, drugs, and alcohol may initially provide a fleeting promise of solace but will ultimately accelerate the disintegration of the individual and the marriage. And, finally, even though the abusive spouse may claim that the abuse is justified or that it springs from love and is done for the victim's own welfare, the audience knows and the abuser frequently realizes that the assault is actually an eruption of repressed hatred.

In the early monologue *Before Breakfast*, for example, O'Neill's self-pitying and vicious Mrs. Rowland begins her day by surreptitiously drinking a glass of gin and searching through her husband Alfred's coat pockets where she discovers a letter from his pregnant mistress Helen. She wakes Alfred, and as he shaves before the bathroom mirror, she subjects him to an unrelenting barrage of ego-shattering criticism. She berates him for being lazy, a drunk, a tramp, a silly would-be poet who will not get a job, and a disgusting failure who does not deserve to live. She attacks his friends for their haughty airs and denigrates his father, a millionaire who wasted his fortune and died owing everyone money. She accuses Alfred of marrying her only because she was pregnant and declares that their baby was luckier to have been born dead than to have lived with such a father.

She is startled but perversely satisfied when Alfred reacts to the abuse by cutting his face with a razor. Then, as he resumes shaving, she destroys his hopes of escape by vowing she will never divorce him and by informing him that his mistress is "no better than a common streetwalker." Alfred is devastated by this abuse. Staring at the mirror and seeing only a total failure who brings catastrophe into the lives of those he touches, Alfred commits suicide by slitting his wrists. Mrs. Rowland hears the thud of his body hitting the floor, sees what he has done, shrieks, and runs madly from the room.

In spite of its brevity and simplistic structure, *Before Breakfast* contains many of the common elements of psychological abuse. Mrs. Rowland's relationship with her husband is complicated by the couple's poverty and by alcohol abuse on the part of both partners. Furthermore, the husband and wife are warped products of significantly different backgrounds. A gap in the partners' social status is frequently a predominant element in the abusive relationships (Walker 1984, 11). However, whereas usually the husband has married into a higher socioeconomic class and has subsequently become violent in order to compete with his more genteel wife, in *Before Breakfast*, these roles are reversed; Mrs. Rowland reacts not only to her husband's infidelity, but also to her own sense of inferiority and inadequacy. The brutality of her attack reflects the self-hatred resulting from her perception that she cannot adequately fulfill her conjugal duties. Since spouse abuse can often be found among couples who have been "rigidly socialized" into the stereotypical roles (Walker 1984, 2), Mrs. Rowland's sense of failure in her marital tasks lies at the root of her abusive behavior. Her inability to please Alfred in the bedroom, her failure to convince him to act like a traditional husband by getting a job, and her bitterness at having to earn the couple's living single-handedly are constant sources of frustration for her. Thus she "unpacks her heart with words" in an effort to punish, if not destroy, her husband.

The characteristic elements of spouse abuse dramatized in *Before Breakfast* are virtually all repeated in O'Neill's mature play *The Iceman Cometh*. Here again the attack occurs after the abusive spouse has experienced years of frustration in which he has become overwhelmed with a sense of powerlessness and in which his sense of shame and guilt has caused him to hate both himself and his wife. By the time he reached adulthood, Hickey, the son of a small-town preacher, had rejected his religion and his family, had dropped out of school, had gained the reputation of being a worthless tramp, and had found acceptance only in bars and brothels. His self-esteem badly battered, he decided to marry Evelyn because she steadfastly believed in the illusion that he could and would reform. But when he proved repeatedly that he could not resist temptation and she invariably forgave him for his escapades, his self-loathing intensified, and he began to hate her because he could not live up to her expectations.

His binges and whoring continued. He contracted venereal disease and passed it on to her; but even that did not disillusion Evelyn, as she did her best to believe his lie that the illness can be contracted from a cup. Describing their life together, Hickey recalls that year after year the suffering and guilt piled up until he could no longer forgive her generosity of spirit because it made him hate himself; thus he began to despise her. Hickey's powerlessness to reform and his repressed anger finally exploded in violence. He knew that he could not simply leave her because even that would not destroy her expectations of him, so to end his pain and guilt, he took the gun he had given Evelyn for protection and shot her as she lay sleeping. In recounting the episode, he tries to justify the murder by claiming he only wanted to bring her peace. But as he stands gazing at her corpse, his repressed sentiments bubble to the surface, and he laughs, exclaiming "Well you know what you can do with your dream now, you damned bitch."

As is the case with many abusive spouses, his anger is quickly abated by the fulfillment of his violent act (Walker 1984, 2) and he becomes contrite. Since his wife is dead, however, he must direct his newly discovered good intentions upon his fellow drunks at Harry Hope's saloon. He concocts a scheme to cure them of their personal expectations so that they too can become contented for the first time in their lives, and he attempts to convince himself that his violent act was a mercy killing. Despite his elaborate rationalizations, his illusion is shattered as he is arrested and led off to jail, and he discovers that only death will bring an end to his torment.

In many ways, Hickey conforms to the profile of the abusive partner. He is poor, and he drinks excessively. Also, his self-esteem is destroyed by his inability to fulfill the stereotypical role of the husband because he cannot assume responsibility. He is unsuccessful in providing for his wife, and he is unable to show fidelity toward her. As a result, he accuses her of sleeping with the iceman so that he does not have to acknowledge that he is mistreating an undeserving person; thus his abuse is an attempt to reduce the gap between her virtue and his vice. If he could convince himself that she too was foul, he could bandage his own self-esteem and avert the violent outcome. However, her virtue remains undaunted, and, paradoxically, he must kill her in order to ease his own conscience.

Whereas *Before Breakfast* deals with psychological abuse and *The Iceman Cometh* treats physical abuse, O'Neill fully integrates both forms of degradation into his midcareer play, *All God's Chillun Got Wings*. Again he traces the roots of spouse abuse to the loss of self-esteem; this time it is caused by the characters' racial background and the crushing pressure exerted to make them conform to the limiting stereotypes of a racist society. Ella Downey, a pretty blonde, and Jim Harris, a black, are attracted to each other as children. As teenagers and young adults, both suffer a series of blows that severely damage their self-esteem. Jim repeatedly fails in his efforts to pass law school exams and thus to prove he is as good as his white peers. Ella gives birth to and then loses an illegitimate child, is rejected by her family and by the child's father, falls into poverty, and is even solicited by a pimp to join his stable.

Although Jim knows that Ella does not love him and although both of the rebels have paradoxically internalized society's racist belief that blacks are inferior to whites, the two marry in an obviously doomed effort to overcome their sense of failure. To underscore her own unconscious racism, Ella tries futilely to deny Jim's blackness by claiming that he has always "been white" to her. Ignoring Ella's racism and denying his own feeling of inferiority, Jim, by passing the bar, hopes to make Ella love him and to prove that he is her equal.

Within a few years, the relationship destroys both individuals. Ella's loss of self-esteem, exacerbated by her marriage to a black man, causes her to become mentally ill and abusive. She can accept Jim as her childhood playmate or her slave; but when he attempts to gain self-respect by asserting his manhood and seeking to earn admittance to the bar, she cruelly reminds him that he failed in high school and that he seldom passed law school exams. Thus like the classic spouse abuser, she cannot tolerate a disparity in social standing between herself and her husband (Walker 1984, 11). Her internalized racial bias will not allow her to accept his advancement; she must try to keep him in a subordinate position.

Jim's sister Hattie is appalled by Ella's vitriolic outbursts. She tries to make Ella appreciate Jim's worth and to acknowledge and accept his blackness by forcing her to admire the ceremonial Congo mask, a symbol of black power, which Hattie has given Jim as a wedding present. Ella is first frightened and disgusted by the artifact. Then, determined to conquer it, she slaps it contemptuously, claiming that Jim will not be "taking any more examinations." When Jim collapses in despair, Ella responds with kindness, reassuring him that he will one day be a fine lawyer and that he will show the world he is "the whitest of the white." Accepting the challenge of this bizarrely unrealistic expectation, Jim promises again to make himself worthy.

Ella's continued self-loathing exacerbates her mental instability. During increasingly frequent periods of insanity, she raves about blackness, fears that her own skin is turning black, and accuses Jim of poisoning her. Then she becomes a whimpering child, terrified by bad dreams and clinging to Jim as her only hope. Hattie urges Jim to leave Ella or at least to place her temporarily in a sanitorium so that he can maintain his own health and sanity, but he refuses. He even quits law school and studies for the bar at home so that he can take care of her. She, in turn, prevents him from sleeping or studying; she threatens to murder him with a carving knife; and when he tries to console and quiet her, she calls him a "dirty nigger." Jim inevitably fails the bar exam, and Ella is wildly gleeful. She cavorts around the room, grabs the Congo mask, places it on the table, and with unrestrained laughter, stabs it. Jim briefly sees her diabolic cruelty, but then forces himself to deny it and to accept his continued abuse. She brags that she wanted him to fail, that she schemed to deprive him of sleep, and that she prayed he would not pass.

The abuse finally ends when Jim relinquishes forever his hope of winning Ella's love by proving himself her equal. In an act of total self-denial, he not only agrees to be her boy and her slave, he also thanks God for giving him this mad child to love.

All God's Chillun Got Wings raises one of the most pressing questions associated with spouse abuse: why does the abused partner refuse to leave the abuser? The answer is quite complex. Often, abused partners are as much victims of their own socialization as they are of their spouses (Walker 1984, 8). These individuals experience what has been termed "learned helplessness" (Walker 1984, 2). They become accustomed to being dominated and come to believe that they cannot function without the abusive partner. Being black, Jim, from his early childhood, has been subjected to white domination. In their teenage years, Ella rejected Jim for his racial origins. In law school, Jim's greatest enemy was his own sense of inferiority. He maintained that he would study for his exams until he knew all of the appropriate material, but when he was placed in a room and forced to compete with whites, his self-defeating tendencies overwhelmed his obvious competence, and he could not perform. This capitulation to racial stereotype further defeats Jim in his marriage. Like the classic abused spouse, Jim feels responsible for Ella's actions and takes the guilt upon himself (Davidson 1978, 50). Feeling embarrassed by the abuse, these partners avoid those individuals who would admonish them for their submissiveness. This is obvious in Jim's reaction to his sister. Hattie, a black activist, encourages Jim to leave his wife, but Jim elects to reject his sister instead. Furthermore, abusers frequently isolate their partners (Walker 1984, 28). Jim admits in conversation with his sister that he and Ella "got to living housed in. Ella didn't want to see nobody, she said just the two of us was enough."

In *Before Breakfast, The Iceman Cometh,* and *All God's Chillun Got Wings,* O'Neill focuses centrally on the causes of spouse abuse and the effects on the couple, but in *Mourning Becomes Electra,* he treats spouse abuse as a catalyst to widespread family violence. Susan Schechter, author of *Women and Male Violence,* argues that spouse abuse is an intergenerational learned response (1982, 12), and we can see this in O'Neill's play, where the abuse becomes a form of vendetta in which each partner victimizes the other in order to vindicate him/herself upon a third party. In this trilogy, O'Neill weaves a web of tangled relationships in which spouse abuse, incest, and adultery lead to madness, murder, and suicide in a chain reaction of family violence.

The destruction of three generations of Mannons was set in motion when David Mannon, eldest son of the wealthy Puritan patriarch Abe Mannon, was disowned by his father for seducing and then marrying a nurse girl, Marie Brantome, whom old Abe himself desired. His self-esteem destroyed by his loss of status, David sank quickly into poverty and abusiveness. He began to drink excessively and grew ashamed of his wife and son Adam. After 29 years, Adam still vividly remembers how his father, coming home drunk, hit his mother in the face. When Adam defended her by cutting his father's head with a poker, his mother wept for the husband she had never stopped loving. Although David subsequently hanged himself, Adam never forgave him. Carrying the desire for vengeance on all of the Mannons into his adulthood, Adam eventually seduces Christine, the wife of his uncle Ezra Mannon, while Ezra is away fighting in the Civil War. He feels particularly justified in this action because Ezra had refused to respond to Marie's plea for help when she was dying of sickness and starvation.

Christine, who bears many similarities to Marie Brantôme, is a vulnerable target. For over 20 years, ever since her wedding night when the consummation of her marriage to Ezra filled her with disgust, she has loathed and feared her husband. She even hates her daughter Lavinia, whom she sees as Ezra's child, the personification of her wedding night. On the other hand, she has developed an unnatural attachment to her son Orin, whom she believes to be all hers since she carried and bore him while Ezra was fighting in Mexico. When Orin grew up and Ezra made him join the army, Christine felt her husband had once again deprived her of life. By entering the adulterous relationship with Adam, she seeks to escape her loneliness, to restore her sense of self-worth, and to degrade her husband.

At the end of the war, Ezra's imminent return threatens Christine's dream of escape. Lavinia, who is terribly jealous of her mother, plays on her worst fears and self-doubts, telling Christine that Ezra will never agree to a divorce and that when she loses her beauty, he will loath her. In desperation, Christine decides that the only way to escape from Ezra is to kill him and that the only way to ensure that Adam will never leave her is to make him an accessory to the crime. She plans Ezra's murder and manipulates Adam into buying the poison for her. Knowing Ezra has a history of heart problems, she precipitates an angina attack by telling him of her adultery with the son of the serving girl. When he calls for his medicine, she gives him the poison instead.

Christine's murder of her husband provokes violence throughout the family. Lavinia discovers what Christine has done and goads Orin into murdering Adam. Then jealous that Christine preferred Adam to him, Orin brags to his mother that he has killed her lover. Distraught that she has lost both Adam and Orin, Christine commits suicide. Orin, in turn, is overwhelmed by guilt and self-hatred. He clings to Lavinia and is terrified by the prospect that she might reject him. Claiming that he has taken his father's place and she has taken her mother's, he tries to bind Lavinia to him by suggesting that they become lovers. Her outraged rejection and cruel denial of his frantic plea affect him as his rejection affected Christine. Like his mother, he commits suicide.

The cycle of violence finally ends only when Lavinia, the last remaining Mannon, decides not to marry and thus not to continue the inevitable pattern of abuse. Instead, she chooses to live alone with the punishing ghosts of the Mannon dead.

In each of the plays discussed above, we see the tragedy of spouse abuse unfold. The roots lie deep within the family backgrounds of the characters, causing them to lose all sense of self-worth and rendering them incapable of establishing mature love relationships. Nonetheless, these psychologically immature couples marry in a desperate effort to prove something or to meet their overwhelming emotional needs. The marriages lead only to further loss of self-esteem, and the spouses become the visible symbols of the characters' own failure. Frustration, self-pity, and hatred build until these emotions erupt in physical and psychological abuse. The violence continues until one or both of the partners are destroyed.

O'Neill's answer to the problem of spouse abuse is not counseling and mutual understanding. His solution is far more pessimistic. He suggests the destruction of the emotionally bankrupt partners can only be averted if they refuse to marry. We realize that Mrs. Rowland could have simply left Alfred. Hickey could have avoided Evelyn's forgiveness by moving out and living at Harry Hope's saloon. Jim could have had Ella institutionalized. But once these doomed marriages take place and the partners become codependent, both are prevented from seizing the opportunity to end the relationship peacefully. Lavinia is the only flawed character who has both the insight and the strength to heed the warning signs and to refuse to marry. She understands that her own self-hatred and evil will corrupt any relationship that she establishes because these feelings are the antithesis of the self-worth and emotional maturity that form the basis of every successful marriage.

References

Davidson, Terry. "Wifebeating: A Recurring Phenomenon Throughout History." In Marie Roy, ed., *Battered Women: A Psychological Study of Domestic Violence*, pp. 2–23. New York: Van Nostrand Reinhold, 1977.

Davidson, Terry. *Conjugal Crime: Understanding and Changing the Wifebeating Pattern*. New York: Hawthorne, 1978.

O'Neill, Eugene. *The Plays of Eugene O'Neill*, 3 vols. New York: Random House, 1954–55.

Roy, Maria. "The Nature of the Abusive Partner." In Maria Roy, ed., *The Abusive Partner: An Analysis of Domestic Battering*, pp. 3–16. New York: Van Nostrand Reinhold, 1982.

Schechter, Susan. *Women and Male Violence*. Boston: South End, 1982.

Schlesinger, Louis B., Mark Benson, and Michael Zornitzer. "Classification of Violent Behavior for Purposes of Treatment Planning." In Maria Roy, ed., *The Abusive Partner: An Analysis of Domestic Battering*, pp. 148–169. New York: Van Nostrand Reinhold, 1982.

Walker, Lenore E. *The Battered Woman Syndrome*. New York: Springer, 1984.

15

Vampires of the Heart
Gender Trouble in The Great Gatsby

PHILLIP SIPIORA

In the late 1850s, Charles Baudelaire published a collection of poems entitled *The Flowers of Evil*. One of these poems, "L'Heauton-timoroumenos" (a title which has no equivalent English translation), is striking for its emphasis on violence and torment, and its depiction of an overpowering force of brutality directed both inward and outward. The speaker viciously brutalizes both himself and an unnamed character (or characters) in an excoriating fit of rage. The poem reads as follows:

> I shall strike you, but without anger
> And without hate, as a butcher strikes,
> As Moses struck the rock!
> And from your opened eye,
>
> To water my Sahara,
> Shall flow the waters of our suffering.
> My desire, swelled with hopefulness,
> Upon your salt tears shall swim
>
> Like a ship which moves to sea,
> And in my heart drugged by them
> With drunken joy your sobs will sound
> Like drums beating a charge in war.

Am I not a faulty chord
in this divine symphony,
Thanks to the hungry Irony
That shakes and cuts me like a sword?

It is in my voice, screeching!
It is my very blood, black poison!
I am the hateful mirror
Where the Fury Scans herself!

I am the wound and the knife!
I am the blow and the cheek!
I am the limb and the wheel that breaks it,
The torturer, and he who's flayed!

I am the vampire of my heart,
One of the lost forever,
Condemned to an eternal laugh
Because I know not how to smile.[1]

This poem draws attention to the experience of painful self-mutilation and wringing self-destruction, a kind of barbarism that finds one form of expression in gender conflict, or the manner in which members of different sexes engage in performative acts.[2] I believe, however, that these conflicts are also representative of larger societal festerings, in particular those which grew out of a national frustration with growing problems in the aftermath of World War I. These problems were social as well as political and even had global reverberations. According to George McMichael,

> Out of the war's catastrophes and appalling waste came little more than a sense of the failure of political leaders and a belief in the futility of hope. No abiding solutions to the world's problems had been found, and the years following the war saw the resurgence of nationalism and the rise of a new totalitarianism. (1985, 1494–1495)

The exploration of various conflicts within F. Scott Fitzgerald's *The Great Gatsby* reveals them to be encapsulations of society in general. Many of the chapters in this volume devote considerable attention to the examination of battered "wives"; however, this chapter attempts to expand that focus and examine the battered lives most of the characters inflict upon themselves and others in the chaotic world of postwar and predepression America.

The nineteenth-century narrator of Baudelaire's poem, obsessed with the spirit of egoism complemented by a violent self-torment—a kind of "auto-vampirism"—anticipates the spirit of many of the characters who inhabit the frenzied, brutal, festering, aimless twentieth-century world of Fitzgerald's classic. This powerful narrative portrays the decadence of America, a society of wrecked hopes and dreams. Roger Lewis summarizes the novel as follows:

> The world of *The Great Gatsby* can seem as sordid, loveless, commercial, and dead as the ash heaps presided over by the eyes of Dr. T. J. Eckleburg. Indeed, this atmosphere is so essential to *The Great Gatsby* that one of the alternative titles Fitzgerald considered for the novel was *Among the Ash-Heaps and Millionaires*. (1987, 48)

Many readers found value in *Gatsby*, however, as it became an instant success when it was first published in 1925. Most critics acknowledge that *Gatsby* represents a multiplicity of perspectives on life in the "roaring twenties" but, in particular, it suggests an atmosphere of hopelessness and helplessness. Fitzgerald himself sardonically called the times and culture of which he wrote the "Jazz Age." In recalling the midtwenties and his mood during the composition of *Gatsby*, Fitzgerald remembers the times as having a distinctly individual flavor, a fervor of solipsism. For him and for so many of his Jazz Age compatriots, "life . . . was largely a personal matter" (Baritz 1970, xvi). Fitzgerald was bothered by the fact that so many reviewers failed to see the sting of individualism in the novel, and said that no one who reviewed *Gatsby* "had the slightest idea what the book was about" (Mandel 1988, 544). Nevertheless, *Gatsby* has become a *chef-d'oeuvre* that has captured the national mood of despair and shattered illusions so many critics see as representative of the modern period in American culture.

The world of *Gatsby* depicts a society populated by individuals devoted to decadence, selfishness, and a disavowal of personal responsibility, particularly in the kinds of behavior that represent gender conflict. The fervor of solipsism, of extreme egotism, that troubled Fitzgerald is one of the primary sources of the pervasive abuses in *Gatsby*. Yet abuse in *Gatsby* is representative of a general malaise of the times. The period as a whole is characterized by dissipation, loneliness, and moral bankruptcy—an attitude toward life that was disseminated by so many major authors of that time, including Ernest Hemingway, T. S. Eliot, James Joyce, and Gertrude Stein. In speaking of the enormous influence that Fitzgerald and these writers exercised, Loren Baritz remarks:

> The writers of the lost generation who occupied the Jazz Age in convincing themselves that they were rootless and aimless seem also to have convinced others. (1970, xvi)

These sentiments are echoed by Edmund Wilson, a close friend of Fitzgerald's and perhaps the most significant "man of letters" in the modern period, who has remarked:

> When all our ideas of honor and loyalty, derived from our social class, from our Renaissance education, from our foolish early fantasies of ourselves, have been broken up and carried off by the currents in which we find ourselves drowning, we are at a loss as to what to fall back on. (1975, 512)

The major (and many minor) characters who populate the world of *Gatsby* reflect this world of drowning, especially in their loss of direction.

The various ways that these characters cannibalize one another constitute a major theme of this chronicle of the roaring twenties. According to John Higgins, there are two major themes running through *Gatsby:* momentarily recaptured love and then disillusion, and the falseness of the American success dream (1971, 75–76). One of the ways in which these themes are revealed is through the characters' malicious brutalizing of one another, particularly the behavior of Tom Buchanan, the most prominent intractable abuser in *Gatsby.* Buchanan is a subscriber to Rousseau's misogynistic views, affirming the belief that women are naturally subordinate to men and should be treated as such, both within the formal institutions of society as well as by individual men (Dobash and Dobash 1979, 65).[3] What makes Buchanan particularly significant is that he is a crude representation of the decadence that permeates *Gatsby,* a world of debilitating social vampirism in which human demons perpetuate the nightmare.[4] Yet the decadence in *Gatsby* also has its "softer" expressions in the words and actions of such characters as Gatsby and Daisy. Even Nick, the "objective" narrator, becomes entrapped in the spirit of materialism and parasitic antipersonalism that pervades the text. By "writing" the cannibalism he encounters, Nick becomes an integral part of the process, as I shall attempt to explain later.

Fitzgerald's world of predation, helplessness, and hopelessness can be uncovered by examining the characters who inhabit East and West Egg and their interrelationships. These characters are depicted in various psychological states, frames of emotional attitudes that promote conflict. According to Bernard Chodorkoff, there are five psychological states that promote violence: a sense of helplessness, a sense of hopelessness, threatened loss of self-esteem, fear and desire to hurt that is unmodulated by feelings of trust and love, and anomie (a breakdown or absence of social norms and values) (cited in Davidson 1978, 36). At various times during the novel, many of *Gatsby's* characters experience all of these psychological states, and their gender relationships and interrelationships further reveal a world characterized by a cycle of abuse: Tom abuses Myrtle and Daisy, Myrtle abuses George, Daisy abuses Tom and Gatsby, and Jordan, in her own way, abuses Nick. It might be said that many characters in *Gatsby* are guilty of "soul murder," a term dating back to the nineteenth century and popularized in the work of playwrights such as August Strindberg and Henrik Ibsen, gender critics who wrote extensively about intra- and interpersonal conflict. According to Leonard Shengold, Strindberg used the phrase to describe "psychic murder, which he [Strindberg] defined as taking away a person's reason for living" (1989, 19). Shengold points out that soul murder thrives in situations of intimate relationship: "The capacity to destroy a soul hinges entirely on having another human being in one's power" (1989, 19). Distressingly, soul murder is a common occurrence:

> A touch of soul murder can be an everyday affair. Every life contains occasions when one is the victim or the perpetrator of an assault on a person's right to a separate identity and a full range of human responses. Few people are without moments of bestiality. (Shengold 1989, 23)

Many of the characters who populate the world of *Gatsby*, however, engage in more than "occasional" acts of intimidation and bestiality. In the world of *Gatsby*, soul murder is a rampant crime, revealed in the ways in which many of the characters subjugate other characters: Tom has power over Myrtle, Myrtle controls George, Daisy manipulates Gatsby, and Jordan attempts to dominate Nick. One characteristic of soul murder is an acute insensitivity to others and the

values they hold; soul murderers demonstrate a flagrant disregard for
In the world of *Gatsby*, soul murder is a rampant crime, revealed in
the ways in which many of the characters subjugate other characters:
Tom has power over Myrtle, Myrtle controls George, Daisy manipulates Gatsby, and Jordan attempts to dominate Nick. One characteristic of soul murder is an acute insensitivity to others and the
values they hold; soul murderers demonstrate a flagrant disregard for
the rights and needs of others.

of interpretation initiates a self-critique in which readers question
their values, particularly with regard to gender conflict. As Sara Deats
and Lagretta Lenker point out,

> Negative examples (in literature) make us aware of the per-
> vasiveness of these harmful ideologies, helping us to question the
> authorization of violence, the masculine hegemony, and the gen-
> der polarization. (p. 9, this volume)

The "realities" in the text refer to realities in life, which is a kind of
text itself. As Jacques Derrida points out, "One text reads another . . . Each 'text' is a machine with multiple reading heads for
other texts" (Derrida 1979, 107). What is important about reading
"vampirism" in *Gatsby* is that this process may initiate the reading of
vampirism into—and possibly out of—our lives. This mode of interpreting, in my view, is an important justification for the "humanizing" effects of critical reading.[5]

One of the most important characteristics of Fitzgerald's best
work is this kind of questioning, this kind of persistent critique that
coerces readers to question values. Yet Fitzgerald was not the first
modernist to probe the vagaries of gender conflict; he was influenced
by his predecessors, both British and American modernists.

One early modernist writer to have an important effect on
Fitzgerald was Joseph Conrad, who spoke of the writer's task in very
specific terms: The writer attempts "by the power of the written word
to make you hear, to make you feel . . . before all, to make you see"
(Eble 1977, 87). One of the things that Fitzgerald learned from Conrad
and makes us see in *Gatsby* is the depiction of the squalor of modern
life as it is brought out in characters' actions and attitudes toward
themselves and others. The way characters mistreat others and mis-
perceive themselves reveals the social and moral destitution of the

times. Like the narrator in "L'Heautontimoroumenos," many of the characters in *Gatsby* are the "wound" *and* the "knife"; the torturer and the tortured; the vampires who must live from the blood of those they meet while themselves providing prey for other vampires. Characters are both vampire and quarry, the blood suckers and the blood sucked. Although the spirit of vampirism pervades *Gatsby*, it is displayed in a variety of ways in the actions and attitude of various characters: Tom Buchanan's destructive behavior differs in many ways from that of Daisy and Gatsby. Characters like Tom and Myrtle, for example, are brutally insensitive, totally uncaring individuals who represent a level of abuse that is qualitatively different from other abusive, solipsistic figures like Jordan Baker and Meyer Wolfsheim. I would like to begin exploring gender conflict in *Gatsby* by examining two intractable, "hard" abusers, Tom Buchanan and Myrtle Wilson, as illustrations of a particularly insidious kind of vampirism informing the novel.

Hard Abuse: Blood and Death

Tom Buchanan is unquestionably the most abusive character in *Gatsby* as he demonstrates a savage brutality that indicates a total lack of concern for anyone other than himself. Buchanan's insensitivity is revealed early in the novel by his racist remarks about "civilization going to pieces." Tom had been reading Goddard's *The Rise of the Colored Empires* and feels threatened by the emerging "colored races." He clearly sees himself as a member of the traditional patriarchy, "a social organization marked by the supremacy of the father in the clan or the family, the legal dependence of wives and children (and "mistresses"), and the reckoning of descent and inheritance in the male line" (*Webster's* 1979). As a self-annointed patriarch, Tom smugly notes that "it's up to us, who are the dominant race, to watch out or these other races will have control of things" (1953, 13). "Control" is very important in the Buchanan order of things. Early in the novel, for example, Tom comments on the fact that Jordan travels a great deal; Jordan's family "oughtn't to let her run around the country this way" (1953, 19). Dominance over others is a way of life for Tom, particularly subjugation that is based on physical force. In this way, Tom typifies the classic "wifebeater," who manifests a continual need to control wife, children, and environment (Davidson 1978, 30). Daisy's public description of her black and blue knuckles indicates how violent he really is and how important it is for Tom to physically dominate the women close to him: "You did it Tom. . . . That's what I get for marrying a brute of a man, a great, big, hulking physical specimen of a . . ." (1953, 12). Tom cuts her off in midsentence, but Daisy's characterization suggests that he is something less than human.

Kenneth Eble, too, characterizes Tom as more animal than human: "Tom Buchanan is gross sensuality, a beast lacking in imagination" (1977, 94). Buchanan's gross "bestiality" is implied early in the narrative, as Nick describes him as a man with a "hard mouth," a "supercilious manner," and "two shining arrogant eyes" (1953, 7). Nick describes Buchanan in very physical terms—an incredibly muscular man, a man who possesses a "cruel body." Even Buchanan's voice is physically imposing, a "gruff husky tenor . . . with a touch of paternal contempt" (1953, 7). Christian Messinger notes that "Buchanan stands as the embodiment of force, a degenerative power source that is running down" (Smith 1982, 77). And from the very beginning of the novel it is clear that Nick, whom many critics consider the "conscience" of the narrative," has little respect for Buchanan. Nick observes that Buchanan always speaks with a tone of contempt in his voice, even with those whom he likes, and we are told that "there were men at Yale who had hated his guts" (1953, 7). Nick's first encounter with Tom in the "action time" of the story (the summer of 1922) shows Tom physically manipulating Nick around in a brief tour of the Buchanan household.[6] These early physical descriptions foreshadow Buchanan's subsequent physical and psychological cruelty.

We first become aware of Tom's psychological abuse in chapter 1, when Tom leaves the company of Nick, Daisy, and Jordan to answer the telephone call of his lover, Myrtle Wilson. Although Tom behaves furtively when the butler whispers to him, it is clear to all present that Tom is carrying on an affair. In fact, when Nick asks what is happening, Jordan remarks that he must be the only person in town who is unaware of Tom's infidelity. Yet Jordan also treats the affair casually, referring to Tom's "situation" as one in which he has "got some woman in New York" (1953, 15). Displaying her disjointed sense of propriety, Jordan righteously comments that Myrtle should "have the decency not to telephone him at dinner time" (1953, 26). Yet Jordan's flippant attitude toward Tom's infidelity in many ways mirrors the social insensitivity of so many of the major characters, particularly Tom. When Tom and Myrtle go to New York, for example, Nick observes that Tom often leaves her sitting alone at a table in a restaurant, as he moves about with reckless abandon. What is important about Tom's refusal to follow fundamental rules of social propriety is that it signifies his far more serious rejection of ethical codes.

Tom Buchanan is clearly a morally bankrupt character. As Christian Messinger remarks, Tom Buchanan is a man "whose power was evident but whose morals and character were cast in sand" (Smith 1982, 77). Moreover, Tom Buchanan totally objectifies Myrtle; she, like his wife Daisy, is just another of his possessions. When Tom and Myrtle accidentally meet Nick in New York, Tom insists to Nick that he meet "my girl" (1953, 24). As his chattel, Myrtle is, in Tom's eyes, subject to any whimsical command. When Tom and Nick stop at George Wilson's gas station, Tom commands her, *sotto voce*, to take the next train to New York, where they will rendezvous. The business of living is play for Buchanan, a man who has never matured—he is an *homme manqué*. In this aspect of his personality, Tom conforms to the portrait of the wife beater as delineated by Terry Davidson: "Underneath his supermacho exterior, her (the battered wife's) husband is a dependent little boy who never grew up—except in brute strength" (1978, 29). Tom's immaturity is reflected in the way he confuses life with sports. As Leverett Smith notes, "Life is Tom's football game, and because he sees it this way, he is more destructive in the adult world" (1982, 79). Tom Buchanan is a sad case of arrested development, forever replaying his heroic days of football greatness on the field of life. Buchanan is unable to separate the acceptable violence of sport from unacceptable behavior in his personal relationships. Tom's physical acts become vehicles for maintaining control over others, particularly women. More than a century ago, John Stuart Mill commented on female bondage in describing men like Tom Buchanan:

> How vast is the number of men, in any great country, who are little higher than brutes. . . . The vilest malefactor has some wretched woman tied to him, against whom he can commit any atrocity. (1970, 16).

More recently, Susan Schechter makes a comparable observation in arguing that the pattern of violent behavior outlined by Mill is very typical: "Violence signifies crossing a boundary in which violation

208

and degradation, previously unacceptable in a loving relationship, are now used as tools of power and coercion" (1982, 17). Tom's infantile personality is reflected in his response to Myrtle's fatal accident: Tom is happy because George's repair shop will have some business. To judge Tom as anoetic—unthinking and uncontrolled by his emotions—is perhaps too kind a psychological evaluation.

Tom's abusive nature is most dramatically represented when he deftly breaks Myrtle's nose in response to her mentioning Daisy's name in the New York hotel room. Tom thinks no more of breaking her face than of smashing a fly against a wall. Tom Buchanan embodies the belief in the legitimation of violence as an acceptable solution to most human problems. In examining analogues to *Gatsby* in medieval romance, Jerome Mandel identifies Tom as the representation of a familiar theme of male brutality toward women:

> The violence that erupts as Tom breaks Myrtle's nose has no place in a medieval Cave of Lovers, but the ordinary world in medieval romance does reflect violence toward women by brutal, possessive men. (1988, 548)

For Buchanan, violence—intended and unintended—is a way of life, a dependence without which he cannot survive. Shortly after Tom and Daisy were married, we are told, Tom ran off with a chambermaid one night and wrecked his car, and in the process her arm was broken, an indiscretion that made the morning newspapers and foreshadows the death of Myrtle, for which Tom must share some responsibility. It is Tom, after all, who first engineers the switch in cars with Gatsby in East Egg that results in Daisy and Gatsby returning from New York to East Egg in a car (Gatsby's) that Myrtle assumes is Tom's. Tom, in fact, orders Daisy, with "magnanimous scorn," to return to East Egg with Gatsby, after he assumes that he has terminated their affair. As Gatsby and Daisy pass by George's station, Myrtle rushes out into the road, mistaking Gatsby for Tom. Daisy is driving, of course, and crushes Myrtle without even slowing down. What makes Tom partially culpable in Myrtle's death is his arrogant insistence in manipulating everyone around him. Tom's maladaptive personality and behavior create the conditions for violence in disrupting everyone's lives with whom he comes in contact.

Buchanan's behavior goes far beyond individual psychological maladjustment, however. According to Richard Godden, it reveals an underlying class conflict that forms a structure for the entire novel:

"Tom Buchanan, having disembodied his own wife for purposes of display, needs to approach denied satisfactions through the body of the working-class female" (1982, 359). Buchanan's behavior surely asks readers to question the authorization of violence under the signature of masculine hegemony. Leo Tolstoy might well have been speaking of Tom when the Russian artist said, "A good portion of the evils that afflict mankind is due to the erroneous belief that life can be made secure by violence" (Roy 1977, 101). The evils that Tom perpetrates result from a defective ego, which motivates him to exploit others. Tom's abusive nature depends upon a cycle of behavior by which he draws attention to himself. His "type," according to Maria, Roy, is rooted in

> an extremely small and very frail self-image that is desperately yearning to be recognized, acknowledged, and fortified; a self-image so negative that it seeks to destroy itself by destroying others. (1977, 4)

While Tom does not destroy himself, he surely destroys others, including Gatsby and George and Myrtle Wilson. Ironically (and sometimes comically), Tom attempts to maintain the pretense that he is an "honorable" man. For example, at the Plaza Hotel, Tom expresses outrage at the notion that Gatsby is romancing Daisy on the grounds that Gatsby's actions indicate a "sneering at family life and family institutions" (1953, 130). Tom's hypocritical statements would be laughable if they were not so pernicious, since Tom's affair with Myrtle is just as responsible for the unraveling of her relationship with her husband George as Gatsby's behavior is responsible for the breakdown in Tom's marriage. Myrtle, in at least a limited way, is very much a victim of Tom's desire to control everyone around him.

Some readers, such as Schechter, believe that class conflict is responsible for ruptured relationships similar to those found in *Gatsby*. Whether Myrtle is or is not a victim of class conflict, she is clearly a victim of Tom Buchanan's brutal nature, which inflicts much more harm than a shattered nose. Tom has drawn much more than blood from her because violence takes many forms, as Schechter points out:

> Brutality is not necessarily confined to hitting, pushing, and pulling out hair. Its extreme, yet not infrequent, forms often leave women severely scarred, physically and emotionally. (1982, 14)

Yet even though Myrtle is Tom's victim, in certain ways she is his counterpart—both are crude, insensitive, and contemptuous of others. In their New York apartment, Myrtle demonstrates her abusive nature in the contempt she displays toward others, particularly those whom she considers inferior. When she complains about the tardiness of the room service clerk, Nick notes that "Myrtle raised her eyebrows in despair at the shiftlessness of the lower orders" (1953, 32). Myrtle is alternately "wound and knife"; she is the "torturer as well as [s]he who's flayed." The physical and psychological abuse that Tom inflicts on her is returned to George in the verbal abuse (direct and indirect) that she heaps on him. In speaking of her husband, for example, Myrtle remarks, "I married him because I thought he was a gentleman . . . I thought he knew something about breeding, but he wasn't fit to lick my shoe" (1953, 35). Myrtle's behavior typifies a familiar scene: An abused individual abuses others in response to her or his mistreatment at the hands of another; the cycle of abuse continues unabated until it is checked by forces more powerful than the abuser. Tom's abuse of Myrtle obviously ends with her death, but there is no suggestion that his abusive tendencies have been checked; they will simply find another outlet. There is no evidence that Tom is a changed person after the deaths of Myrtle, Gatsby, and George. Nick accidentally runs into Tom in New York in October, a few weeks after the bloody events, and Nick quickly realizes that Tom has not changed: "I felt suddenly as though I were talking to a child" (1953, 181). Tom remains in a perpetual state of arrested development.

The kind of intractable abuse represented by Tom and Myrtle, however, is quite different from the vampirism of some of the other couples, particularly Daisy and Gatsby, Jordan and Nick. I would like to now turn to a kind of bloodless vampirism—abuse that is characterized by deception and disillusion.

Soft Abuse: Deception and Disillusion

Tom's liaison with Myrtle obviously offers a parallel to Daisy's affair with Gatsby, although Daisy and Gatsby represent an entirely different kind of vampirism, a more "genteel" form of abuse. Whereas Tom and Myrtle reveal a crudeness in drawing blood, Daisy and Gatsby (and Jordan and Nick) perform a more subtle type of intravenous feeding. These characters slowly suck the lifeblood out of other characters, often in ways that are almost unnoticeable, yet always in the vein of selfishness. Daisy is particularly egotistical in her behavior, which sometimes takes on the quality of a siren.[7] We are given a glimpse of her self-centered attitude in chapter 1, as Nick relates his impression of her:

> The instant her voice broke off ceasing to compel my attention, my belief, I felt the basic insincerity of what she had said. . . . [I]n a moment she looked at me with an absolute smirk on her lovely face, as if she had asserted her membership in a rather secret society. (1953, 18)

Daisy, like Tom, lacks maturity, although she expresses her immaturity quite differently; her "performances" tend toward the illusory and the dramatic. Her experiences five years earlier in Chicago demonstrate these qualities. Before marrying Tom, Daisy had been in love with Gatsby who, of course, was then a poor soldier who suddenly had been shipped overseas. The night before her wedding, Daisy became wildly intoxicated and declared that she had changed her mind about marrying Tom. The next day, however, she married Buchanan "without so much as a shiver" (1953, 78). The point is that Daisy becomes quickly dependent on whomever she is with; and Daisy's decisions are always made on the basis of the exigencies of the moment. For example, she is absolutely obsessed with Tom after their return from Santa Barbara. Jordan notes that Daisy "used to sit on the sand with his head in her lap by the hour, rubbing her fingers over his eyes with unfathomable delight" (1953, 78). Daisy's sudden capitulation to Tom foreshadows her rekindled interest in Gatsby as they renew their acquaintance on Long Island. Nick does not hesitate to function as Gatsby's "pimp" in making the "gonnegtion," and Daisy and Gatsby quickly become lovers. Daisy thus begins to repay Tom for his many "indiscretions," but the significant issue is that her tryst with Gatsby signifies how fragile, how disposable relationships become within the withered emotional climate of the novel. Daisy's behavior toward others, particularly Tom and Gatsby, reflect the artificial world that she brought with her from Chicago—a world of synthetic values, subject to change according to her latest whimsy.

One illustration of the fragility of relationships depicted in *Gatsby* is Daisy's willingness capriciously to substitute one temporary relationship for another. In the Plaza hotel, for example, Daisy quickly shifts her allegiance from Tom to Gatsby and then back again to Tom once she realizes that she cannot publicly maintain both relationships. She states that she never loved Tom, only to retract her words a few minutes later. This denial pacifies Tom, and Daisy, of course, leaves with Gatsby, only to kill Myrtle a short time later. Whereas Gatsby attempts to accept responsibility and protect Daisy by pretending to have been the driver of the "death car," Daisy demonstrates her irresponsibility by failing to admit that she caused the death of Myrtle Wilson. Immediately after the accident, Daisy and Tom plot their strategy. As Nick observes them through a window, he notes that "anybody would have said that they were conspiring together" (1953, 146). They were, of course, conspiring—conspiring to avoid any responsibility for their actions. Daisy is writing off her culpability in Myrtle's death and Tom is writing off his adultery with Myrtle. In predictable fashion, Daisy and Tom leave the country while the blood of Myrtle, George, and Gatsby is still warm. Their selfishness is reflected in their disavowal of any responsibility for their actions. As Nick sums up their characters:

> They were careless people—they smashed up things and creatures and then retreated back into their money or their vast carelessness . . . and let other people clean up the mess they had made. (1953, 181)

Although this judgment of Daisy is certainly plausible, the same might also be said of other characters in the novel, including Gatsby.

In spite of Nick's well-known assessment of Gatsby, "They're a rotten crowd . . . You're worth the whole damn bunch put together" (1953, 154), Jay Gatsby can also be charged with deception and delusion. Like Tom and Daisy, Gatsby is incredibly selfish. Gatsby's egotism is demonstrated in his ostentatious party giving, of course, but his abusive nature is most emphatically revealed by his interpersonal relationships and "philosophy" of life. In a very telling passage, Nick reports that Gatsby has hinted to him that he had raped Daisy five years earlier. Nick recounts Gatsby's story: "He took what he could get, ravenously and unscrupulously—eventually he took Daisy one still October night, took her because he had no real right to touch her hand" (1953, 149). Gatsby "took" Daisy because he, like Tom, has a very weak self-image, a delusional understanding of himself that encourages him to take whatever he wants, by force or otherwise. (There are multiple references to Gatsby's ruthless behavior with other men who interfere with his "business.") Gatsby encouraged the development of his relationship with Daisy in Chicago by misrepresenting himself; he "let her believe that he was a person from the same stratum as herself" (1953, 149). Gatsby's misrepresentations of himself to everyone, including himself, play a major role in the delineation of his character.

And even Nick, Gatsby's only true friend in the 1922 time of the narrative, has reservations about Gatsby,[8] a man "who represented everything for which I have an unaffected scorn" (1953, 2). Although Nick does find reason to admire Gatsby, he also recognizes Gatsby's weaknesses, including the inability to resist his delusions. In speaking of Gatsby's demise, Nick says, "it is what preyed on Gatsby, what foul dust floated in the wakes of his dreams" (1953, 2). It is Gatsby's irrepressible dreams that force him to draw his source of life from others.

Gatsby's delusions significantly determine much of his behavior in the action time of the novel. Gatsby's obsession with the past forces him to believe that it can be repeated. In one of the best-known retorts in the novel, Gatsby shouts back at Nick: "Can't repeat the past? . . . Why of course you can" (1953, 111). Gatsby's romantic dreams cause him to lose all sense of proportion in his behavior; the "colossal vitality of his illusions" sets the stage for the nightmare that will affect at least three other relationships, not to mention his relationship with Nick. Indeed, his infatuation with Daisy prompts him to use Nick in a variety of ways, and Nick is generally quite willing to act as liaison between Daisy and Gatsby. Nick's role of confidant to both Gatsby and Tom places him in the unique role of firsthand observation of both their adulterous affairs.

What makes Gatsby's behavior so unsavory is not only the manner and intensity with which he manipulates others, but also his insensitive attitude toward most of the other characters in the novel, except for Daisy; and even his concern for her is rooted in the pursuit of a romantic vision of life. A dramatic example of Gatsby's delusive insensitivity is his reaction to Myrtle's death. Gatsby is primarily concerned with hiding his (and Daisy's) involvement in the accident and shows little sympathy for Myrtle or interest in justice. Gatsby's behavior is so offensive that Nick is speechless: "I disliked him so much by this time that I didn't find it necessary to tell him he was wrong" (1953, 144). Yet Gatsby's behavior in this situation encapsulates his ethics and conduct throughout the novel. Gatsby lives a life of deception that, ironically, concludes with George Wilson's murder of him because Wilson was deluded into believing that Gatsby killed Myrtle.

Tom, Myrtle, Daisy, and Gatsby are, of course, not the only abusive, "lost" characters in the novel. Jordan, Nick, George, and even minor characters like the McFees are abusive in many ways.[9] Jordan, in many respects, is like Daisy and Gatsby; she, too, is disenchanted with herself and others and is caught up in a world of delusion and deception. Shortly after meeting her, Nick recalls having read something about Jordan and her "cheating incident" in a golf tournament. Jordan's personality and physiognomy suggest to Nick that she is less than forthright: "The bored haughty face that she turned to the world concealed something" (1953, 58). One time she and Nick attend a party, and Jordan leaves down the top of a borrowed car; later, the car is damaged, and Jordan lies about the incident to the owner. Moreover, Jordan is manipulative in her emotional relationships. Nick sums up Jordan's attitude toward men as one based on advantage and deceit:

> Jordan Baker instinctively avoided clever men, shrewd men, and now I saw that this was because she felt safer on a plane where any divergence from a code would be thought impossible. She was incurably dishonest. (1953, 58)

Careless in her driving, Jordan is also careless in her treatment of others. The day after Myrtle's accident, Jordan telephones Nick, informing him that she has left the Buchanans' home. This news annoys Nick, reminding him of Jordan's penchant for avoiding responsibility. Nick becomes very upset when she complains that he was not very "nice" to her the previous evening, an amazing posture considering all that had transpired. Nick decides that he no longer cares about her and allows the relationship to die a natural death. However, Nick sees Jordan one more time and she has not changed; she still looks "like a good illustration," an apt simile for her artificial mode of existence. Their meeting ends with Jordan reinforcing Nick's view of her as an insensitive individual: She tells him that she does not give a damn about him and accuses Nick of dishonesty. Nick shrugs his shoulders and walks away. Jordan's self-centered and abusive nature, as illustrated by her dishonesty, insensitivity, and manipulation of others, cause her to enter into a series of short-term relationships that are destined to fail, just as her relationship with Nick unravels after a few short months.

Nick himself, however, cannot escape the atmosphere of deception and delusion that pervades *Gatsby*, in spite of his attempts to insulate himself from the contamination of the world around him. He dines regularly at the Yale Club in order to get away from "the rioters." He has an affair with a girl who lives in Jersey City, but decides to jettison her while she is on vacation because her brother has given him threatening looks. He walks away from Jordan, in spite of the fact that he still has "some love" for her. And, most important of all, he abandons the East Coast for the more insular world, or so he believes, of the Midwest. Is Nick an "abuser"? Certainly not in the sense that Tom, Myrtle, Daisy, and Jordan abuse those with whom they come in contact. However, Nick is obviously an integral connection in Daisy's affair with Gatsby. Indeed, Nick arranges their early rendezvous, revealing more than a little social dexterity. In one of the novel's more comic lines of dialogue, Nick tells Daisy "not to bring Tom" to her first meeting with Gatsby. Daisy responds (innocently!), "Who is Tom?" (1953, 84). And the lovers are brought together to consummate the art and act of infidelity. Yet Nick is also an accomplice of sorts in the Tom and Myrtle relationship; he participates in the New York apartment scene without publicly or privately suggesting disapproval. One reason for his silence is, of course, his penchant for "reserving judgment," yet the decision to withhold judgment is an ethical judgment in itself. It might be said, therefore, that Nick contributes to abuse even though he himself is not a hard-core abuser.[10]

A Vacated Wasteland

Fitzgerald begins *Gatsby* with the following epigraph taken from his fictional character Thomas Parke D'Invilliers:

> Then wear the gold hat, if that will move her;
> If you can bounce high, bounce for her too,
> Till she cry "Lover, gold-hatted, high-bouncing lover,
> I must have you!" (1953)

This ditty might just as easily serve, however, as an ironic epilogue to the novel. D'Invilliers's concise guide to seduction crystallizes, in a very specific way, the spirit of *Gatsby*, a novel that chronicles a forlorn wasteland, devoid of natural emotions and bereft of humanity. This wasteland, which is psychological space as well as physical space, is inhabitated by those who have suffered psychic death because of the murder of their souls. The vampire of the heart has struck, and both vampire and victim are condemned to a macabre, eternal "laugh" in defensive response to unspeakable physical and emotional mayhem. Yet the victims of soul murder are really ambulatory corpses, their lives having been drained dry by torment—both self and other. Broken marriages and broken relationships become metaphors for the fractured lives that have retreated, either in death or in flight, from an inhospitable landscape. Strewn corpses—physical and emotional— are all that remain of the vacated wasteland, the result of life-snuffing gender conflict.

Tom and Daisy are particularly representative of the discontent of the generation reaching "maturity" in the Jazz Age; they move from place to place in a perpetual state of unrest. They are peripatetic profligates, seeking refuge wherever their antisocial attitudes are tolerated. They have no connection to anyplace called home. As Nick points out when he speaks of Tom and Daisy, "Why they came East I don't know. They had spent a year in France for no particular reason, and then drifted here and there unrestfully" (1953, 6). Daisy and Jordan are symbolically introduced as unfettered vessels, destined to be blown about by arbitrary forces of society. Nick first observes them as "two young women buoyed up as though upon an anchored balloon . . . as if they had just been blown back in after a short flight" (1953, 8). The breakdown of gender relationships in the novel is only a symptom, however, of a more universal malaise, a total breakdown within society. This universal rupture is the result of a multiplicity of causes: social, economic, and cultural, factors too complex for the limited kind of reading this chapter attempts to articulate. What we do know, however, is that these causes dramatically affect interpersonal relations. Psychologically and physically battered lovers and spouses become emblems for the battered lives of the "lost generation."

The conclusion of the novel has been described as follows:

> all that remains are the fleshy Myrtles and the tumescent Toms, the empty Daisys, the fraudulent Jordans, and the unfulfilled Nicks. (Mandel 1988, 556)

Doctor T. J. Eckleburg's eyes peer over a vast nothingness, ironically representing the long-abandoned advertisement for one who, at an earlier time, was able to give sight. Near the end of the novel, Nick erases an obscenity defacing Gatsby's house, as if the decadence and disillusion that Gatsby and most of the other characters experienced could be effaced so easily. East and West Egg still remain the valley of ashes, however, and no effacement can cleanse the waste left by that generation. Yet perhaps the spiritual emptiness that is one legacy of *Gatsby* may leave an affirmative residue. Perhaps the literary expression of hard- and soft-core abuse and conflict may spark a kind of critical reading that is inherently ethical; a kind of questioning that, by calling attention to itself, forces readers to reexamine the attitudes they hold toward the gender conflicts we all face in one form or another. Vampires can be held at bay.

Acknowledgment. I would like to thank my research assistant, Adrianna Palumbo, for her fine work in painstakingly tracking down some elusive source materials for this chapter. Her tireless efforts and acute investigative ability were instrumental to the completion of this chapter.

Notes

1. This translation of "L'Heautontimoroumenos" is based on the work of Bert M-P. Leefmans, although I have liberally altered his translation when I felt that certain changes would result in a "better" reading of the original.
2. The subtitle of this chapter comes from the probing book of the same name by Judith Butler (1990), who argues that "gender trouble" need not necessarily "carry such a negative valence" (ix). According to Butler, "trouble is inevitable and the task [is] how best to make it, what best way to be in it" (ix). Butler's perspectives on trouble and gender are useful, I believe, in forcing us to draw inferences from gender conflict, which reflects a larger system (with subsystems) of ongoing conflict. In other

words, the kinds of represented conflict in *Gatsby* can be ameliorative in calling attention to some underlying causes of those conflicts. My use of "gender" attempts to signal a "way of thinking" rather than a sex-determined form of expression. That is, males may express "feminine" sentiment and vice versa.

3. It is important to note that in societies where women were considered superior to men, there is no history of a corresponding female domination over males. According to Terry Davidson, "When women were sovereign in religious matters—and indeed in all matters—men were not battered by women. Women did not treat men as though a battered–battering relationship was destined and correct. There is no evidence that men were denied fields in which they might act without female supervision" (1977, 4).

4. These characters are reminiscent of Slavonic vampires, mythological half-humans, "who suck the blood of living victims; incubi and succubi, who consort with women and men, respectively, in their sleep and the former of whom may impregnate their victims" ("The Role of Demons" 1973, 403).

5. What I am suggesting here is that there is an "ethics" of reading, which lies in the process of persistent critique. By reading "critically," we subject our values to the same kind of rigorous interrogation we subject literary values to. This position is derived from the work of Derrida (1979), de Man (1986), and, most particularly, J. Hillis Miller (1987).

6. Perhaps a brief outline of the novel's chronology may be helpful: 1892 (Nick and Tom are born, and probably Gatsby too; 1899 (Jordan is born); 1901 (Daisy is born); 1917 (Daisy meets Gatsby); 1918 (Daisy and Tom are married); 1919 (Pammy Buchanan is born); 1922 (the action time of the narrative—three summer months plus October); 1924 (Nick's "time of narration"; he is remembering events that took place two years earlier).

7. See Glenn Settle for a systematic analysis of Daisy as a siren. Settle argues that Daisy represents the archetype of the *femme fatale* in her ability to draw others to her. As Nick says of her in chapter 1, "her voice compelled me forward breathlessly" (1953, 14). There are, of course, many other examples of Daisy's "mesmerizing charms," including her singing at one of Gatsby's parties. Upon hearing her sing, Nick remarks that her voice is capable of "bringing out a meaning in each word that it had never before and would never have again" (1953, 109).

8. The issue of Nick's credibility is obviously an important one in interpreting the novel; indeed, the issue of narrator reliability and credibility has been a major topic in literary criticism over at least the past 30 years. I believe that any narrator's credibility becomes a rhetorical issue; that is, readers respond to narrative revelation according to the ways in which

narrators employ various appeals or techniques in convincing readers that their stories are consistent and believable. Although I believe that Nick is an inconsistent narrator (how do we respond to a narrator who tells us that he is one of the few honest people he has ever known?), I do not believe that his narrative unreliability necessarily undermines or compromises the spirit of the story he tells. Nick Carraway is another character caught in the tenor of the times and people that he reports; he, too, is subject to the same social and personal exigencies in which other characters find themselves. Nick's portrait of himself is obviously a complex issue. However, I do not think that the problematics of Nick's narrative technique(s) diminish the patterns of malaise and abuse that I find pervasive in *Gatsby*.

9. Although the McFees are minor characters, they, like Meyer Wolfsheim, reflect the corrupt values that are so integral a part of *Gatsby*. In the New York apartment scene, for example, the McFees mimic Tom, Myrtle, and Catherine in their collective distaste for those perceived to be "beneath them." In speaking of her former fiancé, Mrs. McFee declares vigorously, "I almost married a little kike who'd been after me for years. I knew he was below me" (1953, 34). Her comment raises the topic of anti-Semitism, which I believe to be a substantive issue in the novel. Although Nick represents himself as a disinterested observer, his descriptions of Meyer Wolfsheim, the "flat-nosed Jew," represent an attitude that in some ways is not too different from that of Tom Buchanan.

10. Richard Godden makes an interesting argument for Nick as misogynist, arguing that Nick continually blames women for things that happen to him and others: "Daisy's 'carelessness,' Jordans 'lies' and Myrtle's body are at least partially generated by Nick's distaste for women" (1982, 365). Godden goes on to argue that Nick uses his writing to "castigate the female body" (1982, 366).

References

Baritz, Loren, ed. *The Culture of the Twenties*. Indianapolis: Bobbs-Merrill, 1970.

Bruccoli, Matthew J., ed. *New Essays on The Great Gatsby* (1985). Cambridge: Cambridge University Press, 1987 (reprinted).

Butler, Judith. *Gender Trouble: Feminism and the Subversion of Identity*. New York: Routledge, 1990.

Davidson, Terry. *Conjugal Crime: Understanding and Changing the Wifebeating Pattern*. New York: Hawthorne, 1978.

Davidson, Terry. "Wifebeating: A Recurring Phenomenon Throughout History." In Maria Roy, ed., *Battered Women: A Psychosociological Study of Domestic Violence*, pp. 2–23. New York: Van Nostrand Reinhold, 1977.

de Man, Paul. *The Resistance to Theory.* Minneapolis: University of Minnesota Press, 1986.

Derrida, Jacques. "Living On/Border Lines." In Harold Bloom *et al.*, eds., *Deconstruction and Criticism*, pp. 75–176. New York: Continuum, 1979.

Dobash, R. Emerson, and Russell Dobash. *Violence Against Wives: A Case Against the Patriarchy.* New York: The Free Press, 1979.

Eble, Kenneth. *F. Scott Fitzgerald.* Rev. ed. Indianapolis: Bobbs-Merrill, 1977.

Fitzgerald, F. Scott. *The Great Gatsby* (1925). New York: Scribners, 1953 (reprinted).

Godden, Richard. "*The Great Gatsby:* Glamour on the Turn." *Journal of American Studies* 16: 343–71, 1982.

Higgins, John A. *F. Scott Fitzgerald: A Study of the Stories.* Collegeville, MN: St. John's University Press, 1971.

Johnson, Norman, ed. *Marital Violence.* London: Routledge, 1985.

Lewis, Roger. "Money, Love, and Aspiration in The Great Gatsby." In Matthew J. Bruccoli, ed., *New Essays on* The Great Gatsby, pp. 41–57. Cambridge: Cambridge University Press, 1987.

Mandel, Jerome. "Medieval Romance and *The Great Gatsby.*" *Modern Fiction Studies* 34: 541–558, 1988.

McMichael, George. "20-Century Literature." In George McMichael, ed., *Concise Anthology of American Literature*, pp. 1493–1497. New York: Macmillan, 1985.

Mill, John Stuart. *The Subjection of Women* (1869). Cambridge: MIT Press, 1970 (reprinted).

Miller, J. Hillis. *The Ethics of Reading.* New York: Columbia University Press, 1987.

"The Role of Demons in Literature." *Funk & Wagnalls New Encyclopedia.* 1973 ed.

Roy, Maria, ed. *Battered Women: A Psychosociological Study of Domestic Violence.* New York: Van Nostrand Reinhold, 1977.

Schechter, Susan. *Women and Male Violence: The Visions and Struggles of the Battered Women's Movement.* Boston: South End Press, 1982.

Settle, Glenn. "Fitzgerald's Daisy: The Siren Voice." *American Literature* 57: 115–124, 1985.

Shengold, Leonard, M. D. *Soul Murder: The Effects of Childhood Abuse and Deprivation.* New Haven: Yale University Press, 1989.

Smith, Leverett T., Jr. "Why Tom Buchanan Played End at New Haven." *American Notes and Queries* 20: 77–79, 1982.

Webster's New Collegiate Dictionary. Springfield, MA: Merriam, 1979.

Wilson, Edmund. In Leon Edel, ed., *The Twenties: From Notebooks and Diaries of the Period.* New York: Farrar, Straus and Giroux, 1975.

16

"Family Dramas"
Spouse and Child Abuse in Faulkner's Fiction

ROSALIE MURPHY BAUM

> As Flaubert took commonplace and boring "material" and of it
> made a thing of beauty, so Faulkner with the sordid and mean;
> the violent, corrupt, depraved.
> ALBERT J. GUERARD (1976, 128)

Richard H. King's study of Southern literature between 1930 and 1955
argues that the Southerner "saw society as the family writ large. . . .
Individual and regional identity, self-worth, and status were determined by family relationships. The actual family was destiny" (1980,
27). This sense of the family as "destiny," of course, was compounded
by the agrarian nature of Southern society, with its lack of "strong
extra-familial institutions" (King 1980, 27) and by the very nature of
family itself, as an internalized and shared system of various relations
among family members (Laing 1971).

Not surprisingly, William Faulkner's fiction is central to King's
study. As Donald M. Kartiganer has suggested recently, "Faulkner is
the premier American novelist of family" (1982, 381).

That a sense of family was both "urgent" and "vital" (Kinney
1984, 155) to Faulkner's perspective is obvious: "the bulk of Faulkner's
people are not so much single, separate persons as collective enterprises, the products and processes of family dramas apart from which

221

the individual actor is scarcely intelligible" (Kartiganer 1982, 381). Such characters include members of the Compson, McCaslin, Sartoris, Snopes, Bundren, Hightower, Sutpen, and Varner lines as well as lesser-known figures in works like *Pylon, The Wild Palms,* and *A Fable.* The "family dramas" that emerge in the Faulkner canon to produce these characters (both as individuals and as "collective enterprises") include innumerable instances of family violence, among them spouse and child abuse (both emotional and physical), sibling violence, and murder. It is clear that many of Faulkner's characters are "both attracted to and repelled by the prospect of violence" (Polk 1980, 114).

Thus, Faulkner's fiction could be considered a compendium of intrafamilial violence and abuse—whether one defines domestic violence and abuse as (1) "physically striking a family member and causing injury," (2) "striking a person with the intent of causing harm or injury—but not actually causing it," (3) "acts of violence where there is the high potential of causing injury," or (4) "acts where there is no actual hitting at all—such as verbal abuse or psychological and emotional violence" (Gelles 1983, 155).

In the many instances of intrafamilial violence and abuse in Faulkner's fiction, the portrayals are usually consistent with the findings of investigators in the field. For example, the violence tends to occur in families that are isolated from the community, in families that are under great stress, in families characterized by severe inequality between the sexes (especially in those that support the notion of the "real man"), and in families that believe in the use of physical punishment in the discipline of children. The abuser's motivation is frequently "a sense of helplessness," "a sense of hopelessness," or "threatened loss of self-esteem" (Chodorkoff, paraphrased in Davidson 1978, 36).

In addition, Faulkner's interweaving of characters' lives within their extended families—that is, the creation of "family complexes, synchronic and diachronic systems whose individual units take their meanings from their transactions with each other" (Kartiganer 1982, 381)—clearly supports research that indicates that family violence occurs most frequently in families whose adults have been mistreated as children. And Faulkner's concern with community and society as well as family clearly supports the models of family abuse that "highlight the *multicausal* nature of marital violence and the dynamic interaction of psychological and wider social variables" (Prescott and Letko 1977, 74).

Faulkner also successfully avoids many of the popular misconceptions about family violence and abuse. His violence is only occasionally alcohol-related and in no way suggests that alcohol itself is the necessary cause of the violence. It can involve the assault of either spouse upon the other as well as of either spouse upon a child and thus does not mistakenly focus only on male abusiveness. It usually occurs in relationships involving "love, attachment, and affection" (Gelles and Straus 1988, 51), not simply in situations of fear, hatred, and deliberate cruelty. And, contrary to the popular impression that family abuse is a lower-class phenomenon, Faulkner's violence can be found—although with different patterns—on all economic and social levels.

Atypically, however, Faulkner's abusers sometimes do not fall into the familiar category of violent people who are "angry, resentful, suspicious, competitive, moody, tense . . . [with] an aura of helplessness, fear, inadequacy, insecurity" (Chodorkoff, quoted in Davidson 1978, 35); or, if they do display some of these characteristics, other qualities are much more pronounced. Surprisingly often these other qualities are ones usually considered admirable, such as personal integrity, a strong sense of history, loyalty to family and kin, concern for the welfare of the weaker, or allegiance to a Southern code, be it the planter's, yeoman's, or poor white's. Sometimes Faulkner's violence is connected with an individual male's need to demonstrate his masculinity, a cause seldom found in family violence according to Linda Gordon (1988, 254–55, 287) but "more frequent than generally realized" according to Terry Davidson (1978, 37). Sometimes the violence stems from a parent's efforts to deal with a stubborn child about religious matters, a motive recalling seventeenth-century tracts on "stubborn" children (Pleck 1987). Sometimes the violent interaction involves siblings, an area that only began to be examined by behavioral scientists in the 1970s (Pleck 1987, 227).

Such recurring patterns of family violence and abuse in Faulkner can clearly heighten reader awareness of this important area of human relationships and gradually help to affect a societal climate that has accepted domestic violence for so many years. Further, Faulkner's portrayals clarify the complexity of such interactions as he graphically reveals the horrors for the victim while often showing understanding of and even sympathy for the abuser. Frequently, his concern is for the child or young adult in the present; but, at the same time, Faulkner is always aware of the child that the abuser once was— in a past that has contributed to his or her being an abuser in the present. This complex and multigenerational perspective on family abuse is clear in all of Faulkner's works; but, because of limitations of space, this chapter can consider only some of the many examples of spouse and child abuse (both emotional and physical) in the Faulkner canon.

Cases of spouse abuse are scattered all through Faulkner's works but tend to be treated briefly, suggestively, rather than dwelt upon. (As Robert Dale Parker's study of Faulkner suggests, Faulkner's novels tend "to withhold and repress" the "most frightening sins, the same sorts of things people repress" [1985, 15].) Emotional abuse, without physical abuse, appears to occur in a number of Faulkner's upper-class and middle-class families; it is likely, for example, between Jason and Caroline Compson, in "That Evening Sun" and *The Sound and the Fury,* and between Horace and Belle Benbow, in *Sanctuary.* As Richard Gelles and Murray Straus explain, however, although emotional abuse is "the most hidden, most insidious, least researched, and perhaps in the long run most damaging form of intimate victimization," it is also the most difficult to define. It is very difficult to determine the line between serious incompatibility and the "belittling, scorning, ignoring, tearing down, harping [and] criticizing" (1988, 67) of emotional abuse.

Still, the "narcissism, repression, and masochism" that form "the controlling matrix" of the Southern Belle's personality in Faulkner (Seidel 1985, 97) suggest an almost chronic state of emotional abuse. The male adulation of women, on the one hand, and the dependence of the powerless female on the male protector, on the other, assured that women and men would remain essentially "abstractions, objects, things to be used" (Brien 1967, 132) and that neither female nor male could establish self-identity. Further, the pressure on the male "to prove early virility, an obligation in which shame and honor played a crucial, if not exclusive role," encouraged "jealousy, malice, and physical and social competitiveness by endowing these basic human sins with the rationale of sensitivity to self-esteem" (Wyatt-Brown 1982, 154, 174). Under such circumstances, "adult, mutual, heterosexual relationships" were "an impossibility," and society was "left with no other option than to continue to pursue its sick and self-destructive course" (Brien 1967, 132). Women like Temple Drake, Narcissa Benbow, and Caroline Compson emerge as victims of a societally acceptable emotional abuse, in which female "helplessness, fear, inadequacy, insecurity" (Chodorkoff, quoted in Davidson 1978, 35) are considered virtues; at the same time, their narcissism, repression, and masochism become abusive. Men like Horace Benbow, Jason Compson, and Quentin Compson experience depression, futility, and despair; they engage in the withdrawal behavior typical of victims of abuse (Flanzer 1982, 21), although, as sustainers of the Southern chivalric code, they are equally abusers.

Faulkner's more detailed portrayal of Gail Hightower, in *Light in August*, clearly suggests Hightower's emotional abuse of his wife, but not for the reasons usually associated with spouse abuse, that is, helplessness, hopelessness, low self-esteem, or simply cruelty. Rather, Hightower's abusiveness stems from an obsessive (and romantic) preoccupation with the past, a confusion between his role as husband and minister in the present and his fantasy life in his grandfather's apparently glorious past. Although Faulkner does not offer any description of the Hightowers' domestic life, Byron Bunch's comments, the townspeople's opinion, Mrs. Hightower's fate, and Gail Hightower's later reflections all suggest a situation of emotional abuse. Bunch sees Hightower's obsession with the past as the "sort of thing that men do to the women who belong to them" and speculates that "that is why women have to be strong and should not be held blameable for what they do with or for or because of men, since God knew that being anybody's wife was a tricky enough business" (1985, 443). The town's view is that Hightower's wife would have been "all right" if Hightower "had just been a more dependable kind of man, the kind of man a minister should be instead of being born about thirty years after the only day he seemed to have ever lived in—that day when his grandfather was shot from the galloping horse" (1985, 443). Both Bunch's and the town's views are, of course, the typical patriarchal view—that wives belong to husbands and that women are essentially passive and dependent in marital relationships. In such a world, they are not surprised that Mrs. Hightower, a "small, quietlooking [sic] girl" whom they hear "weeping in the parsonage in the afternoon or late at night" (1985, 443), eventually seeks sexual solace in hotels in Memphis and finally jumps or falls from a hotel window.

The experienced reader of Faulkner, of course, can safely assume that the situation is more complicated, that the emotional abuse is multicausal in nature. In the latter part of the novel, the reader discovers that Hightower's wife, several years older than he, had pursued him for three years prior to their marriage, "with eyes . . . with almost desperate calculation, like those of a harassed gambler" (1985, 754). She had deliberately selected Hightower as a very "innocent" (1985, 754), naive young man, with "the bright, happy voice of a child" (1985, 756), to help her escape a life she found unbearable and had instructed him in "a campaign of abasement and plotting" and lying to secure his ministerial position in Jefferson. Thus, although Hightower's obsession—the "hunger" of his fantasy of the past—clearly would qualify as emotional neglect and abuse, his wife's own emotional instability is as much the "instrument of her despair and shame" (1985, 762) as is his personality disorder.

Much of the physical violence between Faulkner's spouses—usually mentioned in significant but brief passages—tends to involve both husband and wife as abusers, frequently concerns jealousy or an area in which the husband asserts authority (as is typical of spousal violence according to Dobash [1979, 95]), and is often sexual in nature. Afterward, neither spouse tends to show the "surprise, shock, shame, and guilt" that Dobash suggests is typical of abuser and victim (1979, 95); and the reader senses that violence is part of the everyday language of the relationship. Seldom does the violence seriously incapacitate either spouse. (Mrs. Gant's shooting of her unfaithful husband in "Miss Zilphia Gant" is unusual in Faulkner.)

With minor characters, Faulkner will simply note the spousal violence. The husband is usually the abuser in these situations, the violence often serious but within bounds that the couple has defined. For example, in "Barn Burning," when Mrs. Snopes tries to protest against her husband's plan to burn the DeSpain barn, Abner flings her back, "not savagely or viciously, just hard" (1961, 22). In *The Mansion*, when Minnie, Miss Reba's maid, objects to her husband's giving her money to his girlfriend, Ludus snatches a flatiron from Minnie's hand "and damn near tore her ear off with it" (1959, 80). In *The Reivers*, Boon hits his wife because, although she had washed for him on Monday night, he "didn't want just rewashed clothes . . . [He] wanted a change of clothes that had had time to rest for a while . . . at home, smelling of rest and quiet drawers and starch and bluing" (1962, 260).

Mink Snopes recalls that when he was a child his stepmother was "always either with a black eye or holding a dirty rag to her bleeding where her husband had struck her." At the same time, his father and stepmother are good examples of Faulkner couples who keep their violence within bounds: Mink is surprised one midmorning to find his stepmother still in bed and realizes that his father must have "beat her this time even harder than he knew" (*The Mansion* 1959, 105). Not surprisingly, when Mink himself is a husband, he strikes his wife while his three children watch (*The Hamlet* 1957). These couples are minor figures, lower-class figures, appearing in "Barn Burning," *The Mansion*, *The Town*, and *The Reivers*. They give depth to one of the central concerns of the Faulkner canon—familial violence as "exploitative power" (Roy 1982, 4). Their conscious or unconscious decisions to set limits to family abuse are decisions greatly feared by social and behavioral scientists who observe that when a person is engaging in violence, he or she can easily miscalculate the degree of force being used or, quite simply, lose control, even momentarily.

With more important characters, Faulkner will offer somewhat more detail and create complex situations of family abuse. For example, Laverne Shumann slaps her husband in *Pylon* when she realizes that he plans to enter an air meet in a plane that has "a shot engine and two wrenched longerons" (1985, 907)—just because she is seven months pregnant and they have no money. She cannot bear the risk he is willing to take. Raging, "You rotten pilot, you bastard rotten pilot," she snatches his cigarette from his mouth, then strikes his cheek, "clutching and scrabbling about his jaw and throat and shoulder" (1985, 907) until he physically restrains her. The scene concludes with their having intercourse; and it becomes clear from other scenes in the novel that Laverne, not Roger, becomes violent under extreme stress—in "mindless repudiation of bereavement," in expression of "protest and wild denial" (1985, 908). She does not resort to the pleas and arguments considered typical of the female (Dobash and Dobash, 1979, 94). Rather, she turns to violence and sex, thus supporting Linda Gordon's observation that some "women have been as aggressive, irrational, and self-destructive as men in marital conflict"

(1988, 286). In Laverne's case, of course, she is fortunate in that Roger does not physically fight with her; rather, he uses his greater strength to restrain her.

Another of the more fully developed scenes of spousal violence in Faulkner occurs in *Sanctuary*, with Lee Goodwin and his common-law wife, Ruby Lamar-Goodwin, on the night that Temple Drake spends with them. Lee is obviously drunk; and both he and his wife have clearly been affected by the intense gender play—both between Temple and all of the men (Van, Tommy, Popeye, Lee) and between the University of Virginia "gentleman" Gowan Stevens and the rough "he-men"—which has occurred during the afternoon and evening. Ruby is convinced that Lee intends to bed Temple that night and warns him that she will not let him. She is perfectly prepared to use physical force, a fact which supports the view that women are as ready as men to engage in marital violence (Gelles and Straus 1988, 162). When Lee grips her arm, she curses him, and the two face each other "in a mounting terrific muscular hiatus." Then Lee flings Ruby "aside in a complete revolution that fetched her up against the table, her arm flung back for balance." She strikes at him with a butcher knife (thus engaging in a level of violence unusual for a woman according to Gelles and Straus [1988, 162]). He catches her wrist and holds both wrists as he slaps her: "It made a dry, flat sound." Lee then slaps his wife again, "first on one cheek, then the other, rocking her head from side to side" (1985, 245).

There is no question that this is a couple under great stress. Both are frightened of the exchanges that have already occurred between Gowan and Temple and the other men, and they are fully aware of the possible repercussions in their lives if anything (assault or rape) happens to Judge Drake's daughter. In addition, Lee himself seems to be tempted by Temple; and Ruby is experiencing one of the classic causes of spouse abuse, jealousy (Martin 1983, 59). There is also, however, no question that Lee and Ruby care deeply about each other and about their child. In fact, in the middle of their fight, Lee carefully removes their son from Ruby's arms and lays him safely on the table. But violence has always been a central part of their relationship; it is a part of their language. Earlier Ruby had proudly explained to Temple that Lee is a "Man . . .a real man," the kind of male that Temple's "putty face" has never seen. Ruby believes that a real woman, one who is not a coward, is one who will "crawl naked in the dirt and the mire" to be called a "whore" by a "real man" (1985, 219).

Thus, with Lee and Ruby, as with Laverne and Roger, the physical blow is a gesture of communication for people who care deeply about each other, a situation consistent with the findings of Gelles and Straus, who argue that, contrary to popular myth, love and violence can "coexist in families" (1988, 51). The physical assaults grow out of verbal arguments, thereby supporting the contention of some social and behavioral scientists that physical conflict usually begins with a war of words (Martin 1983, 51). Atypically, however, in both cases, it is the greater physical strength of the male that keeps the exchanges under control rather than leads to more serious violence. Roger restrains Laverne; Lee prevents Ruby from doing serious harm with the butcher knife.

In *The Hamlet*, Faulkner even suggests that the male will on occasion wait for, hope for, violence from the female in order to more clearly define his own role. When Jack Houston, for example, leaves his common-law wife of seven years to return home and marry another woman whom he has not seen for 12 years, his common-law wife curses "him, cursing them both" (1957, 213). Houston hopes that she will "just touch me, hit me, make me mad enough to hit her" (1957, 213). That would make his decision to leave easier. In all of these cases, one could argue, as Richard Gelles does, that the violence (actual or hoped for) is "strikingly rational and coherent" in nature, not irrational as some people think; it is "instrumental" in nature, with the abuser hoping "to achieve some goal or desired end" (1979, 190).

Faulkner also indicates that a couple can take pride in physical violence as a part of their relationship, especially in a case of jealousy and possessiveness. In *The Town*, Sally Priest proudly displays the black eye her husband has given her after she received a triple "panic-size corsage" (1957, 77) from a former boyfriend, Grenier Weddel. Charles Mallison recounts that on the night of the Cotillion Club Ball, first Weddel and Maurice Priest fight, and there is one black eye (Weddel's) and a bloody nose (Priest's). Then, the next morning there is a second black eye, this time Mrs. Priest's. Gowan Stevens explains that Mrs. Priest flaunts her prize, coming downtown both morning and afternoon "so everybody in Jefferson would have a chance to see it or at least hear about it" (1957, 77). And V. K. Ratcliff confirms that Mrs. Priest is "proud she still had a husband that could and would black her eye; proud her husband had a wife that could still make him need to" (1957, 78). According to Davidson, this kind of pride in a visible injury tends to be unusual among middle-class abusers, largely because of "social conditioning"; however, when disfigurement does occur in such cases, it seems to be intentional.

The acceptance of physical violence as a usual part of a marital relationship by so many couples in *Sanctuary, Pylon, The Hamlet, The Town, The Mansion,* and *The Reivers* may be surprising; and the reader may be tempted to dismiss these cases as examples of unusual marital behavior since they involve mostly lower-class couples. The couples in Faulkner who would qualify as middle or upper class more usually engage in emotional abuse rather than physical violence. However, statistics indicate that a surprisingly large number of people accept or approve of "minor" forms of physical violence in marriage, such as slapping, pushing, and shoving (Gelles and Straus 1988; Dobash and Dobash 1979). A national survey taken in the late 1960s by the U.S. Commission on the Causes and Prevention of Violence found that one-fourth of adult men and one-sixth of adult women recognized circumstances in which they thought it would be acceptable for a husband to hit his wife or a wife to hit her husband (Gelles and Straus 1988, 26). A recent survey of spouses (three-fourths middle class, one-fourth lower class) indicated that 66 percent of the men and 50 percent of the women recognized "legitimate" circumstances in which a husband could hit his wife; 48 percent of the men and 54 percent of the women recognized "legitimate" circumstances in which the wife could hit the husband, although only 25 percent would find such behavior "appropriate" or "acceptable" (Greenblat 1983, 244, 255). The victim's behavior was the main reason given by both male and female respondents in this recent survey. The behavior could include actions that angered or frustrated the abuser as well as infidelity or flirtation. Thus, Faulkner's portrayal of lower-class couples is consistent with researched profiles of middle-class couples today.

One final example of spouse abuse in Faulkner, however, involves a patrician Southern lady, Joanna Burden, and a very different source of violence. During the three-year sexual relationship which Miss Burden and Joe Christmas (possibly black, possibly Mexican) share in *Light in August,* much of the racial and class prejudice frequently "at the root of street and mass violence" but usually less "salient in domestic violence" clearly surfaces, with all of the "social fears and hatreds . . . from old traditions" (Gordon 1988, 196). The violence occurs in two stages. In the first, Joe Christmas, a roving manual laborer, first enters Miss Burden's house to steal food and then, with her encouragement, returns night after night "by stealth [as though] to despoil her virginity each time anew" (1985, 571). Each encounter is a dinner engagement, with Christmas sitting alone at the kitchen table, eating the food Miss Burden has prepared for him, and an invited rape in the upstairs bedroom. The sexual interaction is violent. Miss Burden awaits Christmas, her surrender "hard, untearful and unselfpitying and almost manlike" (1985, 571). Christmas feels as though he is struggling "physically with another man for an object of no actual value to either, and for which they . . . [are struggling] on principle alone" (1985, 572). He feels as though he must "despoil [over and over] again that which he had already despoiled— or never had and never would" (1985, 571). During this period, there is nothing personal in the relationship between the two: they seldom talk and know little about each other.

After Christmas has ceased going to Miss Burden's house and she has sought him out, she tells him about her life and family history, and they enter the second stage of their relationship. In this second violent phase, Christmas feels as though he has fallen "into a sewer" (1985, 588). Although he has been casually promiscuous in his adulthood (he is 33), he is shocked and bewildered by Miss Burden's passion, rage, corruption, and nymphomania. He finds her "hidden, in closets, in empty rooms, waiting, panting"; he meets her "beneath certain shrubs about the grounds, where he will find her naked, or with her clothing half torn to ribbons" (1985, 590). Although Miss Burden has devoted much of her life to the struggle for racial equality, she exalts in the possibility that she, the Southern lady, is sleeping with a black. (This motif of a white woman's sleeping with or fantasizing about sleeping with a black also appears in "Miss Zilphia Gant," "Dry September," and "Elly.") Even given the more peaceful third phase of their relationship, the final outcome is not surprising, as Joanna Burden, with eyes "calm and still as all pity and all despair and all conviction" (1985, 607), prepares to shoot Christmas and then herself (1985, 610), before the gun misfires and Christmas finally kills her.

Such a violent relationship can, of course, be dismissed as "sick"; the characters can be considered seriously disturbed. But such labels belong to the days before spouse abuse was recognized as a particular kind of violence, one tied to the power dynamics of the family (Finkelhor 1983, 18–22). Such offenders are considered much less deviant today since it is clear that while people like Miss Burden and Joe Christmas reveal their violent and abusive tendencies within their intimate relationships, they continue to live normally in other areas of their lives and often hold responsible jobs and civic positions, just as Miss Burden and Joe Christmas do.

Faulkner's concern about spouse abuse is clearly reflected in all of his fiction; it is familial relationships (and racial interactions) that offer the "violent, corrupt, depraved" (Guerard 1976, 128) material of his art. But Faulkner's concern about emotional and physical abuse involving children is far greater than his concern about spouse abuse. In fact, many of the abusive spousal relationships are significant primarily because they affect children who are growing up in such an environment or because the spouse abuse appears to be a direct result of the abusive childhoods of the abuser and victim. Faulkner is clearly aware that spouse abuse offers a "childhood conditioning" that will "color" the rest of the children's lives: "all other input will be processed through the mire of the first marriage they ever saw and their earliest role models of husband and wife" (Davidson 1978, 116). His portrayal of family generations also confirms the theory that the "best prediction of future violence" is "a history of past violent behavior," which includes "witnessing, receiving, and committing violent acts" in the childhood home (Walker 1984, 10).

As with spouse abuse, the occurrence of emotional abuse is more usual in the lives of Faulkner's children than is the occurrence of physical abuse. Child neglect—one of the most difficult categories of family violence to define (Gordon, 1988, 118)—is especially prevalent. This neglect may be simple abandonment or inadequate care given prevalent societal norms.

A child's abandonment by one or both parents—sometimes patrician, sometimes poor white—is a special preoccupation of Faulkner's fiction. For example, Caddy deserts Quentin in *The Sound and the Fury*; Popeye is abandoned by his father in *Sanctuary*; Joe Christmas-McEachern, the illegitimate son of Milly Hines, is left at an orphanage one Christmas night in *Light in August*; Joe Brown/Lucas

Burch flees the pregnant Lena Grove in *Light in August;* Jiggs deserts his wife and children in *Pylon;* Laverne leaves her son with Roger's parents in *Pylon;* Thomas Sutpen abandons Eulalia Bon and their son Charles in *Absalom, Absalom!;* Charlotte Rittenmeyer leaves her two daughters in *The Wild Palms;* Jack Houston deserts his common-law wife and children in *The Hamlet;* I. O. Snopes abandons his first wife and son in *The Hamlet;* Temple Drake plans to leave her son in *Requiem for a Nun;* and Byron Snopes sends his four children to Flem Snopes in *The Town.*

As the above list suggests, the abandonment is frequently physical, but many Faulkner children also experience emotional abandonment. For example, Quentin Compson, son of "a weak, nihilistic alcoholic" father and "a cold, self-involved" mother (Minter 1983, 124), cries, in *The Sound and the Fury,* "*if I'd just had a mother so I could say Mother Mother*" (1957, 190). And Faulkner himself, in an interview, calls Quentin's sister Caddy a "fatherless, motherless girl" who has grown up in a home where "she has never been offered love or affection or understanding" (quoted in Seidel 1985, 114). In *As I Lay Dying,* Jewel Bundren is separated from his natural father and feels separated from his legal father; Darl feels that in a basic sense he never had a mother. Henry Sutpen and Charles Bon, in *Absalom, Absalom!,* share no emotional relationship with their father. There is no question that in Faulkner's world the norm is parental abandonment, whether it is physical desertion or the more usual passive neglect of parents who are "simply and completely . . . psychologically unavailable to their children, leaving their children psychological isolates in a complex and harsh world" (Gelles and Straus 1988, 69).

Greatly complicating the evaluation of cases of child neglect in Faulkner are the role of "class and sexual inequalities" (Gordon 1988, 167) and the psychological limitations of one or both parents. Family life like that of Popeye and of the Goodwins' son in *Sanctuary* would be considered inadequate by most social workers, full of examples of child neglect, despite the fact that there is no evidence of hostility or indifference from the parent or parents raising them. Both mothers exhibit deep love for their infants; and Lee Goodwin is concerned about his son. In prison, he tells Horace Benbow that he will feel "easy" in his mind if Benbow will just "promise to get the kid a newspaper grift when he's old enough to make change" (1985, 368).

Yet neither child's parents offer "the minimum standards of the society," a necessary requirement to avoid charges of child neglect (Gordon 1988, 166).

The Goodwins, bootleggers in touch with the Memphis underworld, keep their baby in a wooden box behind the stove (1985, 185), "a series of pale shadows in soft small curves" with a "putty-colored face and bluish eyelids" (221), a sickly child, "flushed and sweating, its curled hands above its head in the attitude of one crucified, breathing in short, whistling gasps" (272). Certainly they do not get him the medical care Horace Benbow thinks he needs or provide him with even a minimally adequate physical and moral environment.

Popeye is tended by a pyromaniac grandmother while his mother is at work in a department store until the grandmother perishes in a boarding-house fire that she has set. Faulkner's description of Popeye's mother after the fire is the kind of tragic description a social worker would give before removing a child from the care of a mother who loves the child deeply:

> She never wholly recovered [from the fire and her fear that Popeye had died in it]. What with the hard work and the lack of fresh air, diversion, and the disease, the legacy which her brief husband had left her, she was not in any condition to stand shock. (1985, 392)

Thus, Popeye, from the age of three, is raised by a mother who loves him but has the "deep emotional incapacity to care for a child" (Gordon 1988, 123) that is typical of many parents in child neglect cases.

But Faulkner's children appear in many other situations of what Leonard Shengold calls "soul murder." The above examples of abandonment and neglect would fall under Shengold's category of child deprivation: "the child has been exposed to too little to meet his or her needs." Many other examples in Faulkner would fall into Shengold's second category, that of child abuse: "the child has felt too much to bear" (1989, 1).

Jack Shumann, in *Pylon*, for example, is regularly teased about his parentage; and it is his mother, who has lived a promiscuous life, who first began the practice. Jack's response is always the same, no matter who taunts him with "Who's your old man today, kid?" The six-year-old lowers his head and rushes at the questioner, "his fists flailing," hammering "with puny and deadly purpose," not caring where he hits (1985, 16). Such taunting by his mother, his legal (and perhaps natural) father's mechanic, and even strangers cannot fail to affect Jack's self-concept, leaving "deep and long-lasting scars," "emotional wounds [that will] fester beneath the surface forever" (1985, 68).

Homes like those of Sarty (Colonel Sartoris) Snopes, in "Barn Burning," and Joe Christmas, in *Light in August*, portray child abuse in very complex family interactions. In both homes the boys are clearly loved by their mothers, who are ineffectual against the dominant personalities and physical power of their husbands. In Joe Christmas's case, his adoptive mother's weakness leads the young boy to despise her, fearing that her dependent and emotional ways will weaken him. As Davidson explains, after reaching the age of five or six, a child in a home in which the father dominates the mother may lose respect for the mother and "identify with the aggressor"; by their teen years, children in such households tend to "depersonalize" the mother, "block her from their consciousness and conscience. She couldn't be worth much if she got herself into such a fix, now, could she?" (1978, 119).

In both homes, however, there is also every reason to think that the boys are loved, even respected, by their fathers. Abner Snopes takes Sarty with him to the DeSpains and to town, trying to show Sarty the economic inequities of life and introduce him to the man-talk at the smith's in town. Simon McEachern and Joe Christmas share "a very kinship of stubbornness" (1985, 508), which McEachern clearly respects. But the boys' fathers are men who, in very different ways, are at war with the world around them and wish to enlist their sons as allies in their own personal struggles. A sympathetic reading of both fathers would suggest that their violence toward their sons is concerned primarily with "moral training and character training" and with the fathers' belief that "they will spoil or harm their children if they do *not* use strict discipline" (i.e., force) (Gelles 1979, 189). With both Sarty and Joe, then, the violence would be basically instrumental. A less sympathetic reading would suggest that both fathers are assaulters, and "assaulters are highly possessive of their victims." They believe that their possessiveness gives them "the right to exert control" (Flanzer, 1982, 19).

In Sarty's case, Abner Snopes is deeply angry about what he sees as his economic and social enslavement by the patricians of the South with their code of honor. He, too, has developed a code of honor, one that requires him to revenge what he sees as the intolerable inequities and social slights of the patrician South. Sarty, however, has developed a sense of integrity consistent with the patrician code of honor: to Sarty, lying, even to those in power, is wrong; to Sarty, burning barns, even of those who enslave him and his family, is wrong. Thus, Sarty experiences his father's disapproval and an occasional blow because Abner Snopes feels that Sarty is being treacherous to his own family, treacherous to "the old fierce pull of blood" (1985, 3). Given the degree to which Snopes fulfills the classic description of the abuser—with his "sense of helplessness," "sense of hopelessness," and "threatened loss of self-esteem"—the household is surprisingly nonviolent. And when Snopes does strike Sarty "with the flat of his hand on the side of the head," the narrator explains that it is a "hard" blow but "without heat"; that is, a blow intended for character development, not to express anger. In addition, Snopes explains to Sarty why he has struck him: "You're getting to be a man. You got to learn. You got to learn to stick to your own blood or you ain't going to have any blood to stick to you," because none of the patricians will ever care about you (1985, 9).

Faulkner shows much less understanding for the religious–obsessional motivation that lies behind Doc Hines's and Simon McEachern's treatment of Joe Christmas. Clearly, Joe Christmas's self-identity is irreparably harmed by his violent background. His grandfather, Doc Hines, has been so outraged by the immorality of his daughter Milly, who becomes pregnant outside of marriage, that he kills Christmas's father as Milly and the young man (who says he is Mexican) are running away together. Then Doc Hines leaves Christmas—"the devil's laidby crop" (1985, 678)—at an orphanage because he finds the boy's "black" blood repellant. McEachern adopts Christmas and uses force in the interest of what he sees as moral development and religious training. It is quite usual for McEachern to beat Christmas with a strap for not having learned his catechism. These beatings are often severe. On one occasion, McEachern beats Christmas—"with slow and deliberate force, . . . without heat or anger" (1985, 509)—until the boy collapses. Yet McEachern, in his fanatical way, cares about both the boy and his religion. After Christmas has recovered somewhat from his collapse, McEachern, a "ruthless man who had never known either pity or doubt," kneels with the boy in prayer. He makes two requests: first, that he be "forgiven for trespass against the Sabbath and for lifting his hand against a child, an orphan, who was dear to God" and, second, that "the child's stubborn heart be softened and . . . the sin of disobedience be forgiven him also, through the advocacy of the man whom he had flouted and disobeyed" (1985, 511). It is highly unlikely however, that many battered children could sort out the kind of "childhood conditioning" Christmas experiences—the confusing mixture of rejection, violence, and affection—and develop normal, caring family relationships in adulthood. Thus, no reader is surprised that Joe Christmas eventually kills McEachern and, later, Joanna Burden.

With the number of cases of abandonment, neglect, and abuse that occur among Faulkner's children, it is quite clear why Noel Polk has commented that "there are practically no children in Yoknapatawpha before Chick Mallison . . . who have anything like a normal, even a reasonable, much less a positive and healthy, childhood. Childhood in Faulkner is almost invariably a terrifying experience" (1984, 67). Faulkner's adults seem incapable of "healthy" relationships, a fact which insures "unhealthy" childhood environments. And the generational pattern is clear. The emotionally neglected child (Popeye), the emotionally abused child (Jack Shumann), the emotionally and physically abused child (Joe Christmas), and the witness of regular spouse abuse (Mink Snopes) learn that "love . . . and violence are synonymous." The children learn to view "violence and extreme aggression in the family" as "a *coping/problem-solving mechanism*" (Flanzer 1982, 9). Further, they do not question "the moral rightness of hitting" between family members after years of "seeing and experiencing violence" in their childhood homes (Gelles and Straus 1988, 91).

Even given the degree of control that Faulkner's characters tend to display in both spouse and child abuse, it is surprising that permanent physical injuries and deaths are not common in Faulkner. In fact, a reader concerned about family violence could worry that Faulkner misleads the public by portraying so many families who engage in physical abuse without experiencing serious physical consequences—especially since most social and behavioral scientists believe that physical violence, by its very nature, is difficult to keep in check. On the other hand, the reader could quickly recall that Faulkner's method is often to withhold the details of events while pointing to their "determining significance" (Parker 1985, 4); and since all of Faulkner's families tend to decline within a few generations, the effect of the emotional and physical abuse is very clear.

Most remarkable in Faulkner's fictional presentation of interfamilial violence is his portrayal of the complexity, the multicausal nature, of spouse and child abuse. Faulkner's interweaving of his characters' lives, within both their nuclear and extended families, and his emphasis on the function of violent behavior within an established family dynamic actually anticipate much of the current research being done in the field of domestic violence. As this discussion of some of Faulkner's works has shown, his dramatizations of intrafamilial violence support all four of the theories most favored today in explanations of spouse and child abuse: the intrapsychic theory, which concentrates on the personality traits of the abuser and abused; the behavioral response theory, which focuses on environmental causes; the social learning theory, which emphasizes learning through role models and social norms; and, most recently, the systems theory, which views the family as two or more people interacting in complex patterns (including the processes described by the previous three theories). Of the four theories, Faulkner's multicausal approach emphasizes the reciprocal action and reaction of each family system—an interplay in which the intrapsychic make-up of each individual, environmental stimuli, and social conditioning all contribute to a kind of violence that is tied to the power dynamics of the family (Finkelhor 1983, 18–22). Faulkner's emphasis, like that of many therapists today, is on the "powerful *interdependence* between family members" (Napier 1980, 273), on the "crippling entanglements" (Napier 1980, 277) between family members, and on the function of violence as "a *coping/problem-solving mechanism*" (Flanzer 1982, 9). That Faulkner's preoccupation with intrafamilial violence occurred years before spouse and child abuse arose as a publicly acknowledged problem in the late 1960s and early 1970s is not surprising to those who argue, like Lionel Trilling and Allen Tate, that "the great writer, the spokesman of a culture, carries in himself the fundamental dialectic of that culture: the deeper conflicts of which his contemporaries are perhaps only dimly aware." Clearly Faulkner's fiction demonstrates the way in which "inner strains, stresses, tensions, the shocked self-consciousness of a highly differentiated and complex society, issue in the dialectic of the high arts" (Tate 1968, 589).

References

Brien, D. E. "William Faulkner and the Myth of Woman." *Washington State College Research Studies* 35 (June): 132–140, 1967.

Chodorkoff, Bernard. Seminar on Violence in the Family. Family Service Association of Detroit and Wayne County. October 2–3, 1975.

Davidson, Terry. *Conjugal Crime: Understanding and Changing the Wifebeating Pattern.* New York: Hawthorn Books, 1978.

Dobash, R. Emerson, and Russell Dobash. *Violence Against Wives: A Case Against the Patriarchy.* New York: Free Press, 1979.

Faulkner, William. *The Hamlet.* New York: Random House, 1957.

Faulkner, William. *The Sound and the Fury.* In *"The Sound and the Fury"* & *"As I Lay Dying,"* pp. 3–336. New York: Modern Library, 1946.

Faulkner, William. *The Town.* New York: Random House, 1957.

Faulkner, William. *The Mansion.* New York: Random House, 1959.

Faulkner, William. "Barn Burning." *Selected Short Stories of William Faulkner,* pp. 3–27. New York: Modern Library, 1961.

Faulkner, William. *Light in August.* In *Novels 1930-35,* pp. 399–774. New York: Library of America, 1985.

Faulkner, William. *Pylon.* In *Novels 1930–35,* pp. 775–992. New York: Library of America, 1985.

Faulkner, William. *The Reivers.* New York: Random House, 1962.

Faulkner, William. *Sanctuary.* In *Novels 1930–35,* pp. 179–398. New York: Library of America, 1985.

Faulkner, William. "Smoke." In *Knight's Gamble,* pp. 3–36. New York: Random House, 1949.

Finkelhor, David. "Common Features of Family Abuse." In David Finkelhor *et al.,* eds., *The Dark Side of Families: Current Family Violence Research,* pp. 17–28. Beverly Hills: Sage Publications, 1983.

Flanzer, Jerry P. "Introduction." In *The Many Faces of Family Violence,* pp. 3–13. Springfield, IL: Charles C Thomas, 1982.

Gelles, Richard J. "An Exchange/Social Control Theory." In David Finkelhor *et al.,* eds., *The Dark Side of Families: Current Family Violence Research,* pp. 151–165. Beverly Hills: Sage Publications, 1983.

Gelles, Richard J. *Family Violence.* Beverly Hills: Sage Publications, 1979.

Gelles, Richard J., and Murray A. Straus. *Intimate Violence.* New York: Simon and Schuster, 1988.

Gordon, Linda. *Heroes of Their Own Lives: The Politics and History of Family Violence, Boston 1880–1960.* New York: Viking, 1988.

Greenblat, Cathy Stein. "A Hit Is a Hit . . . Or Is It?" In David Finkelhor *et al.,* eds., *The Dark Side of Families: Current Family Violence Research,* pp. 235–260. Beverly Hills: Sage Publications, 1983.

Guerard, Albert, J. *The Triumph of the Novel: Dickens, Dostoevsky, Faulkner.* New York: Oxford University Press, 1976.

Kartiganer, Donald M. "Quentin Compson and Faulkner's Drama of the Generations." In Arthur F. Kinney, ed., *Critical Essays on William Faulkner: The Compson Family*, pp. 381–401. Boston: C. K. Hall, 1982.

King, Richard H. *A Southern Renaissance: The Cultural Awakening of the American South, 1930–1955.* New York: Oxford University Press, 1980.

Kinney, Arthur F. "'Topmost in the Pattern': Family Structure in Faulkner." In Doreen Fowler and Ann J. Abadie, eds., *New Directions in Faulkner Studies*, pp. 143–171. Jackson: University Press of Mississippi, 1984.

Laing, R. D. *The Politics of the Family and Other Essays.* New York: Pantheon, 1971.

Martin, Del. *Battered Wives.* New York: Pocket Books, 1983.

Minter, David. "Faulkner, Childhood, and the Making of *The Sound and the Fury*." In Richard H. Brodhead, ed., *Faulkner: New Perspectives*, pp. 117–135. Englewood Cliffs, NJ: Prentice-Hall, 1983.

Napier, Augustus Y., with Carl A. Whitaker. *The Family Crucible.* New York: Bantam Books, 1980.

Parker, Robert Dale. *Faulkner and the Novelistic Imagination.* Urbana: University of Illinois Press, 1985.

Pleck, Elizabeth. *Domestic Tyranny: The Making of Social Policy Against Family Violence from Colonial Times to the Present.* New York: Oxford University Press, 1987.

Polk, Noel. "'The Dungeon Was Mother Herself': William Faulkner: 1927–1931." In Doreen Fowler and Ann J. Abadie, eds., *New Directions in Faulkner Studies*, pp. 61–93. Jackson: University Press of Mississippi, 1984.

Polk, Noel. "Faulkner and Respectability." In Doreen Fowler and Ann J. Abadie, eds., *Fifty Years of Yoknapatawpha*, pp. 110–133. Jackson: University Press of Mississippi, 1980.

Prescott, Suzanne, and Carolyn Letko. "Battered Women: A Social Psychological Perspective." In *Battered Women: A Psychosociological Study of Domestic Violence*, pp. 72–96. New York: Van Nostrand Reinhold, 1977.

Roy, Maria. "The Nature of Abusive Behavior." In Maria Roy, ed., *The Abusive Partner: An Analysis of Domestic Battery*, pp. 3–16. New York: Van Nostrand Reinhold, 1982.

Seidel, Kathryn Lee. *The Southern Belle in the American Novel.* Tampa: University of South Florida Press, 1985.

Shengold, Leonard. *Soul Murder: The Effects of Childhood Abuse and Deprivation.* New Haven: Yale University Press, 1989.

Tate, Allen. *Essays of Four Decades.* Chicago: Swallow Press, 1968.

Walker, Lenore E. *The Battered Woman Syndrome.* New York: Springer, 1984.

Wyatt-Brown, Bertram. *Southern Honor: Ethics and Behavior in the Old South.* Oxford: Oxford University Press, 1982.

17

The Foxes in Hellman's Family Forest

Lagretta Tallent Lenker

American literature's reliance on themes and situations of family life to weave stories that graphically reflect the human condition has become legendary. Lillian Hellman's entry into the ranks of "cultural familiars" such as William Faulkner's Snopeses and John Steinbeck's Joads is the Hubbards (Wright 1986, 143), a family bonded by mutual greed, distrust, and manipulation. Hellman presents this clan in *The Little Foxes* (1939) and *Another Part of the Forest* (1946), plays that constitute an unfinished trilogy[1] set in Bowden, Alabama, beginning in 1880. Hellman emphatically denied that these dramas contain social messages or polemical motives (Wright 1986, 305). Yet time has taught even Hellman's many admirers that this dramatic genius could not be trusted to account accurately for her motives and actions (Wright 1986, 394). We are certain that Hellman conducted extensive research to gain just the right "sense of the period" that she was depicting, especially concerning the financial condition of the postwar South (Carl Rollyson 1988, 123). Against this carefully crafted social and economic backdrop, Hellman presents, deliberately or not, stirring criticisms of social conditions, which in many instances, are recognizable in society today. Most scholars interpret these plays as attacks on personal greed and on the results of the capitalization and indus-

241

trialization of the Old South (Wright 1986, 21, 144). I propose a more personal reading—that the Hubbard saga chronicles the debilitating effects of family violence, especially spouse abuse, from the inter-woven perspectives of husband–wife, brother–sister, and parent–child.

Hellman's fictional family exhibits classic symptoms and behav-iors of actual troubled families described in the literature of medicine, social work, counseling, and other socially oriented disciplines. Su-san Schechter, a clinical social worker and respected author of works about family violence defines the problem:

> Battering is a pattern of coercive control that one person exercises over another. Abusers use physical and sexual violence, threats, emotional insults and economic deprivation as a way to dominate their partners and get their way. (1987, 4)

Lillian Hellman examines manifestations of learned helplessness, ag-gression, manipulation, and violence, all significant factors in docu-mented cases of spouse abuse. Hellman even deviates from the most common situation wherein the male partner is the physical or psy-chological batterer to include both men and women as abuser and abused, violators and victims. Finally, the wealth and power of the Hubbards (however it was obtained) rebuke the stereotype of abuse as being linked with poverty and lower socioeconomic classes. These patterns of pathological behavior and domestic coercion have not been considered previously as a structural element of the plays, and this omission underscores how deeply such behavior is ingrained in our society. A close reading of both plays from the perspective of one concerned with the problem of family violence follows.

Lillian Hellman wrote her portrait of the Hubbard family out of chronological order. This approach is not uncommon. For example, Shakespeare wrote his chronicle history plays of the Yorks, Lan-casters, and Tudors in the same fashion. Authors often compose this way in response to the success of a work whose subject warrants further exploration, and *The Little Foxes* (1939) commanded such strong popular acclaim (although the critical reaction was mixed) that Hellman wrote *Another Part of the Forest* (1946) to show how the Hub-bard clan became the way they appeared in the earlier play (Wright 1986, 203). However, *Another Part of the Forest* did not enjoy the same enthusiastic reception that was accorded *The Little Foxes*. Rollyson reports, "This lack of popularity had little to do with the quality of the play but a great deal to do with its savage tone" (1988, 250–251). Rollyson calls Hellman's writing "ruthless" and pronounces the dramatic exchanges between family members "unpleasant to watch." The savagery of her characters compares with that of Shakespeare's creations, but Hellman's postwar audience was less receptive than Shakespeare's bloodthirsty Elizabethans (Rollyson 1988, 252).[2] Therefore, given Hellman's motives for writing *Another Part of the Forest* and my purposes for this discussion, *Another Part of the Forest* should be considered as the predecessor to *The Little Foxes*.

Another Part of the Forest is a drama of family loyalty and allegiances, or the lack thereof. James Parrish summarizes as follows:

> All of them, the Hubbards (with the exception of the mother, Lavinia) are egocentric, grasping creatures truly interested in no one but themselves. Marcus made the family fortune but keeps his sons working for him at the wage of twenty dollars per week, barely concealing his contempt for them. His affection for his daughter Regina seems to grow more out of his loneliness than out of any real concern for the girl. Regina, on her part, is motivated toward a single end—running away to Chicago with John Bagtry, a member of a genteel family whose fortunes have deteriorated along with the South. She openly dislikes her brothers and seems to agree with Marcus that her mother is crazy. Although she is always kind and solicitous where her father is concerned— she gets his coffee in the mornings and they go on picnics together—I suspect that she does this simply in order to be on his good side. My suspicions were encouraged by the picnic they go on in Act One, since Regina uses the occasion to talk Marcus into letting her go to Chicago, where she hopes to be met by Captain Bagtry. This plot is foiled by one of her brothers and, with Ben's assistance at the end of the play, Regina deserts Marcus, which would seem to confirm my beliefs about her. (1950, 2–3)

This family situation reflects, at least initially, the South as a bastion of the patriarchy.[3] Lawrence Stone describes a patriarchal society:

> Power tends to drift into the hands of the oldest males, and in every family, village, and country . . . there is a constant struggle

to win the approval of, or establish some reciprocal claim upon, some individual—often an old man—who controls the levers of power. (1977, 90)

Lenore Walker relates this concept to family violence:

Men's dominance over women in a patriarchal society is an important factor in spouse abuse. . . . [O]ur data . . . all demonstrate that in homes where the man is more dominant, the woman is more likely to suffer serious battery. (1984, 37)

The patriarch in *Another Part of the Forest* is Marcus Hubbard, a ruthless businessman who has made his fortune by operating outside of the law and accepted social behavior. As family scion, he suppresses his sons, needlessly cutting short their trips to attend to insignificant business (1972, 349) and reducing already meager salaries in response to requests for a raise (355). He constantly criticizes Ben and Oscar and then flaunts his own freedom while controlling their lives. He belittles Ben, his eldest, for not being more knowledgeable about music:

BEN. I've been too busy, Papa.
MARCUS. At what?
BEN. Working my life away for you. Doing a lot of dirty jobs. And then watching you have a wild time throwing the money around. But when I ask you to lend me a little . . .
MARCUS. You're a free man, Benjamin, a free man. You don't like what I do, you don't stay with me. (*Another Part of the Forest* 363)

His relationship with his daughter, although appearing more loving, manifests equally manipulative characteristics. Marcus dotes on Regina, who humors him in hopes of getting her own way. Critics delight in finding Oedipal–Electra undercurrents as father and daughter brush dangerously close to crossing the lines separating family love from sexual attraction and encouragement (Faulk 1978; Wright 1986; Rollyson 1988). Wright gets specific: "In fact, Marcus as the *ogre pater familias* is a walking anthology of Freudian flaws: son castrator, wife enslaver, daughter covetor" (1986, 206).

As Wright suggests, Marcus's mistreatment of his wife Lavinia parallels his abuse of his sons. Marcus is a prototypical overbearing husband. He thwarts Lavinia's hopes to fulfill a lifelong dream of

teaching and helping poor children by continually postponing discussing the matter with her. After years of failing to convince Marcus
to accept her plans, Lavinia states pathetically, "You get to be fifty-
nine, you don't be happy then, well, you got to find it. I'm going to be
a very happy, happy, happy, happy—" (367). The audience, thus,
knows of Lavinia's unhappiness and also of her actual fear of her
husband: "I've always been afraid of him, because once or twice—"
(399). Lavinia's voice trails off, leaving unspoken the anticipation of
the physical violence that has almost certainly plagued her marriage.
This account and the patriarchal nature of the household, with its
implicit code tag Marcus as a recognizable personality type—the violent husband identified by Margaret Elbow:

> The controller may manipulate, and if manipulation fails, then
> demands and force may follow. He must have his way. He must
> control the situation. He seems to know no limits. (Davidson
> 1978, 201)

At the start of the play, Marcus firmly controls the household and
everyone in it. Interestingly, the seemingly weak Lavinia becomes the
agent of change (Rollyson 1988, 243). The genteel Lavinia represents
"good blood" mixed with the Hubbard bad (Faulk 1978, 61). Although
she seems to genuinely love her family, Marcus's total disregard for
her feelings infiltrates her children's attitude toward their mother.
Her *modus operandi* becomes one of "learned helplessness," Lenore
Walker's apt term for the attempts of women such as Lavinia to cope
with their situation:

> Women's experiences of the noncontingent nature of their at-
> tempts to control the physical and psychological violence would,
> over time, produce learned helplessness and depression as the
> repeated batterings, like electrical shocks, diminish the woman's
> motivation to respond. (1984, 87)

Yet Lavinia, characterized by her family as "crazy," does have a re-
course that eventually leads to her escape from the damaging bonds
of her family. She alone knows of Marcus's true involvement in a
suspicious business deal during the Civil War that directly resulted in
the deaths of 27 "home town" soldiers whose vengeful families still
feel the pain of the episode. Only after a particularly nasty family
quarrel does Lavinia gain the courage to reveal what she knows to

Ben—information that dramatically shifts the balance of power in the household. This accomplished, Ben convinces the now-fearful Marcus to sell him the family business for one dollar, and Lavinia prepares to leave to "do her work." Before departing, Lavinia has a poignant scene reminiscent of another downtrodden woman who prepares to go on a "journey." Shakespeare's Ophelia, shortly before her death, gives appropriate flowers to her loved ones as remembrances of her. Similarly, Lavinia distributes appropriate gifts to her family before leaving home (Faulk 1978, 61). But Lavinia's fate differs from that of Ophelia, who commits suicide, and also from the traditional endings of women who are unsuccessful in marriage or flaunt the traditional feminine role—madness or death (DuPlessis 1985, 16). Lavinia departs to find personal fulfillment and to rid herself of the domestic atmosphere of fear and violence that heretofore has been her lot (421). Although Lavinia anticipates self-actualization at last, she and Marcus leave their unhealthy relationship as a legacy to their children. Walker's conjecture that "The best prediction of future violence is a history of past violent behavior . . ." (1984, 10–11) proves prophetic. The three Hubbard children are depicted as adults in *The Little Foxes*. Together they represent the next generation of an abusive–abused family.

In *The Little Foxes* Ben, Oscar, and Regina Hubbard are described 20 years later, sans mother and father. Each lives a life that may be directly related to their early environment. Ben, the eldest, never marries. His life centers around the family business, and his gods are those of power and money, a continuation of Marcus Hubbard's idolatry. As the primogenital heir to the Hubbard fortune, Ben would be a "good catch" for any southern belle. Instead, he remains single, perhaps a conscious or even unconscious reaction to his parents' version of domestic bliss. Ben's bachelorhood, however, does not keep him from using the marriages of his brother and sister to strengthen the Hubbard financial and social status. He even speculates that his niece (Regina's daughter, Alexandra) and nephew (Oscar's son, Leo) may marry to solidify the family position (155). But these arranged, advantageous marriages often bring trouble—especially for unsuspecting partners lured into the Hubbard web.

In *The Little Foxes*, Oscar Hubbard has married Birdie Bagtry, the faded, aristocratic symbol of the once-glorious Old South. Although Birdie's marriage has saved her home from passing into the hands of strangers (the plantation Lionnet now belongs to her husband's family), Birdie's life has become a nightmare of physical, psychological, and alcohol abuse. She is a woman completely dominated by her husband and his conniving, condescending family. What little dignity she has left after years with the Hubbards comes from the universal acknowledgment that she is the only aristocrat in the family (144). Her only pleasures are her niece Alexandra, whom she tries to protect from the Hubbards, and music, a passion she must conceal from her husband. Nevertheless, the family's important guest, William Marshall of Chicago, prefers Birdie's talents as a pianist to the Hubbards' business conversation. Yet Birdie's repressed domestic life renders her story a genuine *künstlerromane manqué*—the depiction of an artist who never develops, in Birdie's case, because of societal and domestic constraints.[4]

Birdie offers a prototypic example of the female victim of both physical and psychological spouse abuse. After admitting that indulgence in alcohol has been her coping mechanism for years, Birdie tells Alexandra that she has not had a "whole day of happiness" in 22 years (189). This is the pitiful fate of a woman who served as a "commodity"—a patriarchal vehicle for the transfer of property from one family to another, not an uncommon occurrence throughout history (Stone 1977, 89). Furthermore, Birdie's husband Oscar exemplifies the social learning explanation of spouse abuse, since he has learned to mistreat his wife by watching his father abuse his mother. In addition, his propensity for abuse intensifies because Birdie is considered "above him" in education and social position, a syndrome of the abusive situation noted by Terry Davidson (1978, 27).

Lastly, violence as the accepted method of "handling things" is a well-established pattern with Oscar. In *Another Part of the Forest*, his father must pay "hush money" to keep Oscar out of trouble after he is identified as a participant in the beating of a black man (351). And Oscar, as an adult, loves to shoot for the mere pleasure of killing things (*LF* 151). This savage temperament, covertly and overtly, poisons Oscar's relationship with his wife. For example, when Mr. Marshall visits the family and pays particular attention to Birdie, Oscar checks her enjoyment of this unexpected attention: "I said get yourself in hand. Stop acting like a fool" (141). This psychological degradation proves minor compared with Oscar's physical battering of his wife. In the only show of force that actually occurs onstage,

Oscar slaps Birdie viciously after she attempts to interfere with the family's plans to have Alexandra and Leo marry (160). Birdie reacts in a manner typical of the battered wife—she lies to protect her husband (Davidson 1978, 52), telling Alexandra that she has only twisted her ankle (160). Further conversations with Alexandra reveal that, as often occurs in an abusive situation, this physical violence has happened before (186). The family surely knows of Birdie's suffering (186), yet no one intervenes. As Ben explains to Alexandra, "Married folk frequently raise their voices, unfortunately" (181). So, Birdie's hell is a disturbingly conventional, even accepted, one in a society and family that know better than to interfere.

The family situation of Marcus Hubbard's daughter proves less typical. The central relationship of the play features Regina and her husband Horace Giddens, the handsome, successful banker handpicked for her by her opportunistic family in *Another Part of the Forest* (419). Horace is a reformed despoiler (Faulk 1978, 54). He no longer can bear the greed of the Hubbards and regrets ever having profited at others' expense (*LF* 183). When *The Little Foxes* opens, Regina and Horace are estranged, presumably because of his heart problems, although other factors soon emerge (274). Mutual mistrust has been a long-standing norm in the Giddenses' household. But with Horace's change of heart, Regina is left alone, center stage, as the prime manipulator and aggressor. As her father's psychological heir, Regina proves that the role of the abuser is not the exclusive property of men.[5] Although many authorities hold varying opinions on the prevalence of physical or psychological battering of men by women, Regina fits seven of the eight items on Walker's profile of the psychological abuser (1984, 27–28):

1. Isolation of victim—when Horace arrives home from Johns Hopkins, Regina relegates him to an upstairs bedroom where, because of his heart condition, he exists in virtual isolation (*LF* 191) in Hellman's perhaps unintentional parody of Charlotte Brontë's "mad woman in the attic" found in *Jane Eyre.*
2. Induced debility producing exhaustion—when Horace first returns home, Regina forces him to discuss the financial "deal" she is eager to enter into with her brother. This debate weakens Horace's condition and although he repeatedly asks for postponement, Regina does not relent. (*LF* 172–178).

3. Monopolization of perception including obsessiveness—Regina is obsessed with reaching her financial goals and forces this subject on her sick husband (see 2, above).
4. Threats—Regina implies that if Horace does not cooperate, she will join her brothers' scheme of arranging a marriage between Horace's beloved Alexandra and her first cousin, the insipid Leo (*LF* 173).
5. Degradation—Regina's first line of offense when Horace rejects her plans is to hurl charges of womanizing at him (*LF* 174).
6. Drug or alcohol administration—as we shall see, Regina does not administer but withholds a lifesaving drug when Horace suffers a massive heart attack after their major confrontation— a very effective form of abuse.
7. Occasional indulgence that keeps hope alive—Regina's summoning Horace home gives him encouragement: "Alexandra said you wanted me to come home. I was so pleased at that and touched. It made me feel good" (*LF* 173).

However, as with most abusive partnerships, Horace's hope turns out to be a chimera. The climax of this relationship occurs in a scene of "drawing room brutality" (Wright 1986, 151). As the couple argue, Regina continues her heartless attack, calling the sick man a "small town clerk" and "a soft fool" (*LF* 194). After taunting Horace with the revelation that she has despised him for ten years, Regina watches intently as her wheelchair-bound husband clutches his throat and reaches for his medication. In his weakened condition and agitated state, Horace drops the medicine that can save him. When the bottle smashes against the table, Horace implores his wife to send upstairs for another bottle. Hellman's stage directions convey Regina's reaction:

> Regina does not move now. He stares at her. Then, suddenly as if he understood, he raises his voice. . . . He makes a sudden, furious spring from the chair to the stairs. . . . When he reaches the landing, he is on his knees. His knees give way, he falls on the landing, out of view. Regina has not turned during his climb up the stairs. (*LF* 195)

Regina's response in this scene is reminiscent of Shakespeare's Regan, who passively effects the torture of Gloucester in *King Lear*, and one wonders if Hellman deliberately patterned her abusive wife after her Shakespearean namesake. These two manipulative women are remembered as among the cruelest in all of literature for their calculated inactivity as others suffer harm that they could have prevented. Regina's brothers instinctively suspect her involvement in Horace's death (*LF* 203, 205), and critics concur that Regina hastens, if not actually causes, Horace's demise (Faulk 1978; Rollyson 1988; Wright 1986). Nevertheless, Regina does succeed in gaining the control of the family business venture that she so desperately desires, and the audience senses that the soon-to-be-rich Regina will attain her long-standing goals of moving to Chicago and buying only the best things (*LF* 205). However, Regina does pay a high price. Her daughter, Alexandra, whom she hopes will share her "good life," rebels against her mother, hating Regina for her cruelty to Alexandra's father. Alexandra, seen by most critics as the play's only proffered hope for smashing the Hubbard family mold, predicts that Regina's future will not be as happy as she hopes. In response to her mother's offer of companionship and consolation during the time of grief after Horace's death, Alexandra closes the play with the prophetic query, "Are you afraid, Mama?" (207).

Regina's despicable behavior cannot be ameliorated. But just perhaps that familiar villain, the patriarchy, is at work in Regina's life, also. As a woman growing up after the Civil War, certain negative stereotypes affect her relationships, especially those with her own family. We know that she is a capable woman—even Ben, her arch-rival, acknowledges her abilities (*APF* 415). Yet Marcus, her doting father, despite his preference for his daughter, follows tradition and leaves his money to the male heirs (*LF* 194). Thus, Regina must marry well to secure her own future. As a commodity in the power game, she is expected to strengthen the family position *and* provide for herself. After this "ideal" marriage, she must be relegated to a supporting role, watching men of lesser ability conduct the business, while she appears only as the gracious hostess. Jean Baker Miller, a noted Boston psychologist, proposes that aggression is often the only avenue open to capable women trapped by society in inferior positions (1976, 14). This aggression, which often manifests itself in women considered "domineering," leads to Regina's schemes and machinations. Thankfully, most domineering women do not go this far, but Regina sees this type of behavior as her only hope for achieving self-actualization, for gaining the right of choice for her own life. Rollyson interprets both *Another Part of the Forest* and *The Little Foxes* as focusing on the right of individual choice, or the lack thereof (1988, 246). The restoration of choice is also the goal of marriage and family counseling as interpreted by Nicholas Mazza (see ch. 3). Ben, Oscar, and Regina Hubbard are trapped in their family roles; as they presently live, choice is an impossible dream for them and their unsuspecting marriage partners, Horace and Birdie.

The chronicle depicted by these two dramas is one of learned family violence. Hellman recognizes that abusive behavior exists in cyclical form[6]—that the sins of the father are manifested in the sons and even the daughter. No one escapes Marcus Hubbard's legacy, especially those who unsuspectedly marry into the clan. Critics agree that Hellman saw Regina's and Horace's daughter Alexandra as a hope for breaking the cycle. The playwright intended to portray Alexandra's flight from her family and her subsequent achievements in another drama. The play was never written, perhaps because of other commitments or loss of interest on Hellman's part. But possibly this writer who so cogently limned this Hubbard family portrait instinctively knew that the odds were against the third generation of Hubbards breaking the cycle. The saga ends as it begins, in brutality and abuse.

The noted psychologists Russell and Emerson Dobash (1979) stress that in order to combat domestic violence, the study of individual cases must be universalized to scrutinize our society as a whole. Lillian Hellman presents this opportunity through drama. Each time these plays are performed or read, audiences must face the problem; hopefully, some will remember the message.

Notes

1. Hellman intended to write a third play depicting the adult life of a third generation Hubbard, Alexandra Giddens. For a discussion of this play and why it remained unfinished, see William Wright (1986, 203); Richard Moody (1972, 161); and Doris Faulk (1978, 57).
2. Throughout this chapter, comparisons are made between Hellman's work and that of William Shakespeare. Wright presents evidence that Hellman intentionally imbued her plays with Renaissance dramatic echoes (1986, 208).

3. This important facet of Southern life is described by social historians such as W. J. Cash (1941, 52); Steven M. Stowe (1987, 154); and I. A. Newby (1978, 42, 320–22).
4. I am indebted to Professor Sara Deats for this apt phrase. For a full discussion of women as undeveloped artists because of stereotypical constraints, see Rachael Blau DuPlessis (1985, 1–19).
5. For an excellent discussion of the battered husband controversy, see Maria Roy (1982, 63–71).
6. For an alternate view, See Blair Justice and Rita Justice (1990) and Cathy Spatz Widom (1989).

References

Cash, W. J. *The Kind of the South*. New York: Alfred A. Knopf, 1941.

Davidson, Terry, *Conjugal Crime*. New York: Hawthorne, 1978.

Dobash, R. Emerson, and Russell Dobash. *Violence Against Wives: A Case Against the Patriarchy*. New York: Free Press, 1979.

DuPlessis, Rachel Blau. *Writing Beyond the Ending*. Bloomington: Indiana University Press, 1985.

Faulk, Doris. *Lillian Hellman*. New York: Frederick Ungar, 1978.

Hellman, Lillian. *The Little Foxes*. In *Lillian Hellman: The Collected Plays*, pp. 138–207. Boston: Little, Brown, 1972.

Hellman, Lillian. *Another Part of the Forest*. In *Lillian Hellman: The Collected Plays*, pp. 341–421. Boston: Little, Brown, 1972.

Justice, Blair, and Rita Justice. *The Abusing Family* (rev. ed.). Insight/Plenum, 1990.

Miller, Jean Baker. *Toward A New Psychology of Women*. Boston: Beacon Press, 1976.

Moody, Richard. *Lillian Hellman, Playwright*. New York: Pegasus, 1972.

Newby, I. A. *The South: A History*. Holt, Rinehart and Winston, 1978.

Parrish, James, A. *How Real Is Lillian Hellman's Realism?* Unpublished essay, circa 1950.

Rollyson, Carl. *Lillian Hellman: Her Legend and Her Legacy*. New York: St. Martin's, 1988.

Roy, Maria. *The Abusive Partner: An Analysis of Domestic Battering*. New York: Van Nostrand Reinhold, 1982.

Schechter, Susan. *Guidelines for Mental Health Practitioners in Domestic Violence Cases*. National Coalition Against Domestic Violence, 1987.

Shakespeare, William. *King Lear*. In David Beavington, ed., *The Complete Works of Shakespeare*. London: Scott, Foresman, 1980.

Stone, Lawrence, *The Family, Sex, and Marriage in England 1500–1800*. New York: Harper & Row, 1977.

Stowe, Steven M. *Intimacy and Power in the Old South*. Baltimore: Johns Hopkins University Press, 1987.

Walker, Lenore E. *The Battered Woman Syndrome*. New York: Springer, 1984.

Widom, Cathy Spatz. *The Intergenerational Transmission of Violence*, reprinted as *Occasional Papers of the Harry Frank Guggenheim Foundation*, no. 4, 1989.

Wright, William. *Lillian Hellman: The Image, the Woman*. New York: Simon and Schuster, 1986.

18

From Victim to Victor
Walker's Women in The Color Purple

EMMA WATERS-DAWSON

A persistent characteristic of Alice Walker's fiction is the use of a Southern Black woman as a protagonist challenging convention. Also, inherent in her fiction is a black feminist perspective, depicting women suffering stressful situations: loveless dull marriages, stifled creativity, jealous or cruel spouses, sexual and racial victimization, capitulation to ignorance and tradition, and a myriad of other problems. Yet, the female protagonist's principal source of strength appears to be the knowledge, gained through experience, that suffering is the maternal legacy of the African-American woman, and that survival is effective revenge for the pain. In *The Color Purple*, Alice Walker recommends self-love as a panacea to combat abuse in any form, whether it be that of gender, race, or class.

In the essay "In Search of our Mothers' Gardens," Walker describes three types of black women: the physically and psychologically abused black woman, the black woman torn by contrary instincts, and the new black woman, who recreates herself out of the creative legacy of her maternal ancestors. Significantly, Walker also utilizes these types in *The Color Purple*. The novelist does this by weaving taboo subjects and customs, such as spouse abuse and incest, into creative literary patterns. In her fiction, she is primarily

255

concerned with black women and shows "oppressed figures searching for their own voices in the context of social and psychological
conditioning that would deny them expression" (Byerman 1985, 128).

Walker adapts the classic American stock situation of a rags-to-
riches climb achieved after apparently endless incidents of abuse. She
thereby affirms her creative vision that positive change, rebirth, and
spiritual beauty may emerge from misery and suffering. In its presentation of the positive possibilities for women, however, her book
more closely resembles the contemporary novel than the classic
American success story. Kalamu ya Salaam, in "If the Hat Don't Fit:
An Appreciation of Women Writing," makes the following comment
on the tendency of African-American women writers to work literature into new areas:

> In the context of Black literature, women and those who are
> sensitive to women are offering critiques of society that stretch
> beyond class and race, and this stretching is both healing and
> necessary . . . female authors are making these important cre-
> ative strides not simply because they are reacting to . . . oppres-
> sion and exploitation in general, and to their own particular op-
> pression and exploitation as women. In other words, they are
> fulfilling their historic mission. (1989, 93)

Although Salaam fails to identify the "historic mission," I surmise
that he refers to contemporary black women writers' use of controversial issues as a vehicle for cultural empowerment. Walker, for example, adheres to the significant characteristics of the African-American
literary tradition as identified by Mary Helen Washington. In noting
the African-American women novelists' conformity to characteristics
often manifested in novels written by male authors, she identifies the
terms *invisibility,* the *black mask,* and *double-consciousness* as having
special meaning in this tradition (1987, xvii). Certainly the operation
of these terms in Walker's characterizations of men and women is
evident in *The Color Purple.*

In probing the mysteries of God and everyday life, Walker utilizes the epistolary form. This technique allows the narrative to be
developed through letters written by one or more of the characters
and permits the author to weave loose ends together in a creative
manner. Keith Byerman observes of the female protagonist's letter
writing that "one so degraded as Celie denies herself even the most

private speech act" (1985, 162). Yet, she survives the cruelties of her life by recording every detail in letters. With childlike innocence and language, she writes to God about events whose implications are too tragic or horrible to relate to anyone else. In Celie's narration of a forced sexual act in a letter to God, Walker dramatizes a young woman's entrapment in an apparently inescapable, vicious cycle of abuse. In addition, Walker renders the dialect of the rural black South in Celie's use of black folk English. Always preferring to describe her characters' speech as "Black folk English" and not dialect, a word she feels has been traditionally employed in a condescending, racist way, Walker uses no self-conscious apostrophes and contractions to assure the reader that, of course, she really knows what the proper standard English and grammar should be (Steinem 1982, 89). Finally, Walker shows the harsh treatment of black women by *some* men.

Celie's narration of rape, for example, vividly illustrates not only Walker's depiction of physical and psychological abuse, but also the plight of a young girl torn by contrary instincts:

> He never had a kine word to say to me. Just say You gonna do what your mammy wouldn't . . . He start to choke me, saying You better shut up and git used to it. But I don't never git used to it. (Walker 1982, 3)

The epistolary form Walker utilizes allows the reader to be inside Celie's head as the protagonist records and comments on the events that happen to her. Although she is invisible to Pa as a human being experiencing pain and degradation, Celie reveals to the reader her emotional and psychological distress at sexual relations with the man she assumes to be her father. This abnormal dimension of sex is repulsive to Celie; in the absence of paternal kindness and in her response to her father's warning to "tell no one but God," she describes her physical and psychological abuse to Him in one letter after another. The letters reveal the apparent hopelessness of her life as well as her unnatural situation. They also affirm her ability to mask her true feelings, as writing about her experiences allows her to articulate in written form what Pa had forbidden her to voice to anyone. Therefore, Celie represents simultaneously the first two types of oppressed black women that Walker refers to in "In Search of Our Mothers' Gardens": the physically and psychologically abused black woman and the black woman torn by contrary instincts. Also, her assumption of a mask to hide the pain she feels and her invisibility in the eyes of Pa and Mister reflect the traditions of African-American literature.

In Celie, Walker certainly selects an unlikely character through whom to explore the possibility of redemption. Uneducated and psychologically abused, she is also deprived and physically abused as well. The character of Celie becomes a supreme example of Walker's faith in human potential. Gloria Wade-Gayles comments:

> I identified with readers who found the opening scene of the novel unnecessarily repulsive. . . .
>
> Before we can recover from the brutality of this scene, we are introduced to another abusive Black man whose name, symbolically, is simply "Mister" and whose verbal, psychological and physical abuse of Walker's heroine Celie lasts for decades. Celie's pain is profound and wrenching and all of it is created by Black men. No pretty pictures of purple flowers growing in an open field and no emotional homecomings can redeem . . . (1986, 50)

Celie is raped by her mother's husband, taken out of school because she is pregnant, and deprived even of the two offspring she is forced to bear; furthermore, she becomes sterile, unable to have more children, and is married off to a widower, Mister, who needs a hard worker to take care of him and his many children.

Yet, Celie survives the harshness of these experiences and recreates herself concurrently, partly by recording every detail of her life in letters. Barbara Christian observes that letters are "a principal source of information and facts about the everyday lives of women and their own perceptions about their lives," a source of both "objective" and "subjective" information (1985, 93). Although Celie initially writes of her experiences rather than actually voicing them, the reader views Walker's protagonist through the character's feelings about herself and her situation, rather than through the eyes of an "objective" narrator. Concerning Celie's therapeutic behavior, Byerman remarks, "speaking forth carries with it its own authority," giving evidence of "an interiority and humanity that others have denied her" (1985, 166).

Yet, Celie's redemption in the classic rags-to-riches success story no longer seems remarkable or neoromantic when we examine Walker's statement that she is committed to exploring not only "the oppressions, the insanities, and the loyalties, but the triumphs of Black women as well" (O'Brien 1973, 192; Washington 1979, 133). Celie, in *The Color Purple*, is only one of Walker's triumphant protagonists. Gloria Snodgrass Malone states of Walker's fiction in general that she "presents . . . a montage of miserable characters, most of whom are black and female" (1979, 8). Nevertheless, these women, who often represent the utter extreme of hardworking, spiritless, and occasionally unattractive human beings, attempt redemption through Walker's exploration of intrafamily relationships. In her exploration, Walker examines the presence of violence and its effect on children. Evan Stark and Anne Flitcraft discuss the relationship between woman battering, child abuse, and social heredity. They cite B. F. Steele, an authority on violence, who writes that "the single most common element in the lives of violent or abusive adults is the experience of being neglected or abused to some degree by caretakers during the earliest years" (1985, 156).

Pa strikingly reflects Walker's exploration of this element as well as the cruelty that one individual may inflict on another. Yet, Walker demonstrates this point not by examining the violence the abused child Celie may inflict on her own children, but by constructing a pattern whereby the abused child becomes the battered wife in marriage. Malone states, "The cruelty of the black man to his wife and family is one of the great tragedies. It has mutilated the spirit and body of the black family and of most black mothers" (1979, 194). Walker meaningfully introduces the idea of the black man's abusive behavior at the novel's beginning through the character of Pa; yet, it is not until the novel's end that Pa blames racism for his abuse of his family. When Celie finds out that Pa is not her real father and visits him after many years, he tells her that her natural father's failure to cooperate economically with the white race led to his lynching, a story he claims was too sad to share with the young girls, Celie and Nettie. In explaining *his* "thorough" understanding of the system, he reveals his own exploitation, which perhaps led to his abusive behavior:

> But the fact is, you got to give 'em something. Either your money, your land, your woman or your ass. . . . So what I did was just right off offer to give 'em money. Before I planted a seed, I made sure this one and that one knowed one seed out of three was planted for *him*. Before I ground a grain of wheat, the same thing . . . (Walker 1982, 154)

Pa asserts himself in his family environment by abusing his wife and Celie when the Jim Crow society prevents his exercising entrepreneurial skills in his own way. In the tradition of African-American literature, Pa characterizes the double-consciousness that appears to be inherent in those of African descent living in America. He realizes his inferior plight as a black man restricted by his skin color as well as by the legal and social limitations existing in the America of his day. Yet, Pa also understands the economics of survival and adapts the system to his advantage. Through Pa's abusive behavior, Walker explores the double-consciousness of the black psyche.

Walker, however, dismisses racism as a justification for cruelty and discusses black men in general in an essay "In the Closet of the Soul." She discourages emulation of either the dominant patriarchal or inferior matriarchal system by African-Americans even though a desire to project dominance, impose subordinance, and accept an inferior status is consistent with being descendants of slave *owners* as well as slaves (1986, 32). Walker's depiction of the "master's mentality" in Pa is graphic, cruel, and disturbing. Referring to his rape of Celie, he warns her when she is a child, "You better not never tell nobody but God. It'll kill your mammy" (Walker 1982, 3). By Pa's standards, the incest and adultery that he has committed are not *his* violation of taboo; rather he projects his guilt upon Celie, making her fear that a violation of his command will kill her mother. On this point, Byerman comments, "He presumes that his rules of order transcend those of the social order" (1985, 162). Pa's conduct, representative of Walker's depiction of the black male, attempts to answer the question of why *some* black men abuse their families and cause pain, developing "the theme of the black man's mistreatment of his wife and family and the reasons, both conscious and unconscious, for such cruel behavior" (Malone 1979, 194). From such a cycle of vicious family abuse the protagonist Celie must seek to redeem herself.

Celie's story reveals a vivid picture of the physical and psychic abuse she, her mother, and Pa's new wife suffer during his sexual assault of women. Celie describes Pa's sexual advances toward her mother soon after childbirth and her mother's death in a screaming and cursing rage as well as the young new wife's zombie state after similar sexual abuse. In her depiction of three physically and psychologically abused women within the family unit, Walker suggests, in only a few pages, the collective suffering of black women as well as the stifling of individual aspiration.

Although Pa is specifically an abusive husband and father, he also illustrates more generally just how despicable one individual may be in his treatment of another. He illuminates his insensitive nature even further when Mister tries to negotiate with him for the rights of marriage with Nettie. In her letters, Celie describes how Pa informs Mister that he will never allow him to marry Nettie because she is too young, but that he offers Celie, insisting that she has given birth twice already and would thus be ideal for a widower. In this verbal exchange between the two men, the reader perceives the male's value of women. The verbal exchange, incidentally, occurs within earshot of Celie and illustrates her invisible status to both Pa and Mister. Ironically, a man like Pa, whose sexual abuse of Celie has resulted in two pregnancies and births, values virginity and physical attractiveness highly. However, despite his view of Celie as "ugly," he praises her ability to work hard. Byerman comments, "The discussion between the two men takes the form of negotiations over livestock; the deal is closed when a cow is included with the woman. Celie literally has become a commodity, one with a low exchange value" (1985, 163).

Walker prepares the reader for similar circumstances in Celie's married life by focusing on the disorganization, instability, and abuse of her childhood. In marriage, Celie, nonetheless, manifests her potential for creativity in figuratively becoming a tree:

> He . . . beat me like he beat the children. Cept he don't never
> hardly beat them. He say, Celie git the belt. . . . It all I can do not
> to cry. I make myself wood. I say to myself, Celie, you a tree.
> That's how come I know trees fear man. (Walker 1982, 22)

Ironically, in this instance, Celie's creativity permits her to become indifferent. Moreover, her indifference is essential to her survival; it is another example of the black mask of the African-American literary tradition. In this instance, the black woman assumes a mask not against the white racist world, but in the sanctity of her own home, as self-protection against an abusive husband. In discussing personality problems in the batterer's wife, Natalie Shainess observes:

> . . . in most marriages, the partners, are, in some way, psycho-
> logically and emotionally on the "same level." People pick mates
> responsive to their own . . . neurotic needs. Relationships in
> which beating takes place are sometimes characterized as follows:
> One partner may be overly submissive; one may be attacking,

overly demanding, and sadistic. For the most part, there is a kind
of sex role division, with the woman being the submissive partner . . . (1977, 115)

Celie, who has been forced into the role of the submissive partner,
experiences a mock death in order to survive and ultimately to discover herself. In discussing similar loss of control experienced by the
battered wife, Terry Davidson states:

> The battered wife has been at the mercy of someone else's
> mood fluctuations and predictable or unpredictable temper to the
> point where she feels she has no control over her own life. No
> one seems to care about *her* moods. Indeed, she has to deny
> them, stifle them.
>   Living this kind of life results in generalized fear and emo-
> tional paralysis . . . (1978, 57)

Despite her paralysis, however, Celie fashions out of her personal
contemplations a work of functional art in order to survive. This
attempt at survival seems almost instinctive. Yet, so pervasive is the
cruel influence of Pa and Mister that critics often focus on their conduct as opposed to the survival of the female.

Noted African-American literature scholar and critic Trudier Harris voices one of the most perceptive and thorough objections to the
novel in "On *The Color Purple,* Stereotypes, and Silence." She writes:

> I couldn't imagine a Celie existing in any black community I know
> of. . . . What sane black woman, I asked, would sit around and
> take that crock of shit from all those folks? How long would it
> take her before she reached the stage of stabbing somebody to
> death, blowing somebody's head off, or at least going upside
> somebody's head? But the woman just sat there, like a bale of
> cotton with a vagina . . . waiting for someone to come along and
> rescue her. I had problems with that. (1984, 155)

Harris's difficulty with *The Color Purple* and her reaction of loathing
demonstrate that the perspective that Walker advocates would entail
a radical revision in the way men and women think about each other
and themselves. Also, such a dismissal entails a refusal to accept
Walker's personal declaration that her intent is not to divide the sexes,
but to pinpoint how outside forces (the oppression of race, sex, or
class) may function to divide and conquer the relationships of the
black male and female in the insular folk community.

Enlarging on the simplified explanation of racism that Pa subtly implies as the reason for his abuse of black women, Walker provides additional explanation of Mister's motivation. Through him, the reader realizes that the sexist socialization of the male as well as class oppression may contribute to his mistreatment of black women. Celie's recording of the events of Mister's life preceding his marriage to her, for example, helps to explain his mistreatment of her. The reader quickly becomes aware that the sexist socialization of the male is responsible for his behavior. In an essay "In the Closet of the Soul," Walker herself responds to the hostile reaction of some people to the character of Mister. She states that of the negative reviews she has seen, there has been a relative absence of an analysis of Mister's past. In fact, she continues, Mister's father is the son of a white slaveowner who shows contempt for Old Mister and his mother. Old Mister's parentage, thus, accounts for the run-down plantation, the slave–master attitude, and the contempt Old Mister reflects toward Shug Avery (1986, 32). Walker here examines the sexist paternal legacy that Mister inherits from his mulatto father and from his white grandfather. Mister is depressed by his inability to marry the woman he really loves, Shug Avery, because she is, according to Mister's father with his negative conception of blackness and beauty, "black as tar . . . nappy headed" with "legs like baseball bats" (1982, 49). Mister, therefore, resents Celie because she is not Shug and becomes increasingly bestial in his treatment of her. Furthermore, Celie indicates that Mister's first wife received similar abuse from him until, tiring of his abuse and infidelity, she takes an abusive lover who shoots and kills her in front of her son Harpo. Of violence in Walker's fiction Malone comments, "Pervasive in the works of . . . Southern writers is a climate of violence inherent in the traditions and conflicts present in the history of the South" (1979, 195). The atmosphere of brutality Malone refers to stems from the history of a patriarchal, racist society that perpetuates a continuous cycle of oppression. The characters of Pa, Mister, and Old Mister illustrate that they believe in the economic exploitation and social domination of women by men. They believe in and practice sexism against black women even though they are oppressed in the larger Jim Crow society. In a study, "Men Who Assault Their Wives," M. Faulk attempts to understand the dynamic relationship of the offender to the victim by categorizing five types of relationships: (1) dependent, passive husband; (2) dependent and suspicious; (3) violent and bullying; (4) dominating husband; (5) stable and affectionate group. Of the five types, Pa, Mister, and Old Mister appear to be combinations of the violent and bullying and dominating husband, for Faulk describes these types as men who "attempted to solve their problems or gain their end in many aspects of their lives by violence and intimidation . . ." and as husbands who "had a great need to assert themselves and would brook no insubordination from their wives . . ." (1977, 121–122).

Walker develops a pattern of abuse and victimization as the novel continues, depicting the world of the story as harsh and unconventional, yet in her probe of the characters' internal lives, the novel is psychologically convincing. Ironically, Mister, like almost all men in the novel, is from a solidly patriarchal background where, according to Michelle Wallace's definition in *Black Macho and the Myth of the Superwoman*, "Men are accustomed to unquestioned authority" (1978, 136). Although Walker does not judge the black man innocent for his participation in the persecution of the black woman, her exploration into the motivation behind his behavior refutes the assertion that she intends to divide black men and women.

According to Malone, Walker only "uses violence to stress the urgency of the problems she explores and to illustrate the depth of the despair which emanates from the deep-seated, unfulfilled desires of her characters" (1979, 195). Similarly, Zaron Bennett evaluates Celie's treatment from the perspective of a black male. He states:

> For Celie it doesn't matter even a little bit that the racist nature of this country produces and supports the circumstances that oppress black men. The problem for all black folks at the individual level is the elimination of a problem of external origin that plays hell with the internal functioning of our very lives. (1986, 44)

Individuals seek to eliminate problems that interfere with their external functioning as well, for Celie's physical abuse prevents both sound mind *and* body.

Mister has not been able to fulfill his lifelong desire because of his father's negative influence. Perhaps in despair and rage, he strikes out at other victims of circumstance, Celie and his first wife. Thus, a combination of crushed pride, battered ego, great ignorance, and rage at himself, his life, and his world—all stemming from his socialization in a patriarchal, racist society—prompts Mister to become so abusive to the women in his life. Maria Roy examines the relationship between power and violence. Her assessment is quite similar to Walker's fictional depiction. Roy states:

> Violence is the end product of pent-up frustration, denial of perceived legitimate rights over a period of time, and the constant erosion of self-esteem. It is an eruption similar to the explosive outpouring of volcanic lava following a period of dormancy. It builds, reaches a peak, and then falls, rising then falling, ticking then exploding like a kind of human time bomb. Violence is . . . accumulated aggression that failed to be defused. It is related to power because it is a consequence of the absence of power—conceived and born of impotence. (1982, 3)

Terry Davidson concurs with Roy's assessment in observing:

> Abusive behavior stems from anger and frustration. If it is strongly violent, and the abuser loses control of his judgment and behavior, then it is very likely his rage comes from deep within and is related to old hurts and insults from childhood—not really from the present situation or person. (1978, 46)

Brownfield's attitude toward Mem, his wife, in an earlier Walker novel, *The Third Life of Grange Copeland*, could very well be a description of Mister: "His rage and his anger and his frustration ruled. His rage could and did blame everything on her" (Walker 1982, 55). Malone supports this assertion in observing that while Walker "does not ignore the humiliations and degradations upon (blacks) by their white oppressors, she primarily stresses the cruelties that the characters inflict upon each other" (1979, 196).

Although Walker focuses on Celie, most of the females in the novel offer examples of women who are physically and psychologically abused and torn by contrary instincts. The other women in the novel provide an interesting contrast to Celie. Shug, for example, is ostracized because she does not fit the conventional mode of behavior for a woman of her time: she smokes, drinks, curses, has given birth to three children out of wedlock, and wanders over the country singing blues. Sofia, Celie's daughter-in-law, is imprisoned for "sassing" the mayor's wife; and, Squeak, Harpo's girlfriend, is beaten and raped by her white uncle when she attempts to get Sofia released from prison. Although these women sometimes behave in a manner not consistent with their deep-rooted emotions, they do so in order to survive themselves or to help another woman survive. Marjorie Homer, Anne Leonard, and Pat Taylor examine the informal sources of assistance in family, friends, and neighbors when the battered wife finally seeks to escape a cycle of abuse. They report:

> . . . there were . . . constraints which reduced the degree to which women turned to relatives and friends for help. These included feelings of shame, ideas about privacy and the need for independence, the need to protect family members, friends and neighbours from the man's violent behaviour and the unwillingness of some of those approached to become involved. Women who overcame these constraints spoke warmly of the support they received. (1985, 93)

The women characters in *The Color Purple* overcome such constraints and affirm Walker's conviction that the private and public world can be transformed. In this cruel and violent story of redemption, what matters to most of the women is revealing the truth to those who seek it, taking only what one needs from other people, being freed from the suppression of one's will or talent, and choosing for oneself. The desire for individual choice is the determining factor when Celie finally asserts herself to Mister after years of abuse and musters the courage to proclaim, "You a lowdown dog . . . It's time to leave you and enter into the Creation" (Walker 1982, 170). In a review of *Our Nig*, Marilyn Richardson states, "the confrontation by which the black character claims a distinct sense of self is one of the classic recurring scenes in all early black writing" (1983, 15). Although Richardson's observation refers to early black literature, its application is obvious in this situation, where after years of abuse by Mister, Celie finally realizes that she must begin to embrace life, in spite of the pain and sorrow. Indeed, most of the characters in the novel grow and change. Through the women in *The Color Purple*, Walker depicts a confidence in the human spirit. These women recreate themselves from the debris of human passions and neglect resulting from physical and psychological abuse in a life torn by contrary instincts. They seek to find some dignity by asserting their personalities and needs through art forms that women traditionally practice: thus, Shug and Squeak sing the blues; Celie designs fashion pants; and Sofia acts as a surrogate parent. These female art forms are the bits and pieces allowed black women by a sexist and racist society and are the fragments from which Celie seeks to reconstruct herself and redeem herself from a cycle of abuse. Illustrating the value of the network of female nurturance, Shug becomes for Celie a means of salvation. Though Mister brings his lover to his home, she becomes a healing force, for she promises Celie that she will not leave until she knows Albert has stopped his physical abuse of Celie. Shug, thus, becomes a figure of salvation for Celie and raises her up from an emotional depth, for, in encouraging Celie's creativity, she offers a source of hope.

The redeemed character of Mister also develops and gains a new insight, sensitivity, and an appreciation of Celie for herself. Wade-Gayles offers an insightful analysis and summary of both Celie's and Mister's characters in relation to the evaluation in their relations to each other. She states:

> In our hostile response to negative images of abusive men in the first third of the novel, we fail to celebrate the beauty of growth and change in all of the characters—most especially in Celie and Mister. . . . When Celie changes, Mister changes. At the end of the novel he is a sensitive man in the process of redefining with Celie's help, as Celie has done with Shug's help, what it means to be a human being capable of loving self and loving others. He is humanized, not feminized. . . . Significantly, he is pleased with himself. (1986, 53)

For the female and male characters in *The Color Purple*, spiritual redemption evolves through the self. Through Mister's illustration of the new man he has become and through Celie's acceptance of the absence of Shug in her life, Walker presents her belief that the individual cannot depend on man or woman to provide the love that the self must foster. Individuals must struggle to recreate and subsequently redeem the self in the face of adversity. Despite adverse criticism, novelists such as Alice Walker must continue to explore the psyche of the black woman and female self-expression in words or in art as part of the development of black feminine consciousness.

References

Bennett, Zaron. "*The Color Purple:* Personal Reaction." *Catalyst* premier issue: 43–44, 1986.

Byerman, Keith E. *Fingering the Jagged Grain: Tradition and Form in Recent Black Fiction.* Athens: University of Georgia Press, 1985.

Christian, Barbara. *Black Feminist Criticism: Perspectives on Black Women Writers.* New York: Pergamon Press, 1985.

Davidson, Terry. *Conjugal Crime.* New York: Hawthorn Books, 1978.

Faulk, M. "Men Who Assault Their Wives." In Maria Roy, ed., *Battered Women*, pp. 119–126. Atlanta: Van Nostrand Reinhold, 1977.

Harris, Trudier. "On *The Color Purple*, Stereotypes, and Silence." *Black American Literature Forum* 18(4) Winter): 155–161, 1984.

Homer, Marjorie, Anne Leonard, and Pat Taylor. "Personal Relationships: Help and Hindrance." In Norman Johnson, ed., *Marital Violence*, pp. 93–108. Boston: Routledge & Kegan Paul, 1985.

Malone, Gloria Snodgrass. "The Nature and Causes of Suffering in the Fiction of Paule Marshall, Kristin Hunter, Toni Morrison, and Alice Walker." Ph.D. dissertation, Kent State University, 1979.

O'Brien, John, ed. *Interviews with Black Writers.* New York: Liveright, 1973.

Richardson, Marilyn. "The Shadow of Slavery." *The Women's Review of Books* 1(1) (October): 15, 1983.

Roy, Maria. *The Abusive Partner.* New York: Van Nostrand Reinhold, 1982.

Salaam, Kalamu ya. "If the Hat Don't Fit: An Appreciation of Women Writing." *Catalyst* (Winter): 89–93, 1989.

Shainess, Natalie. "Psychological Aspects of Wife Battering." In Maria Roy, ed., *Battered Women.* Atlanta: Van Nostrand Reinhold, 1977.

Stark, Evan, and Anne Flitcraft. "Woman-Battering, Child Abuse, and Social Heredity: What Is the Relationship?" In Norman Johnson, ed., *Marital Violence*, pp. 93–108. Boston: Routledge & Kegan Paul, 1985.

Steinem, Gloria. "Do You Know This Woman? She Knows You: A Profile of Alice Walker." *Ms* 10 (June): 35–37, 89–92, 1982.

Wade-Gayles, Gloria. "Anatomy of an Error: *The Color Purple* Controversy." *Catalyst* premier issue: 50–53, 1986.

Walker, Alice. *The Color Purple.* New York: Harcourt Brace Jovanovich, 1982.

Walker, Alice. *In Search of Our Mothers' Gardens.* New York: Harcourt Brace Jovanovich, 1983.

Walker, Alice. "In the Closet of the Soul: A Letter to an African-American Friend." *Ms* 15(5) (November): 32–35, 1986.

Walker, Alice. *The Third Life of Grange Copeland.* New York: Harcourt Brace Jovanovich, 1970.

Wallace, Michelle. *Black Macho and the Myth of the Super Woman.* New York: Dial Press, 1978.

Washington, Mary Helen. "An Essay on Alice Walker." In Roseann P. Bell, Bettye J. Parker, and Beverly Guy-Sheftall, eds., *Sturdy Black Bridges.* Garden City, NY: Anchor Press/Doubleday, 1979.

Washington, Mary Helen. *Invented Lives: Narratives of Black Women 1860–1960.* Garden City, NY: Anchor Press/Doubleday, 1987.

19

Women as Outsiders in the Movies and Television

Harriet A. Deer and Irving Deer

It would be unfair to suggest that one might find in the popular arts any widespread conscious approval of spouse abuse. Most popular programs and films appear to reflect the general public's position that beating one's spouse, especially one's wife, is bad form. Nevertheless, looking at the treatment of some highly popular heroines in the popular arts in the past 50 years, we can detect a conformity to closed patriarchal patterns of value within which it is possible to justify abusing women, because any self-assertions on their part are seen as disruptions of "the natural order of things." In that view women are supposed to function as submissive companions of men, conforming to male ideas of what constitutes the natural order, those things that sustain the egos of the men who rule society. Heroines as diverse as Scarlett O'Hara, Gracie Allen, and Lucille Ball all try to assert their own egos. We can get some idea of the way the popular arts sometimes promote spouse abuse, perhaps unintentionally, by briefly examining what happens to these three heroines as a result of their small feminist rebellions.

By far the most complicated heroine, and the most fruitful for our concerns, is Margaret Mitchell's enduringly attractive melodramatic heroine, Scarlett O'Hara. *Gone with the Wind* is a paramount illustration of the acceptability of spouse abuse. The central scene in the film is a marital rape, in which Rhett carries Scarlett, clad in her red dressing gown, up the wine-colored stairs to assert his masculine rights over her body. The importance of the scene is suggested by its use for the original publicity posters of the film, and the extent of the scene's popularity is shown by the reissue of the poster to advertise the film's rerelease on the occasion of its fiftieth anniversary, and the use of the scene in the previews for the rerelease. That a marital rape scene, with its glamorization of masculine superiority, should be at the core of the film seems to imply an ambiguous treatment of Scarlett. On one hand, she is a heroine whose vitality and determination seem to merit our admiration; these qualities enable her and her sisters to survive the war, to rebuild the family estate, to succeed in business, and to save Ashley and Melanie. She further saves Melanie from dying during childbirth, and protects Melanie and herself from possible rape and murder by shooting a Yankee deserter who is looting Tara. She is also the only member of the family who can cast aside the hierarchical traditions that would prevent her from working on the land, even for survival.

On the other hand, however, Scarlett is presented as a flirtatious, mendacious, and misguided woman. She exploits men heartlessly in order to achieve security. She costs her husband his life when Southern tradition compels him to avenge her honor after she has been attacked when she recklessly travels into a camp of former slaves and carpetbaggers. She pursues and nearly succeeds in corrupting Ashley Wilkes. Most important of all, she refuses to acquiesce to the Southern ideal of womanhood, represented by Melanie, and to recognize Rhett's greatness and appropriateness for her. Scarlett seems a prototype of the popular heroine whose independence is both admirable and culpable.

The novel/film seems calculated to affirm the stereotype of a woman who will be destroyed unless she submits to male dominance. The spirited Scarlett is destined for the masculine Rhett, but she loves Ashley. Ashley, however, is in many ways soft and, like a woman, subservient to the traditional Southern values of family and hierarchy, as shown by his marriage to his cousin Melanie ("Oh, if only the Wilkeses didn't always have to marry their own cousins!")[1] (Howard 1980, 62). Although he admits that Scarlett excites him, he tells her directly that he is going to marry Melanie because she shares his values and is an appropriate wife (Howard 1980, 90). Throughout the story, Scarlett casts aside obvious happiness with Rhett. She avoids commitment to him until she has lost her second husband. Then, being essentially bought by him, she fails to recognize either his commitment to traditional Southern values, which he reveals throughout the entire story, or his stereotypical masculine appropriateness for her own high-spirited femininity. Not until the rape scene does she recognize the value of Rhett's mastery. She wakes the morning after the rape, and the camera catches her smiling contentedly, a clear confirmation of two old stereotypes: one, that "what every woman needs is a good screw," and two, that she wants and somehow invites it.[2] However, she recognizes Rhett's value too late; he has already made plans to travel to Europe with their daughter. He might have been stopped had she been able to admit her "errors," but since her pride prevents her from speaking, she loses her chance for happiness. The moral of the story is clear from that moment forward: masculine superiority is necessary to redeem female independence and rebellion.

The moral of the story is made more explicit through the treatment of Melanie. She is the ideal woman of antebellum society. In the film we see her twice shown against the background of a church-shaped window as if she were a religious icon herself—on the stairs at Tara when she drags herself from childbed to defend herself and Scarlett against rape by a Yankee deserter who is looting Tara, and later in Atlanta when she comes to comfort Rhett after his daughter's death.[3] Melanie seems subservient and ineffectual, but she has the traditional strength of the unselfish helpmate, supporting Ashley, bearing his children with great difficulty, tolerating Belle Watling and recognizing her goodness despite the fact that Belle is a prostitute, evoking from Scarlett the unselfishness of which she is sometimes capable. She is the martyred servant figure, the image of the strong but self-sacrificing woman of Southern patriarchal tradition. Although Melanie dies in childbirth and Scarlett lives, Melanie achieves serenity and fulfillment while Scarlett achieves only loneliness and frustration.

The overwhelming popularity of *Gone with the Wind* and the uncritical acceptance of the subservience and spouse abuse it promotes give the novel and a film a special importance and imply that they may embody wider social values of which spouse abuse is merely one indication. Whether through a nostalgia for the antebellum South or because of a renewal of interest in this period in the 1930s, Margaret Mitchell's *Gone with the Wind* became instantly successful upon publication in 1936. By the 1980s, the book had sold over 16 million hardback copies, many millions more in paperback, and had been translated into 27 languages and published in 37 different countries (Taylor 1986, 113). The David Selznick film, which was released in 1939, may have been even more popular. Among a host of other awards, it won Academy Awards for best picture, best actress, best supporting actress, best director, and best screenplay (Michael 1969, 351). In 1989, 50 years after its original release, the People's Choice Awards, which are based on popular votes, honored it as the general public's favorite film of all time.

The popularity of both the film and the novel, on the other hand, has from the beginning caused concern among those who noticed their "idealization of the Old South and racist revival of neo-Confederate sympathies for antebellum social and racial relations" (Taylor 1986, 114). As Helen Taylor points out, the racist implications of both film and novel have caused a rift between some white and some black feminists. The white feminists see "Scarlett O'Hara's mingled determination, competence, and vulnerability [as] . . . qualities with which women readers identify" (Taylor 1986, 115).[4] But some black feminists (and Taylor) "would argue that for a reader to celebrate the text's feminism must involve both turning a blind eye to its white supremacist Southern propaganda and entering into an unholy alliance with the crudest Southern chauvinism and the activities of the Ku Klux Klan" (Taylor 1986, 115).

Taylor's argument is well-taken. The novel itself shows that the "good life" that has disappeared is based on the ownership of humans as property and on the subservience of women to their men. Unlike her mother, Scarlett shows independence; thus she cannot hope to marry Ashley Wilkes, who represents the chivalrous values of the Old South and loves Melanie. Melanie is the primary ideal in the novel, managing to express independence when necessary (in her interaction with Belle Watling and in her attempts to bear children, as well as in her emergence from the childbed to confront a marauding Yankee soldier) but always observing the conventions of the Old South. Scarlett is practical and uses human beings for her own political or practical agenda—marrying Charles Hamilton to get even with

Melanie for marrying Ashley, then marrying Frank Kennedy to get the money for Tara. Her wartime relationship with Rhett is based on his ability to bring her fine things from Europe. Later, however, she learns that she cannot simply buy everything she wants, but must learn to submit to the patriarchal system; she finds that she cannot have Ashley and discovers that she really wants Rhett to master her. She finally loses Rhett, who is capable of mastering her, because she discovers too late that she has loved an illusion, and that Ashley will never consider her as more than a flirtation and impropriety. Scarlett is heroic in her mercenary courage, yet she is punished for going outside the boundaries of the "old South" values. Those who fight paternalism are evil—for example, the carpetbaggers and the freed blacks who turn to rape and pillage, while the blacks, like Mammy and Big Sam, who stay on the plantation are good. Scarlett is bad because she recklessly goes into a black encampment and is nearly raped, the implication being that she has asked for such treatment. She thereby forces the good white men to defend her in proper KKK style, resulting in the death of Frank Kennedy and the near death of Ashley Wilkes. Scarlett is punished; she loses her daughter Bonnie, an unborn child, and Rhett because she pursues roles reserved for men in the antebellum society in which Rhett, Ashley, her father, and the other "gentlemen" in the world from which she comes believe. These are the views condoned and supported by the film and the novel. Scarlett is too manly, too successful a businesswoman, too independent, too much in pursuit of power and gratification of her own ego to be tolerated in a male-dominated society.

The major point we have been trying to make is that even though the popular arts generally do not treat spouse abuse directly as some kind of appropriate behavior, they nevertheless sometimes promote values that make spouse abuse seem an acceptable way of responding to breaches of the patriarchal code. Most people are like the O'Haras, the Wilkeses, and Rhett Butler in the sense that they also want unity, order, and purpose in their lives, and they see deviation from that unity and order as threatening and dangerous. They consider those elements of society that violate closure and unity destructive, often evil, and, as such, deserving of punishment. In a world where women are still considered subordinate to men, if not actually their property, women are sometimes taken to be both causes and articulations of the disruptions that men often experience. The treatment of women in *Gone with the Wind* supports this view. Two other popular heroines we will discuss briefly represent different stages of this patriarchal conception of society.

The character that Lucille Ball played in the "I Love Lucy" television series is an example of the heroine who is treated as the child–woman. She tries in an ineffectual way to establish her credentials as a successful adult member of society by trying to earn a living, manage finances, manage a family, and join Desi's band. She spends a great deal of time attempting to escape from the consequences of her generally childish grasp of the activities that she is trying to conduct. These attempts are often excuses to perform old vaudeville routines. For example, her efforts to earn a living give the performer an excuse to launch into her famous "Veggie Vitamin" syrup routine, a thinly veiled version of Red Skelton's "Guzzler's Gin Commercial" routine. Both have to keep sampling their wares during retakes of the commercial, both become inebriated, and both use the inebriation as a catalyst for hilarious mimes of drunkenness. In another routine, she thinks she has permanently disgraced herself and tries to leave home. Sitting on a park bench, she performs a number of fine "hobo" mimes, reminiscent of another Red Skelton creation, "Freddy the Freeloader." She finally decides to join the Salvation Army, which gives her an opportunity to mime the player who does not know how to handle the size of the bass drum.

The routines, however much they may echo the catalogue of standard vaudeville routines, create a subtle effect when placed in the context of the housewife who is searching for an identity. The routines involve masculine roles only somewhat adapted for a comedienne, so that we are aware that the roles Lucy tries to play are inadequate and inappropriate for her situation. Despite their humor, they imply the problem of the twentieth-century woman who is searching for an identity. The implication is, however, never allowed to develop. Lucy's idea of the world is always shown to be naive, and she has a greater ability to get herself into difficulty than to extricate herself from it. She must therefore always depend on her husband or an older couple, Fred and Ethel, to rescue her. She needs control, and at the end of each episode, she accepts the wisdom of those who control her. She indulges in imaginative flights of escape, but she remains the child–woman who initially rebels against but finally confirms the patriarchal society.[5]

Gracie Allen, playing the fictionalized wife of George Burns on the "Burns and Allen" show, appears on the surface also to represent the child–woman. From one perspective, her "controls" seem even more overt than those of Lucy. George is the "straight man," who sets up the jokes and brings the show to an end. Moreover, he watches the action from a television set in his den, spying on the secrets of Gracie and her friend Blanche, and descending from his second-floor den to bring the plot under control when it threatens to run amok. One might be tempted, then, to think of George as a godlike paternal figure who keeps order, saves Gracie from herself, and perhaps saves us from Gracie. However, aspects of the Burns and Allen television show (as distinguished from the radio show)[6] suggest that beneath the conventional surface of patriarchal control lurk considerably more sophisticated and ambiguous concepts.

First, George's control over Gracie is problematic. He tolerates her, he sets up lines for her, he asks questions about her relatives, but he is never sure what the response will be. Gracie's language is serendipitous. We never know which word in a sentence Gracie will pick up as the point of reference. Her resistance to the rules of reference is monumental. Even the famous sign-off ("'Say Goodnight, Gracie,'" says George. "'Goodnight, Gracie,'" she responds) is an example of willful distortion of the reference intended in the imperative, "say," and the appositive, "Gracie." We never have any idea where her stories about her relatives will lead, but we know that in a peculiarly traditional way, she will make a cogent point at the end of her story— but not necessarily the point we were anticipating. Moreover, George, rather than insisting on order, obviously adores the disorder Gracie introduces into the world. He sets up the lines and then waits with some malice toward the audience until the insanity appears. Or is it insanity? Gracie's stories and verbal responses generally have a peculiar logic that forces us to confront the stereotypes that hedge in our own responses to the world. When George asks a question, he is exposing us to disorder, he is putting us at the mercy of a world of *non sequitur* improvisations, he is stretching the limits of predictability, and he is, in a small way, pointing to the limits of our ideas of order.

It is difficult to associate such behavior with a controlling God figure. George's delight in disorder seems more appropriate for a Devil figure,[7] an association made irresistible because of George's omnipresent cigar, which gives him an aura of smoke and fire. His "control" of Gracie seems more on the order of the prankster who lets loose disorder than the patriarch who defines order. Perhaps the device of George observing the mayhem on his television set in the den serves to remind us in a quiet way of the limits of patriarchy. The creativity of improvisation reminds us that control is not a very creative illusion. Gracie, who seems on the surface a child to be controlled, is in reality a creative improviser, a full partner in the exploration of irrationality, a being set free rather than confined by the very "straight man" lines George delivers to her. Although she pretends to be a child–woman, one senses that she may, in fact, be an exceptionally independent woman masquerading as a child.

The Burns and Allen show, then, seems potentially an example of a show in which patriarchal convention appears to be observed but, in reality, is violated. Unfortunately, the potential is never totally realized. Gracie and George pursue disorder and upset the routines of the world, but, in the final analysis, they do not reject patriarchy. At the end of each show, Gracie always accedes to George's final authority. If George says it is time to end the madness, then Gracie obeys the command. "Say Goodnight, Gracie," may be the cue for a violation of grammatical reference, but it is nevertheless a command that Gracie obeys. The show reveals an awareness of the sterility and full conformity of the patriarchal structures that govern many marriages, but it preaches freedom only as a *sub rosa* activity.[8]

Gone with the Wind seems to be and is for some people a novel/film that glorifies the independent woman. Yet in both subject matter and underlying ideology, it points out the dangers of independence and of nonconformity to patriarchal values, and, as we have argued, actually promotes spouse abuse. *Full Metal Jacket* is in some important ways the opposite of this. It has no major female characters and seems to degrade women in almost every line; yet, as we will argue, it actually promotes a vision hostile to spouse abuse.

Full Metal Jacket has no women characters except a few minor prostitutes, a young female enemy sniper, and a few dead bodies of young and old women partially covered with lime in a pit. All are, or have been in the past, primarily objects for men to master or control. Moreover, the language of the film is overwhelmingly sexist. The drill sergeant who dominates the first half of the film can hardly say a word that does not foully degrade women. He violates women with every breath. He also insults his men by calling them "ladies," treating them as objects that he defines and creates, not allowing them to say a word or do anything he specifically does not instruct them to do. Every degradation he heaps on his men—and there are a great many—whether he ridicules them because of race, class, religion, the way they talk or look, or any other reason, finally boils down to a degradation of their manhood, by stressing their "ladylike" qualities.

He cannot even imagine a relationship with a woman that can be anything but perverse. He reduces the recruits' civilian girl-friends to "Mary Jane Rottencrotches," and describes their romantic relationships as "grab assing" and "finger banging" (Kubrick, Herr, and Hasford 1987, 13). He forces them to drill to cadence rhymes about their parents' interest in fornicating (Kubrick *et al.* 1987, 11–12). He requires that they give their rifles girls' names and think of their rifles as replacements for their "Mary Jane Rottencrotches." He sees loving their rifles as a proper replacement for love of any woman, and to drum that idea into them, to create them in the image he wishes them to exemplify, he makes them go to bed with their rifles, pray to their rifles, and drill again and again to cadence rhymes that give them the illusion that drilling, being a good soldier, especially learning how to use their rifles to kill well, are all replacements for the joys of sex: "Gimme some . . . gimme some . . . PT . . . PT . . . Good for you . . . good for you" (Kubrick *et al.* 1987, 12). And then again, "Eskimo pussy is mighty cold! Mmm, good! Mmm, good! Feels good! Feels good!" (Kubrick *et al.* 1987, 29). And after they begin to resemble his desired image, the chants continue: "I don't want no teenage queen. I don't want no teenage queen. I just want my M14" (Kubrick *et al.* 1987, 42).

Hartman's reduction of all sex to perverse sex is an important form of his general reductionism. He reduces everything to his single aim, to mold the new marines under his control into perfect killers. If he can engrain in them the instinctive association of killing with sexual gratification, he feels he will succeed. To reinforce the idea that killing gives supreme gratification, he establishes killing as the basis for religious and patriotic fulfillment as well as for sexual gratification. We can see this in the prayer he requires the recruits to recite in bed with their rifles held at port arms in front of them. The prayer mixes sex, religion, and patriotism together so that all of these motivations can be gratified only if the soldiers can shoot well (Kubrick *et al.* 1987, 13, 18).

Hartman's incredible reductionism is exemplified in the scene in which he asks the platoon sitting on bleachers facing him if they know who Charles Whitman was. Only Cowboy knows that Whitman was the "guy who shot all those people from that tower in Austin, Texas, sir!" (Kubrick *et al.* 1987, 38). Hartman then asks them to identify Lee Harvey Oswald. Most of the recruits know that Oswald was the man who shot President Kennedy. What interests Hartman about both of these men is how well they used their rifles. "Whitman killed twenty people from distances up to four hundred yards . . ." and "Oswald got off three rounds with an old Italian bolt action rifle in only six seconds and scored two hits, including a head shot!" (Kubrick *et al.* 1987, 38). He is very proud that both men learned to shoot so well in the Marines (Kubrick *et al.* 1987, 40). He sees no other way of evaluating the actions of the two men, recognizing only this one narrow way of looking at each event. As in his treatment of his recruits, he here represses any personal vision or act or statement that cannot be reduced to his purpose. This is a desire for unity with a vengeance.

Although the repression to which he subjects Leonard backfires and results in his own death, the second half of the film indicates that the training he gave the other recruits was effective. Joker is perhaps the central character of the film's second half, and from the beginning he seems capable of seeing situations from different perspectives. In fact, he gets the name "Joker" early in the film because he sees the humor in the Sergeant's obscene diatribes. He persists in wearing two contradictory symbols, "Born to Kill" on his helmet and a peace symbol on his shirt, a contradiction for which he is threatened with court martial by a colonel who, like Sergeant Hartman, wants to reduce everything to the unity of killing well. Joker hesitates in crucial moments when he is torn between the kind of behavior Hartman and the war demand and a more humane way of perceiving situations. We can see this, for example, when he hesitates before joining the rest of the platoon in beating Leonard for eating jelly doughnuts and getting them in trouble with the sergeant. He also hesitates before killing the young Vietnamese girl sniper who has been mortally wounded. He is torn between killing her to alleviate her suffering and killing her because she has killed his best friend Cowboy.

Joker, therefore, represents someone capable of openness, of multiple perspectives, who is pressured first by Hartman, and later by the colonel, Animal Mother, and finally by the war to reject all possible ways of looking at any situation except those that affirm killing the enemy and sheer animal survival. Joker may initially hesitate before beating Leonard, but under pressure from his platoon buddies, who are merely following the sergeant's dictates, he finally gives in and hits Leonard harder and more times than anyone else, and then puts his fingers in his ears to block out Leonard's cries of pain. He also may hesitate before shooting the young sniper, but he does shoot her, with a grimace on his face that suggests he is succumbing to hatred for her rather than feeling sympathy for her suffering.

Kubrick visually reinforces these two scenes by presenting them both as symbolic rapes. The men falling on Leonard in his sleep, holding him down on his bunk, and preventing him from screaming by gagging him with a towel are violently assaulting him physically, as in a rape. The scene in which the men are looking down at the gasping and panting Vietnamese girl even more graphically resembles a rape scene. However, we are aware that she is pleading to be killed, not begging for sex. And we recognize the perversity of reducing the scene to a rape, just as we had earlier recognized the perverse reductions by Hartman of every form of sex and all moral or humane feelings to a single, narrow-minded, destructive purpose. Kubrick shows Joker and the other members of the platoon being consistently reduced to the ideal marine image that Hartman envisions for them. By the end of the film, Joker is singing the Mickey Mouse Club song with all the men and fantasizing about a gigantic sexual orgy with Mary Jane Rottencrotch, the very vision and attitude Sergeant Hartman has striven so hard to instill in him. Joker has accepted sheer physical survival as the only thing that matters.

But because Kubrick constantly shows us the multiple possibilities in the situations he presents, possibilities that Joker had earlier only dimly recognized, we become aware of the reduction being dramatized. We never succumb ourselves to the incredible desire for a unified, destructive purpose for which Hartman stands.

Unlike the men, we recognize that treating women as objects to be mastered as they master their rifles is no sign of nobility, manhood, or patriotism. Kubrick's strategies are such that he exposes the destructive values that underlie the profanity and debasing chauvinism of the troops. Whereas the popular works discussed earlier either accept or at best somewhat subvert the patriarchy, Kubrick subjects it to questioning, forcing us to see what it is, requiring us to recognize the constraints and inadequacies of the systems by which we structure our society. Kubrick's work represents a creative new direction for the popular arts, in which they can become forces both for the critical reappraisal of our patriarchal values and for shaping new visions in which all individuals, men and women, can be regarded and valued for themselves.

Notes

1. This is a composite script by Sidney Howard, with minor additions by F. Scott Fitzgerald and Ben Hecht. It has a few scenes that Howard wrote that are not in the final screenplay. During filming and editing, there were some changes and considerable cutting, since, according to Harwell, the composite script he gives us would have been over five hours long (1980, 38). In this script, the line is attributed to Scarlett, but in the film the line is spoken by a guest at the barbecue at Twelve Oaks. In the Howard script, Gerald O'Hara makes Ashley's duty to marry his cousin explicit, as well as his disapproval of any match between Scarlett and Ashley, partly because of the Wilkes's tradition of intermarrying with their cousins.
2. We noticed a recent example of this on a television rerun of the James Bond movie, *On Her Majesty's Secret Service*, in which the father of the character played by Diana Rigg offers James Bond a million-pound bribe (which he refuses) to provide his daughter that service, in order that she learn how to obey her father and behave properly.
3. The church window is established as an appropriate extension of the religious nature of the Southern cause when the written titles for the "Siege of Atlanta," which describe Atlanta praying as the Yankees come nearer, are displayed against the background of a church window. That window is the same shape as the windows in which Melanie is framed (see Howard 1980, 156)
4. According to Taylor, Margaret Mitchell wrote Thomas Dixon, the author of *The Clansman* (on which *Birth of a Nation* is based) and other books which glorified the KKK and their racist attitudes, "I was practically raised on your books and loved them very much." (Taylor draws this quotation from

Q. On which legislative committees do you presently serve?
A. I am currently a member of the Appropriations Committee, the Rules and Calendar Committee, the Youth Committee, the Small Business and Economic Development Committee, the Environmental Regulations/Regulated Industries Committee, the Environ Chairman of the Transportation Subcommittee of Appropriations.
Q. You have the reputation of being a state official who is genuinely concerned with both child abuse and spouse abuse. After your election to office, when did you become involved with the prob lems of family violence?
A. Actually, I became involved with the problems of child abuse before I ever considered running for public office. In fact, I decid ed to run for election as a direct result of my concern for abused children.

Before becoming a state representative, I was President of the League of Women Voters in Tampa. The Junior League of Tampa wanted to form a child abuse council for seeking local solutions to the problem of child abuse and they asked the League of Women Voters for assistance in the project. I agreed to work with them and was sent to our state capitol in Tallahassee to lobby for the money needed to fund a family protection team specializing in crisis intervention.

I had always been interested in state government. When I saw that I was effective working with state offices, I became en couraged enough to run for the position of state representative.

nd you won on your first attempt?
eat a rather well-known incumbent.

hat is the state of Florida presently doing to aid victims of
ily abuse and violence?
e state's primary effort in this matter is through the funding of
estic violence centers, which offer refuge and counseling for
sed spouses and children. These centers, by the way, are
ed by a fee added to the cost of each marriage license.
many of these domestic violence centers are presently in
tion?

w have 29 centers and we should have more. In the 1987–88
year, our centers served a total of 6733 clients. In 1988–89,
nters cared for 7859 clients. That's a one-year increase of
han 18%. During the first seven months of the present

Margaret Mitchell's letter to Dixon dated 15 August, 1936, collected in *Margaret Mitchell's Gone With the Wind Letters, 1936–49.* For a longer consid eration of the connection between *The Clansman, Birth of a Nation,* and *Gone with the Wind,* see Gerald Woods [1984].)

5. Patricia Mellencamp discusses similar issues at greater length and with somewhat different conclusions (80–95).

6. The radio show has none of the "God–Devil" implications of the television show, since both the television set with which George spies and his cigar that brings its own diabolical suggestions are visual devices and are there fore absent from the radio show. However, the "straight man" function we discuss was always part of the Burns and Allen routines, and it is at the core of the ambiguity concerning Gracie. It seems possible, then, that the format of the television show merely spells out some of the latent pos sibilities of the radio show.

7. Filmmakers recognized this diabolical quality when they cast George Burns as God in *Oh God.* Unfortunately, they could not resist rendering the joke explicit in *Oh God, You Devil.*

8. In discussing George and Gracie, Mellencamp approaches the prob lematics of George's control through a Freudian analysis of jokes, but seems to see George as essentially someone who controls not only Gracie but all the other possibilities of meaning and interpretation of any particu lar program (1986, 82–87).

References

Howard, Sidney, *GWTW: The Screenplay.* Richard Harwell, ed. New York: Macmillan, 1980.

Kubrick, Stanley, Michael Herr, and Gustav Hasford. *Full Metal Jacket,* the screenplay. New York: Alfred A. Knopf, 1987.

Mellencamp, Patricia. "Situation Comedy, Feminism and Freud: Discourses of Gracie and Lucy." In Tania Modleski, ed., *Studies in Entertainment.* Bloomington and Indianapolis: Indiana University Press, 1986.

Michael, Paul, ed. *The American Movies: A Pictorial Encyclopedia.* New York: Galahad Books, 1969.

Taylor, Helen. "*Gone with the Wind:* The Mammy of Them all," In Jean Rad ford, ed., *The Progress of Romance in the Politics of Popular Fiction.* London and New York: Routledge & Kegan Paul, 1986.

Woods, Gerald. "From *The Clansman* and *Birth of a Nation* to *Gone with the Wind:* The Loss of American Innocence." In Darden Asbury Pyron, ed., *Recasting: Gone with the Wind in American Culture,* pp. 123–136. Miami: Florida International University Press, 1984.

20

The Future of Our Past

Interview by C. Gordon Deats with Represen[t]
the Honorable Mary Figg, State Representativ[e]
Florida Legislature

Editor's Note: Florida ranks third nationally in number[
children reported in child abuse and neglect cases. [
lem is enormous and frightening. Nevertheless, m[
adopted to provide assistance to those who live in[
environments. For example, a percentage of reven[
riage license obtained in Florida is allocated by law[
for abused spouses and children. These funds h[
ters across the state, but much remains to be d[
State Representative Mary Figg has dedica[
in crisis. The interview with Representative F[
ducted by C. Gordon Deats on June 15, 1990[
activities on behalf of troubled families and n[
Florida's future regarding the problem. This[
the hope of strengthening the resolve of[
painful issue.

Q. Representative Figg, how long have [
the Florida legislature?
A. I was first elected in 1982 and I've be[
for a total of eight years of service.[

s[
c[
Q. A[
A. I [
Q. W[
fa[
A. Th[
dor[
abu[
fun[
Q. How[
oper[
A. We n[
fiscal[
the ce[
more[

fiscal year, the centers have served 5542 clients of which 3233 are children, and there is presently a list of 1650 people waiting to be admitted into the program.

Q. What is the state of Florida presently doing to prevent or discourage family violence?

A. Our state is funding family violence intervention programs across the state. These programs help families to get counseling and avoid violence. Generally, the programs work with husbands and fathers who have already shown a capacity for violence. In fact, 90% of those participating were ordered to do so by the courts.

Q. How many programs have been organized?

A. We have about 30 in operation and each program is divided into groups of around 12 participants. Hillsborough County (Tampa) is divided into 17 groups.

One significant action Florida has taken to diminish both spouse and child abuse is to deny efforts to make abortions more difficult to obtain. Many battered wives are beaten by their husbands while they are pregnant. Abused children are almost always those who are not wanted. Conceivably, some abortions will prevent the abuse of both a wife and her child.

Q. If the state of Florida were to do nothing at all about family violence, what potentially dangerous consequences do you foresee resulting that would threaten the general population?

A. If suddenly we were to do absolutely nothing, we would, in a very short time, experience a surge in crime. We would have more domestic violence. We would have more children die as a result of abuse. Without counseling, more people might turn to drug consumption and the cost of those drugs would result in more burglaries and more armed robberies. And probably because of the general increase in violent crimes, there would be more of our law enforcement officers wounded or killed while trying to perform their duties.

Q. Ideally, what should the state do to solve, or, at least lessen, this problem of family violence?

A. Whether we seek an ideal solution or a pragmatic solution, the answer is the same: we need to educate, educate, educate, and educate. We need to educate young parents. They cannot expect, for example, a six-month-old child to respond to potty training, and you'd be surprised to find that many do. The baby doesn't learn as fast as they think it should so they become stressed. Young parents need to learn the realistic pattern of child development so they won't make impossible demands on toddlers and infants.

We need to provide further training for our workers with the state's Health and Rehabilitation Service so they can do a more thorough job of maintaining surveillance of the children who have been adopted and those placed in foster homes.

We need to educate members of the judiciary. Some judges still believe that spouse and child abuse are family matters and should not be the concern of the state.

We need to educate our police officers. Outside of the family members, they're the ones who will most likely be injured during an outburst of domestic violence. Our police need to be better trained in the handling of family fights and they need to be persuaded that those fights are not to be considered merely husband-and-wife spats, but are frequently symptoms of a need for psychological treatment.

Q. What impedes Florida from following your recommendations?
A. Certainly Florida needs a broader tax base because, of course, the training needed and the facilities needed all require money. At the present we just cannot provide the funding to mount an effective campaign against family violence.

Our larger problem at the present is that the state government lacks the will to confront the circumstances aggressively so we can begin to find remedies for the problems of family violence. The lack of will is the more serious problem because if we had the will to stop family violence, we would certainly find the money to do the job.

Q. Representative Figg, are you optimistic or pessimistic about Florida's ability to solve the problems of family violence in the future?
A. I do not at all doubt that we can greatly diminish our problems of family violence if we set our sights on that goal with determination.

I have to be optimistic. I have children and they will be having children. The Figg family will still be around in Florida for many years into the future. And in that future, I hope that we will be living in a better Florida with fewer problems of family violence.

Index